ASTR
AND
ART OF HEALING

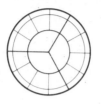

ASTROLOGY
AND THE
ART OF HEALING

A. T. Mann

UNWIN PAPERBACKS
London Sydney Wellington

First published in paperback by Unwin Paperbacks, an imprint of
Unwin Hyman Limited, in 1989.

Unwin Hyman Limited
15–17 Broadwick Street, London W1V 1FP

Allen & Unwin Australia Pty Ltd
8 Napier Street, North Sydney, NSW 2060, Australia

Allen & Unwin New Zealand Pty Ltd with the Port Nicholson Press
Compusales Building, 75 Ghunzee Street, Wellington, New Zealand.

British Library Cataloguing in Publication Data

Mann, A. T. (Tad), *1943*–
    Astrology and the art of healing.
1. Alternative medicine. Astrological aspects
I. Title
133.5'861
ISBN 0-04-440248-1

Set in 11 on 13 point Palatino by Cambridge Photosetting Services
Made and printed in Great Britain by
Richard Clay Ltd, Bungay, Suffolk

To the memory of my dear healing friends,
John Da Monte, Rosemary Russell and David Tansley

Contents

Preface

The tradition of astrology and healing is almost as old as the existence of astrology itself since all early people attributed changes in their health to the operation of the planets and the gods which moved them. Every age has adapted the basic concepts of astrology to suit its prevailing beliefs, and as a result astrology contains the wisdom of the past encoded in a symbolic language which is very popular to this day.

A primary dilemma in all books about the applications of astrology is that the author cannot assume any astrological knowledge on the part of the reader, and therefore is often placed in a quandary about whether or not to encapsulate the entire workings of astrology for the benefit of such beginners in the cosmic art and science. At the same time, such a book as this is intended for sophisticated astrologers. In order to satisfy both audiences, for this book is intended for anyone who is interested in extending understanding of the human condition to ever higher and more relevant levels, the majority of basic material relating to the structure and practice of natal astrology is greatly simplified. It would be helpful – if such background information is required for a deeper and richer sense of astrology – for the reader to consult my earlier book *Life★Time Astrology* (1984), which presents my unique system for modelling the life process from conception to death using a time scale of sublime simplicity.

This book is structured in such a way that the tables, which will be indispensable to practising astrologers and those therapists who wish to use the ideas presented to their full, are placed in Appendices. There are tables for determining the meaning of planets in signs of the zodiac; an index of more than one thousand medical and psychological conditions and their astrological correspondences; the techniques from LifeωTime Astrology by which you can date the registration of planets and sign and house entrances in the horoscope; a technique for rectifying incorrect or unknown birth times; and a list of addresses where computer horoscopes can be obtained for those who do not know their entire horoscope positions. It is hoped that the body of the text will be easy to understand by all levels of students and instructors of astrology.

1
The Modern Health Crisis

It is very apparent that contemporary attitudes towards health and healing are drastically inadequate, to the extent that they are overtly dangerous to the population of the earth. Rather than observing a trend towards a worldwide improvement in health there is an alarming deterioration at every level. The current plagues of stress-related diseases such as ulcers, colitis, high blood pressure, cancer and heart disease are rampant, but even they pale in the light of the spectre of AIDS.

The cause of the 'trial by pestilence' which is affecting us lies deep within modern society, and nothing is more symbolic of the degeneration of the modern world than medicine. The doctors whose responsibility it is to heal us are signally responsible for the decline in public health on a massive scale. There are a number of reasons why doctors and our attitudes towards them are a problem. As Richard Grossinger pointed out in his brilliant *Planet Medicine*,[1] western medicine has concerned itself with the organic causes of illness. The pathology of disease is the series of mechanically determined steps in the deterioration of an average ill individual, and cure is achieved by a path by which all physicians should be able to cure the particular identified disease. Isolated cures are insignificant and only generalised cures applicable to the majority are accepted.

An individual afflicted by a stomach ulcer expects to go to his doctor and receive a label describing what is wrong and a prescription which will make the symptoms go away. If this is accomplished, the doctor has met the expectations of the patient and the patient is happy. But psychotherapists know that stomach ulcers are caused by an inability to express feelings. The stomach is the natural organ which relates to feelings, which we digest and process just as we do food. When strong emotions cannot find expression in the outer world, they create outbursts within the body, specifically the stomach. The more dramatic the inner emotional life, the greater the turmoil within, and the stronger the symptoms of ulcer would manifest. In a very real sense symptoms are an essential communication by the body to a mind which is not willing to respond. No matter how effective the drug given, its only purpose will be to eliminate the symptoms. The primary emotional causes of the ulcer are not addressed, hence they will not be changed or eliminated. The organism as a whole will suffer, yet the body-mind, unable to communicate emotional imbalance in the place most natural to it, will find somewhere deeper within the organism where it can express itself. The minor but common problem of unexpressed emotions can interrupt the function of the major organs, and indeed affect the entire organism. This extreme situation leads ultimately to chronic ill health, a condition which exists in many of us to some degree or other. We have been taught to suppress our natural connection with the earth, our inner being and the central forces which affect life and death.

The paradox which lies at the heart of this issue is that the scientific revolution created the illusion that chemistry and technology could by themselves eradicate illness, when in reality *they often create illness*. Most medicines cannot, and are not designed to, affect the causal being of an individual. Therefore, it is rare to get better with drug therapy. (When patients get better it is their own body which cures them, not the drugs.) The cause remains as strong as before, but the body has spent untold energy dealing with the drugs placed in its way. When imbalances cannot be expressed in their natural places, they create havoc elsewhere, with the result that further symptoms emerge which are unnatural means of expression. As the condition worsens, the ultimate step is to have a surgeon remove the offending organ. When part of the stomach containing the ulcer is cut out, so the logic goes, there is no way that the ulcer can return! As can be observed around us, the removal of organs only benefits the bank accounts of surgeons.

The terrifying infiltration of western society by pharmaceutical drugs is analogous to the pollution of the environment by pesticides. In both cases chemicals are thought to be necessary, but the side-effects are underestimated and they continue to be used even after the true extent of their adverse effects on the environment and food chain are known. The ecological problem is a backlash of pesticide use and pollution by industrial wastes, just as modern ill health manifests to most people who consume food additives and prescriptive medicine. While it cannot be denied that medicines can save lives, it is also true that in most cases we die of the cumulative side-effects of the cure rather than the disease. Cancer sufferers often die from the chemotherapy treatment. 'Global medicine presents the same ultimate ecological problem as global agriculture (with its pesticides) and global petroleum economy.'[2]

At the present time, alternative methods of healing provide a new way for understanding and treating disease. The emphasis is shifting from *curing* symptoms with prescription medicine and surgery towards a holistic *healing* which integrates personal, emotional, mental, environmental and even spiritual factors. What is needed is a *human ecology* to integrate with the essential planetary ecology.

It is clear that true healing is the body-mind curing itself. Doctors, healing techniques, diet, exercise and other therapies may initiate the healing process, support it, or direct it, but the ultimate health mechanism is the body-mind itself. The body knows what it needs and is capable of correcting most imbalances that have not degenerated too far, if only it can operate freely within optimal conditions. As cancer cures aided by visualisation have proven, the body-mind can even reverse extreme imbalances. The great dilemma is that we are our own worst enemies and impede the natural curative process.

Alternative Therapy and Complementary Medicine

What is the alternative to the medical establishment? Recently, methods of healing have been rediscovered which have been in existence for many hundreds of years and new therapies have been created. Acupuncture is a dramatic example, and others include homoeopathy, nutrition, osteopathy, chiropractic, radionics, psychotherapy, many forms of bodywork, massage and herbalism. These healing arts differ from traditional medicine in that they claim to be 'holistic', which means that the whole person is considered part of the problem and of the cure. But how do holist therapies work?

For example, a homoeopathic practitioner considers much more than the 'presenting' symptoms of a new patient. It is necessary to know the entire medical and psychological history, as well as present symptomatology, in great detail. The remedy is chosen to reflect, as much as possible, the entire range of symptoms. In homoeopathy the causes as well as the symptoms are treated. Behind the need for reconstructing an entire 'health picture' is the understanding that homoeopathic remedies transmit behavioural patterns which change the quality of life and subsequently eliminate or correct the imbalances which have produced disease. Until the imbalance has been rectified, it is fruitless to try to eliminate symptoms as they would merely come back stronger next time. Gradually the cure is effected, together with an equivalent change in overall life patterning and habits. Homoeopathy is a primary example of holistic healing.

Even when the primary goal of a therapy is to eliminate presenting symptoms and thereby cure the patient, a therapy is not truly holistic. Holistic healing is much more than any one therapy can offer – it is an attitude to life.

Is it true that alternative medicine is superior? What reason is there to suggest that simply because one is receiving acupressure or reflexology, or is taking herbal and homoeopathic remedies, one is being assisted towards greater wholeness of body–mind–spirit?[3] There is no reason, yet this assumption appears rampant within holistic health circles. The issue is the confusion of tools of care with an approach to life. Instead of the fragmentation into myriad specialities which do not overlap upon each other as exists in traditional allopathic medicine, the movement known as complementary medicine makes the assumption that true healing only happens with the entire organism, yet the care is often not holistic at all. It is not an automatic assumption.

When encountering the world of alternative therapies, it is often difficult to find the appropriate therapy with which to begin. There are few referrals from medical doctors, primarily due to economical considerations. The haphazard information available about alternative therapies is contradictory because each one claims to be holistic and capable of curing all afflictions.

One is left with the necessity to try to find an appropriate alternative therapy unaided.

Typically, we search for a personal recommendation, such as the acupuncturist our sister successfully went to last year. Once visiting the acupuncturist, the treatment will be a holistic attempt to correct patterns which are deeply ingrained. The problem is that, while acupuncture is a holistic therapy, it may not be the only or the best therapy for every affliction. If your spine is out of alignment due to incorrect posture, athletic strains or early imbalances, acupuncture may reduce pain or begin to correct the bodily structure, but bodywork such as osteopathy or chiropractic is more likely to be correct and effective.

Many people are led to therapies which are not appropriate for them, for lack of any clear direction. What is needed is a model for choosing the most effective therapies for any individual. Astrology provides a model which can be used to determine which therapy or combination of therapies is most appropriate.

Many therapies contain the holistic principle as central to their methodology, including acupuncture, homoeopathy, osteopathy, chiropractic, iridology, biofeedback, herbalism and many forms of bodywork such as Feldenkrais, Rolfing, Polarity Therapy, Reflexology and Biodynamic Massage. These represent a small number of the more popular alternatives. With such a wide range of alternative therapies available, all of which are holistic, there is an understandable confusion among those new to alternative therapies as to which one is appropriate.

The variations among therapies are profound. Some can offer a cure after only a few sessions, while others can take years of dedication. There are therapies which are powerful in their impact and depth – such as Rolfing – which offer quite rapid alterations of habits and posture, while vitamin therapies can bring very gradual change over a period of years. Different therapies are appropriate for different people, and the rate at which change can be tolerated varies dramatically. The choice is quite bewildering.

There is a similar profusion of psychotherapies, most of which claim to be appropriate for everyone, which make it equally difficult for the individual wanting help to decide where to begin. The result of such a variety of alternatives is strikingly similar to the difficulty of choosing specialists in traditional medicine.

The term 'complementary medicine' rather than 'alternative therapy' is becoming popular, but there is a definite difference in meaning. Complementary medicine includes those practitioners who attempt to integrate their approach with orthodox medicine and the medical profession, while alternative therapy includes many whose ideas and techniques are distinctly different and do not usually court the approval of medical doctors, preferring to take a separate direction altogether. Therapies must work together with some of the effective elements of traditional medicine and also with each other in order for an effective healing process to be initiated, and therefore the only possible integration includes both complementary medicine and alternative therapy.

Most people who use alternative therapy or complementary medicine do so because traditional techniques have failed. The basic problem is that orthodox medicine treats and sometimes cures symptoms, but does not create or encourage changes in the behaviour patterns which brought the symptoms about in the first place. Given the complexity of our modern world, the state of our health is also very intricate, with the labels used for generations becoming inaccurate and misleading. It is increasingly difficult to attach disease names to modern ills. The problem is vividly illustrated by the search for the causes of elusive low-grade infections, cancer, leukaemia, AIDS and the numerous influenzas which are endemic to our society. Modern illnesses are not caused by bugs which infect us but are instead the result of cumulative influences ranging from food additives, pesticides, refined food, environmental toxins, antibiotics and a score of others. In response to the problems caused by such changing rules, the new holistic therapies have as their primary goal the introduction of change determined by the individual, in contrast to change imposed by a doctor. It is integrative rather than interventive.

Astrology and Healing

Astrology is a very powerful model for the human life in time, and has been utilised to that end for thousands of years. At the present time astrology is undergoing a profound change, not least in the domain of medical astrology. The emerging link between astrology and biology provides ways for astrology to integrate its mechanism of time cycles with health, healing and the ecological process. This book will cover the ramifications of these ideas on traditional medical astrology and will also present a few unique applications of astrology and healing. The following paragraphs show the range of issues and approaches to be covered in *Astrology and the Art of Healing*.

Each sign of the zodiac is related to body parts, internal organs or systems, psychological mechanisms and stages of the process of growth in life. The various types of therapy can also be correlated to the signs of the zodiac.

Chapter 5 is devoted to the Wheel of Therapies, in which each therapy is categorised by the sign whose action it most fully reflects. By knowing which planet is responsible for a particular type of blockage it is quite easy to determine which therapies are likely to be effective because they will be seen by the sign in which the planet resides. Tensions can arise from the action of the planets Mars, Uranus or Pluto, to name a few. When they are active, they will bring the body part in which they reside into prominence and produce symptoms. Afflictions of the stomach, particularly ulcers or cancers, are emotionally related diseases which are signified by the sign Cancer, which rules the stomach, and have their origin in the structure of the home and family system reflected in the stomach. Virtually all stomach trouble is related to family system issues. The therapies related to Cancer are psychotherapy, family therapy and the Bach Flower Remedies. Each sign has associated therapies which are appropriate for its influences. The Wheel of Therapies is a way of understanding how therapies act together to provide the potential for wholeness.

Life★Time Astrology (1984) describes my unique astrological model of the life process in time from conception to death as seen around the periphery of the horoscope. A direct method for determining the dating of planets at the times in life when they are active is described, together with the general orientation of this revolutionary new astrological system which for the first time integrates astrology, the mathematics and mechanism of biological time, modern ideas of biology and genetics and the higher awareness of transpersonal psychology. In practice, Life★Time Astrology is a sublime tool because the entire life process can easily be seen around the horoscope wheel and the arduous dating of events in traditional astrology is superseded.

Life★Time Astrology divides the entire life from conception to transcendence into four octaves, as a multidimensional model of life in time. Through the model it is easy to understand how disease originates, which therapies to choose for particular problems, and also how cures work.

Many contemporary therapies will be presented, evaluated astrologically and their applicability demonstrated with sample horoscopes. While it may once have been true that every person has a particular therapy which is most effective for them, the modern world is so complex that we require a progression of therapies throughout our lives which may vary quite dramatically according to the time and circumstances. The demands of each stage of our development may be supplemented by appropriate therapies. Whereas the process of self-discovery by trial and error can be long and arduous, it is not necessary to be random about the selection of alternative therapies.

The idea of 'open confidence' in therapy will be presented and its implications to the healing process described. Typically, there is a closed confidentiality between therapist and client which ensures that information presented in a therapeutic session goes no further than the two participants. The practice dates back to the Freudian relationship of therapist and patient, and is now an obsolete way of approaching therapy. The limited use of information and feelings evoked during therapy is often not only counter-productive, but overtly sustains problems which need to be brought out into the open. Open confidence is a new concept in bringing the issues of therapy, whether psychotherapeutic or medical, into the open and to the attention of all therapists working with an individual. This is essential for preventing the common occurrence where the acupuncturist works on energising a person every Tuesday morning, and then the psychotherapist directs his energies to calming her down every Tuesday afternoon. For an integration of therapies, there must be a willingness on the part of therapists and clients to extend the therapeutic model to include all therapists. Even the family of the client must be encouraged to expand its awareness of the problems of the system and ways in which the problems are being approached.

A series of astrological diagnoses will illustrate horoscopes of a wide range of people who have imbalances or illnesses, as well as those suffering from cancer, leukaemia, AIDS, sexually transmitted diseases and anorexia nervosa. The entire mechanism of birth is shown to be a critical and undervalued factor in subsequent mental, emotional and physical health.

The modern healing art of Astro★Radionics, developed by the author, will be presented and shown to diagnose and treat an individual at a distance through the energy pattern of the horoscope. The mechanisms and philosophy of this subtle healing art will bring a new perspective on anatomy and health.

Astrological Medical Texts

Many books present information and techniques of medical astrology, and *Astrology and the Art of Healing* is not meant to be a substitute for these texts but rather a more integrated context in which to use their information. A brief review of some of the more influential books will give an idea of the variety and breadth of existing work in the field. Most are valuable sources and provide basic information beyond the scope of this book. As you will see, the range of approaches is varied.

The Astrological Judgement of Diseases (London, 1655) by the great astrological herbalist Nicholas Culpeper is a classic work used by generations of doctors as a standard text. Culpeper combined a profound knowledge of herbs (*Culpeper's Herbal*, 1649) with an understanding of the Greek medicine of Galen and his books seek the forewarning of disease from birth charts and the methods of cure for those already ill. Culpeper's work is valuable for the principles of his work and his astrological classification of medicinal plants.

The *Encyclopedia of Medical Astrology* (New York, 1933) by Dr H. L. Cornell is old fashioned and incredibly convoluted, but its almost one thousand pages is a valuable guide for starting an investigation of medical astrology. Much useful information is included and the correlations between illnesses and the spinal points according to chiropractic are unique.

Astrology, Nutrition and Health (Massachusetts, 1977) by Robert

Jansky is informative, if brief, and focuses on the correlations between nutrition and astrology by way of rulerships attributed to vitamins and minerals. The case histories are treated as purely medical and the study of sexuality and violence uses the mid-points, a very elaborate system for analysis. Jansky has written a series of such books on medical astrology.

By far the best and most exhaustive study of medical astrology is *The American Book of Nutrition and Medical Astrology* (San Diego, 1982), in which Eileen Nauman presents her 'Medi-Scan Technique', a questionnaire which allows the state of a person's health to be studied in an organised fashion in conjunction with astrology. The very informative sections on the astrological and medical functions of vitamins, minerals, herbs and cell salts are excellent. The only drawback is that Nauman uses the Uranian planets which have been mathematically predicted but never found to exist physically.[4] Uranian astrology is often very accurate but the hypothetical nature of the planets is not accepted by all astrologers. The book is a landmark work on medical astrology and will remain as a standard. The example case histories shown are clear and use traditional techniques of natal astrology and transits.

The many books comprising the *Textbook of Astrology: The Munich Rhythm Theory* (Munich, 1978) are extensive in their integration of astrology and homoeopathy, but the overall system for interpretation is awkward and rambles, leaving the student with more unanswered questions than sound principles for practice.

The text which bridges the gap between natal, medical and psychological astrology is the *Combination of Stellar Influences* (Aalen, 1972) also called CSI, by Reinhold Ebertin. This is the handbook of Cosmobiology, an integrated study of astrology and biology. Ebertin lists correspondences so that astrologers learn to apply the information from the horoscope to the intelligent and beneficial application of the cosmogram in the treatment of illness, which will be coloured by mental reservations, anxieties or aggressions.[5] Ebertin demonstrates that the horoscope has great potential advantages for the psychotherapist or homoeopath, as well as the medical doctor. Cosmobiologists are encouraged to treat their clients as doctors do their patients, by presenting the problem flatly, without possible causes or solutions. The information is essential but the bedside manner leaves something to be desired.

Illnesses signify many things about a person, and their causes are always connected to the whole organism rather than isolated incidents. In this model, disease is inseparable from health and is an essential communication between an individual and his or her world. Ebertin investigated in particular detail the flow of afflictions through families and hereditary lines, and his son Baldur Ebertin, a practising psychotherapist, has continued the brilliant work.

The format of CSI and the intelligence behind it is a great contribution. Ebertin placed the greatest importance on the relationship of planets to each other, and devalued the significance of planets in signs or houses. CSI is comprised of the seventy-eight possible combinations of planets to each other, i.e. Sun/Moon, Sun/Mercury, Sun/Venus ... ASC/MC. Each combination occupies two facing pages (Figure 1) and contains its primary Principle, Psychological Correspondences (positive, negative and neutral), Biological Correspondences, Sociological Correspondences and Probable (event) manifestations. On the opposite page, the planetary pair is compared to all the other planets, so that a total of over 1,100 such pictures is included. The biological and psychological qualities relating to each planetary combination can be seen as corresponding aspects of each other, reflecting our experiences as we function on the psychological and biological levels simultaneously. To suggest such a separation is not only artificial but misleading.

Since the 1950s it has become fashionable to correlate psychology with astrology, and indeed many believe passionately that astrology and psychology are primary to the exclusion of other branches of astrology. In their mind, medical astrology or predictive astrology are counter-productive and damaging to health and well being. The psychological viewpoint is clearly demarcated by the following assumptions.

- First, the world of the psyche is central to being and it is from the psyche that outer events issue, therefore psychology is more important than the mundane realities of the world.
- Second, as the object of life is to utilise 'free will', any prediction will inhibit or eliminate such freedom of action by

Principle
Irritability and inhibition, tension.

Psychological Correspondence:
+   The ability to cope with every situation, the power to pull
    through and to endure, perseverance and endurance, inde-
    fatigability, will-power, determination.

-   Unusual emotional tensions or strains, irritability, emo-
    tional conflicts, rebellion, the urge for freedom, a provo-
    cative conduct, an act of violence.

C   A self-willed nature, tenaciousness and toughness, ob-
    stinacy, strong emotional tensions or stresses.

Biological Correspondence:
Inhibitions of rhythm, heart-block, Cheyne-Stokes' breathing. -
Unrhythmical processes. - A sudden loss of limbs (a chronic
illness in this sense); operations accompanied by the removal of something. (Removal of intestinal parts, spleen,
amputation etc.)

Sociological Correspondence:
Violent people.

Probable Manifestations:
+   Growth of strength caused through the overcoming of diffi-
    culties, difficult but successful battles in life for the purpose
    of overcoming a dangerous situation. (Operation).

-   Kicking against tutelage and against the limitation of freedom,
    the tendency to cause unrest within one's environment, a
    quarrel, separation, the use of force, interventions in one's
    destiny, the limitation of freedom.

Figure 1 A page from Ebertin's

0867= ☉   Physical exposure to severe tests of strength, the power of resistance, rebellion, inflexibility. - Separation.

0868= ☽   Strong emotional tensions and strains, states of depression, inconstancy. - The sudden desire to liberate oneself from emotional stress, separation from members of the female sex.

0869= ☿   The making of great demands upon one's nervous energy, the ability to hit back hard under provocation, the ability to organise resistance, the act of separating oneself from others. - Necessary changes.

0870= ♀   Tensions or stresses in love-life often leading to separation.

0871= ♂   An act of violence, the occasionally wrong use of extraordinary engergy, undergoing great efforts and toil. - A violent or forced release from tensions or strains, the stage of challenging others for a decisive contest or fight. - Injury, accident, deprivation of freedom.

0872= ♃   The ability to adapt oneself to every situation, a fortunate release from tensions. - A sudden turn (in destiny), the misfortune to get into difficulties. - Losses, damage to buildings, motor damage.

0873= ♆   The inability to face emotional stresses, falsehood or malice caused through weakness. - A resolve to resign oneself to the inevitable, the abandonment of resistance, weakening strength, separation, mourning and bereavement.

0874= ♀   An act of violence or brutality. - The desire to overcome a difficult situation through extraordinary effort. - Rebellion against one's lot in life, harm through force majeure.

0875= ☊   The inability to integrate oneself into a community, provocative conduct. - Joint resistance to a common opponent, separation.

0876= A   Being placed in difficult circumstances, the fate of standing alone in the world. - The suffering of difficulties caused by others, experiencing emotional suffering together with others, mourning and bereavement.

0877= M   Making the highest demands upon one's own strength, rebellion, provocation. - The act of separating oneself from others.

Combination of Stellar Influences

either preventing natural events from happening, or affecting an individual's destiny through the power of suggestion inherent in the prediction itself.

- Third, the emotional life is the most important aspect of being, and psychology is the science of the emotional world.
- Fourth, the process of psychotherapy is subjective, personal, evocative and inherently haphazard and does not lend itself to the structure of astrology. Astrology seeks to identify patterns while psychology is content with being.

It might seem that psychology and astrology are in conflict, but there are many bridges. More and more psychotherapists are using astrological material as the basis for their work in an attempt to discover the basis of psychology when personal explorative work does not provide clear direction.

The reason why Ebertin's work is so valuable is that he shows the psychological and biological principles as integral components of all combinations of planets. Although there are many more books about psychological astrology than medical astrology, it would be valuable to state some of the more influential.

Dane Rudhyar was the first important psychological astrologer, as demonstrated in his classic *Astrology of Personality* (New York, 1963). He linked depth psychology with the concept of holism and developed a symbolic astrology of cycles. Rudhyar investigated and altered the distinction between good and bad aspects, felt that all variety of events should be interpreted constructively, and integrated many diverse ideas under the umbrella of astrology. In *Astrology and the Modern Psyche* (Reno, 1976), he analysed the horoscope and psychology of Freud, Jung, Adler, Assagioli and others from the view that they *were* their psychological concepts.

Stephen Arroyo made waves with *Astrology, Psychology and the Four Elements* (Vancouver, 1975) which presented an energetic approach reminiscent of Jung's concept of libido. Arroyo created a new attitude among astrologers with his direct notes on counselling, the education and training of astrological counsellors, and his attempt to create an anecdotal language for the integration of modern psychology and astrology.

Liz Greene's *Relating* (London, 1977) presented astrological concepts within a Jungian framework of psychological types related to the elements, the contrast and coincidence of inner and outer selves by way of analyses of the cycles of the outer planets, Saturn and Uranus. Greene uses astrology exclusively as a counselling tool, although not using it overtly in her psycho-analytic practice. She discourages prediction and encourages the freedom from self-imposed restraint. In 1986, she stated publicly that all astrologers should be trained as therapists and have undergone therapy themselves. Her stance has hardened the resolve of psychological astrologers and forced the confrontation between psychology and traditional astrology.

Thus the humanistic astrologers stated their case. Presently, astrologers must choose between the traditional and psycho-logical approaches, which leaves medical astrology as a largely forgotten wing. Modern astrology needs healing within itself just as it needs to bring back *healing* as a description of its integrated function.

The traditional astrological view is appealing and can be accurate, but a unified approach as presented in this book will perform the dual function of bringing psychology back into connection with biology, and provide a structural basis for astrology at all levels of being.

2

Astrology as a Healing Art

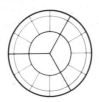

The Planets

The elements of medical astrology are the planets, the signs, the houses and the aspects. The planets are related to physical mechanisms and body systems. A general list is as follows:

Sun	Health, vitality, heart, circulation, the body, the cell
Moon	Fertility, bodily fluids, blood-serum, lymph, digestion
Mercury	Nervous system, the senses, speaking and hearing organs
Venus	Glandular products, hormones, kidneys, veins
Mars	Energy, body heat, muscles, sexual organs
Jupiter	Nutrition, organ systems, blood, liver, gall
Saturn	Skeletal system, heredity, stone formation, old age
Uranus	Body rhythms, pulse, breathing, peristalsis, synapses
Neptune	Solar plexus, aura, paralysis, drugs
Pluto	Regeneration, immune system, miasms, genetics, metabolism
ASC	Birth, physical appearance, the environment
MC	Brain function, ego-consciousness

The significance of the planets can be extended into other functions. The growth of psychology was supported by the planetary typology of the ancients, the correspondence of planets with general psychological types such as saturnine, jovial, lunatic, martial, venusian, mercurial and sunny. All of these words have entered the popular language as ways of describing certain people or ways of behaving.

THE THEORY OF CELESTIAL INFLUENCE

The model for cosmic order proposed by Rodney Collin involved a connection between the planets and endocrine glands which modulate all bodily activity through their secretions. Using the metaphor of 'man as the microcosm', he saw the planets spiral outwards from the Sun within the human body just as they do in space. Figure 2 shows the planets spiralling outwards from the

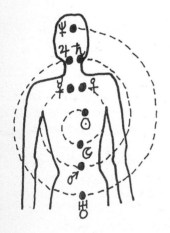

Figure 2 The Spiral of Glands outward from the Heart

Sun/thymus gland. What is intriguing about the connection is that the cycles of the planets correspond to the ages after conception at which the planets come into maximum activity. The horoscope shows where, around the circle of ages graded logarithmically/biologically, the planetary positions register. The sequence is an important model which yields great understanding of the connection between biology and astrology. The developmental stages of life fit within the three octaves and bring clarity to the life process.

Placing the heavenly bodies and the human functions thus synchronized in the order of their frequency round the circle, another strange parallel emerges. The first two functions, creation of physical form and involuntary movement, which begin before birth, do so without the need of air. Only at the third milestone or birth, does the shock of air enter. Two more functions follow, voluntary movement and the power of thought. Then, at the sixth milestone, yet another shock, the full emotional impact of impressions based on light, leads on to the further functions of maturity and to the potential function of consciousness.[1]

Each gland controls many nerve plexi in a threefold octaval arrangement corresponding to the three major systems in the body – cerebrospinal for consciousness, sympathetic for unconscious operation, and parasympathetic for instinctive control. The glands are active throughout life but their activity focuses at specific times when their function is primary. The planetary positions and relative strengths at the important birth time determine the individual 'type'. Collin likened the process to a series of spinning wheels like a complex combination safe which, at birth, is set to a particular code of numbers. Whenever any of the numbers are consequently activated, the glandular system in question becomes over or underactive. The unfolding of the endocrine gland system around the circle is quite precise.

Table 1   Glandular Release Cycles

Planet	Gland	Registration age
Moon	Pancreas	58 days after conception
Mercury	Thyroid	130 days after conception
Sun	Thymus	80 days after birth
Venus	Parathyroid	10½ months old
Mars	Adrenals	2 years 1 month
Jupiter	Posterior pituitary	12 years 6 months
Saturn	Anterior pituitary	29 years 6 months
Uranus	Gonads	84 years
Neptune	Pineal	165 years
Pluto	?	270 years

The *Moon cycle* activates the pancreas 58 days after conception (Table 1). The pancreas in turn activates the lymphatic system, which is responsible for the human immune response, and digestion, corresponding to the water balance affecting emotions. The Moon symbolises the feelings as derived from the relationship with mother, qualities inherited from mother and her ancestors, habit patterns, family systems, fluids in the body and waste products, and the water which composes much of the body. The Moon is related to the stomach and breast through its association with its ruling sign Cancer.

The *Mercury cycle* at 130 days governs the operation of the thyroid gland regulating combustion and body heat, corresponding to first involuntary movement and individual blood circulation. Mercury is communication, intellect, mind and naturally functions through the nervous system and chemical message transmission. The respiratory system is also mercurial through its association with the lungs in Gemini.

The *Sun cycle*, 365 days after conception or 85 days after birth, activates the thymus gland setting the growth in motion and the focus and reception of light. The Sun is life force, vitality, consciousness and disease resistance, and also shows qualities, strengths and weaknesses inherited from father and paternal ancestors.

The *Venus cycle* occurs 10½ months after birth with the parathyroid gland governing mediation and stabilising mechanisms, promoting muscle tone and nerve formation. Venus is the inherent sense of harmony of the organism, its ability to maintain equilibrium, and its appearance, particularly the hair.

The *Mars cycle* at 25 months after birth activates the medulla and cortex of the adrenal glands, heightening sensitivity and producing the 'fight and flight' mechanism. Mars is physical activity and movement, the muscular system and particularly the red blood cells which provide energy to the body.

The *Jupiter cycle* at 12½ years, at the peak of the growth in life, controls involuntary muscles and the nutritive pattern of the body by the posterior pituitary gland. Jupiter governs growth in general, the distribution of fat, the liver and the arterial system.

The *Saturn cycle* at 29½ years signals the end of growth, crystallisation of the skeletal system and the increase of abstract thought. By this time it is clear what the limitations of physical and mental bodies are, and establishing control over the mental–physical body is important. Saturn describes grandparents, particularly those from whom hereditary patterns are received, and the relationship of the minerals to the body and its functions. These qualities affect the reaction to ageing of the body.

These first seven planets, the classic planets of the ancients, are the only ones to make their cycles within a human lifetime. The outer planets have much longer cycles, and as a result govern the collective, generational and civilisational qualities carried by the individual. In medical astrology the outer planets correspond to the *miasms* identified by Hahnemann, the generational afflictions we all carry within us which may or may not be activated by the events of our life. These miasms typically lie dormant at the core of our health and are carried genetically from our parents and ancestors.

The *Uranus cycle* of 84 years relates to the gonads which regulate sexuality, modulated by the Venusian parathyroid and the Mars adrenals. Uranus often represents the expressions of energy which are thrust upon the individual such as accidents and surgical interventions, which are extreme and sudden alterations of bodily rhythms.

The *Neptune cycle* of 165 years relates to the pineal gland, the 'third eye' of eastern mysticism governing extrasensory perception, sensitivity and psychic equilibrium, as well as the reaction to drugs. Neptune is the imaginary life, fantasy, visualisation and the ability of the body to assimilate toxins or to accommodate anaesthetics.

The *Pluto cycle* of 265 years has no gland associated with it, although the entire immune system is appropriate. Pluto is related to abnormal cellular growths and the excretory functions.

The glands work together in regulating the entire physical, emotional and mental bodies. Health is often the synchronisation of the inner glandular workings of the body and their outer form in the world. The relative strengths of glands reflect the astrological position of their equivalent planets in the horoscope.

The planets are archetypes and subpersonalities on the psychological level, both the characters in life outside us and ways of behaving within us, glands and bodily systems on the physical level, chakras on the psychospiritual levels and ways of behaving on the emotional level. Their interaction through geometrical aspect connections within the centre of the horoscope is the web of relationships through which our life energy travels or is blocked. The pure energy of conception is channelled and directed into higher and higher forms as we gain a body, then directed in behaviour within the family and tested in the world outside in maturity. Through this concept it is possible to see exactly where, when and how energy can be turned back onto the individual – often the primary cause of illness. Illness can be diagnosed from the horoscope and the entire concept of the dating of the creation and release of disease is at the core of astrological healing.

The Four Elements

The elements fire, earth, air and water are metaphors for the ways in which an individual functions. Fire is energy, the spirit body and the intuitive psychological function; earth is substance, the physical body, and the sensation function; air is mind, communication, the mental body and the thinking function; and water is emotion, the emotional body and the feeling function. Every human carries these four levels of being and illness may manifest at any or all of these levels. For example, some afflictions are emotionally caused, such as depression. Others are mentally caused, the so-called psychosomatic illnesses or worry, anxiety and neuroticism. Still others are overtly physical, such as accidents, muscle strains and functional problems. The base category is the energetic or spiritual problems which underlie the others and create a lack of energy. There are ten planets in astrology and it is easy to see which and how many planets are in each of the four elements. Sometimes an element will have no planets, in which case the function carried by that element will be deficient and will force compensation.

The Signs of the Zodiac

Zodiac signs represent parts of the body, conditioning qualities through which the planets act, times of the year, and the twelve-fold stages of the archetypal developmental process of nature. Although many astrologers place the primary weight upon the sign in which the Sun resides, in medical astrology the planets affect all the signs in which planets are located, although obviously some more than others. The signs locate the parts of the body where dysfunction is likely to manifest. As the founder of homoeopathy, Samuel Hahnemann, noticed, many illnesses or afflictions are seasonal in nature, implying that they may be due to the Sun passing through a sequence of signs and activating the parts of the body in succession.

It is also important to recognise that the signs of the zodiac are not isolated but intimately related to their opposites. The functions of the throat of Taurus are reciprocal to the sexual organs of Scorpio, as the castrati could testify. All signs are continuously acting with their opposites. When one sign is activated, the opposite sign always receives an equal and opposite reaction, although often internalised. As an example of this action, the stress of dealing with a paternal Capricornian outside world produces tension which will be felt in the inner body as a Cancerian stomach upset or ulcer. Sometimes opposite signs produce very similar effects. Both Gemini (lungs and arms) and its opposite Sagittarius (sciatic nerve and thighs) tend to produce lung trouble, breathing problems and broken limbs. Leo is the heart and Aquarius the circulatory system, and tensions which come from self-conscious Leo tendencies can generate heart trouble and circulatory dysfunction. One of the most obvious but least recognised is the mental stress of Aries created when Libran relationships do not work out as well as expected. The entire healing practice of reflexology or metamorphic technique uses foot massage as a way for stimulating not only the digestive tract

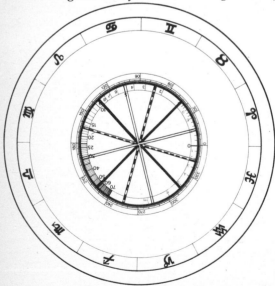

Figure 3 Three Crosses

of Virgo, but also the entire organism. Each pair has its unique dynamic within the mechanism of opposites.

Beyond the connections between opposite signs of the zodiac, in medical astrology the *crosses* or quadruplicities (Figure 3) are also critical. The crosses are the fixed cross (Taurus, Leo, Scorpio and Aquarius), the cardinal cross (Aries, Cancer, Libra and Capricorn) and the mutable cross (Gemini, Virgo, Sagittarius and Pisces). By determining which cross is particularly activated at a time of crisis, the medical astrologer can go further in discovering the root cause of many chronic conditions. Usually, the cross with the greatest number of planets is the one most likely to be affected, but the whole horoscope must be considered. In determining which cross is strongest, the positions of the ASC and MC must also be considered.

Each sign of the zodiac has a cell salt which supports its mechanism, and often health can be restored by correct administration of the appropriate cell salts. The correlations are included in the following table of signs. (The dates of each sign are approximate.)

Aries – cardinal fire sign   21 Mar to 21 Apr

Kali Phos and Nat Phos

Aries governs the head, the cranium and particularly the cerebrum, the motor centres of the brain which regulate all mental and physical activity. Afflictions of Aries are headaches, neuralgia, cerebral haemorrhages, mental deficiency and epilepsy. Aries is opposite Libra.

Taurus – fixed earth sign   21 Apr to 21 May

Nat Sulph and Calc Sulph

Taurus governs the ears, nose and throat, the adenoids, tonsils and larynx, the cerebellum, and the thyroid gland in association with Mercury, and determines the consumption and elimination of food. Afflictions of Taurus are inflamed tonsils or adenoids, goitre, diphtheria, croup, sore throat or problems with teeth. Taurus is opposite Scorpio.

Gemini – mutable air sign

Kali Mur and Silica

21 May to 21 Jun

Gemini governs the arms, hands, lungs and shoulders and the central nervous system, while having governance over the respiratory function. Afflictions of Gemini are bronchitis, tuberculosis, nervous disorders, pleurisy and other lung disorders. Gemini is opposite Sagittarius.

Cancer – cardinal water sign

Calc Fluor and Calc Phos

21 Jun to 21 Jul

Cancer governs the stomach, breasts, the sternum, the diaphragm, and also coverings (meninges) of the brain, lung and heart, and processes and sustains the body. Afflictions of Cancer are digestive disorders, ulcers, gastric complaints, dyspepsia, meningitis, dropsy and disorders of the lymph glands. Cancer is opposite Capricorn.

Leo – fixed fire sign

Mag Phos and Nat Mur

21 Jul to 22 Aug

Leo governs the heart, the dorsal spine, the vena cava and the coronary arteries, having domain over the vital and circulatory system. Afflictions of Leo are heart disease, arterial sclerosis and back pains. Leo is opposite Aquarius.

Virgo – mutable earth sign

Kali Sulph and Ferr Phos

22 Aug to 21 Sep

Virgo governs the abdominal region, digestive juices, the spleen, the intestinal tract and the duodenum, the lower lobes of the liver, and its function is digestive and assimilative. Afflictions of Virgo are peritonitis, malnutrition, diabetes or hypoglycemia, colitis, diarrhoea, diverticulitis, colic or bowel irregularities. Virgo is opposite Pisces.

Libra – cardinal air sign   21 Sep to 21 Oct

Nat Phos and Kali Phos

Libra governs the kidneys, the suprarenals, the lumbar region of the spine, and as the centre of gravity of the body is regulative and balancing. Afflictions of Libra are primarily malfunctions of the kidneys' ability to eliminate poisonous waste from the body, inflammation of the kidneys, nephritis, lower back pain, oedema, skin rashes or eczema, blood disorders, acidosis or Bright's disease. Libra is opposite Aries.

Scorpio – fixed water sign   21 Oct to 21 Nov

Calc Sulph and Nat Sulph

Scorpio governs the bladder, urethra, genital organs, the rectum and descending colon, the sigmoid flexure and prostate gland, and its functions are eliminative and generative. Afflictions of Scorpio are prostate gland enlargement, all sorts of ailments which stem from a malfunctioning colon, venereal diseases, bladder infections, diseases of the womb, cervix or uterus, menstrual problems, constipation, haemorrhoids, cystitis, hernias or sterility. Scorpio is opposite Taurus, and often nasal catarrh, throat infections, adenoids or polypi are indicated.

Sagittarius – mutable fire sign   21 Nov to 21 Dec

Silica and Kali Mur

Sagittarius governs the thighs, hips, femur, ilium, coccygeal and sacral regions of the spine, sciatic nerves, buttock muscles and the great saphenous vein, and is locomotive and supportive. Sagittarius afflictions are hip disease, locomotor problems, sciatica, rheumatism, backache, gout, paralysis, pelvic disruptions, spasms and cramping. Sagittarius is opposite Gemini, and hence relates to the expiration of air as Gemini is its inhalation.

Capricorn – cardinal earth sign   21 Dec to 21 Jan

Calc Phos and Calc Fluor

Capricorn governs the knees, the skin, the skeleton and the gall bladder, and its function is protective and structural. Capricorn afflictions are rheumatism, arthritis, broken bones, eczema and other skin diseases, partially caused by the reflex action from the Cancerian stomach. Capricorn is opposite Cancer.

Aquarius – fixed air sign

Nat Mur and Mag Phos

21 Jan to 21 Feb

Aquarius governs the ankles, tibia, fibula, achilles tendon and the circulation system which supplies the body with oxygen. Afflictions of Aquarius include varicose veins, sprained ankles, dropsy, blood poisoning, cramp, toxaemia, coordination and circulation problems. Aquarius is opposite Leo.

Pisces – mutable water sign

Ferr Phos and Kali Sulph

21 Feb to 21 Mar

Pisces governs the feet and toes, the system of lymph glands and hence the immune system, and functions as a discriminative and distilling function. Afflictions of Pisces include poisoning, drug overdoses, drug reactions, mucous conditions, catarrh, swollen glands, poor circulation, pneumonia, deformed feet, bunions or fallen arches. Pisces is opposite Virgo.

Houses

Houses describe the sequence of developmental stages of life, from conception to old age and death. They are the timing phases of life which structure our lives and reality. In traditional medical astrology they determine how conditions manifest, but this particular issue is the primary subject of Chapter 4 about Life★Time Astrology and will be covered in more detail there.

Aspects of Life

Aspects (Figure 4) are the geometric interconnections which provide the 'web of relationships' by which planets connect with each other, by which events at various times of life interweave, and describe the inner dynamic and energetic working of the life process. The aspects are determined by dividing the circle of 360° by the numbers 1, 2, 3, 4, 6, 8 and 12. The resultant aspect angles have a range of values which they impart to the planets which subtend those angles. When the angular relationships are those

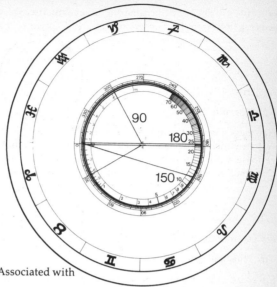

Figure 4 Hard Aspects Associated with
Medical Astrology

divisible by 2 (180°), 4 (90°) and 8 (45° and 135°), they are considered difficult and creative of tension, while the aspects divisible by 3 (120°), 6 (60°) and 12 (30°) are considered harmonious and stabilising. The quality of the aspect of unity, the conjunction of 0° is dependent upon the nature of the two planets involved. The 150° aspect, the inconjunct, is of particular significance in medical astrology as an aspect denoting frustration or chronic dilemmas. In medical astrology the *hard aspects* of 0°, 45°, 90° 135°, 150° and 180° are considered to produce illness and radical imbalance. These aspects are typically involved when there are blockages on any level. They are difficult, central and often painful, but simultaneously hold the key to growth and higher development. Illness usually signals times in life when drastic changes are necessary but resisted. The energy in a person's life travels through the aspect lines in the horoscope, easily by sextile and trine aspects and in a more resistant manner through the hard aspects (Figure 5).

* * *

Because each component of the astrological horoscope provides part of the whole picture of an individual's life in time, it is very useful as a model for placing the various therapies. The

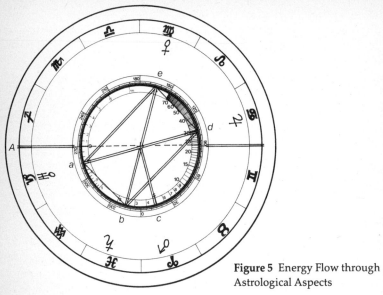

Figure 5 Energy Flow through Astrological Aspects

horoscope indicates which planets (and their equivalent glands or organ systems) are dominant, weak or isolated from the whole. This information permits the possibility of determining which parts of the psychophysical organism is most likely to be affected throughout life. The signs activated by planets, especially the malefic planets, indicate the body parts most likely to be affected, the aspects determine the extent or severity of the ailment and the degree of stress in operation on the individual, and the houses show the time of the developmental stage of life when the activity takes place.

Astrological healing arts are based on the use of astrology as an organising system for understanding, using and integrating alternative therapies. The astrological horoscope is a symbolic pattern in time which describes the whole person, according to the ideas of *Life★Time Astrology*[2] – a system which applies the concept of biological time to the life process and creates a revolutionary new model which allows the horoscope to be understood on physical, emotional, mental and spiritual levels. The life process as seen in the horoscope is an essential organising device for the use of healers, psychotherapists and any others who work with people. Using astrology as a guide, many have been directed to appropriate therapies and therapists. A more detailed and systematic synthesis of these ideas is leading to a new dimension of therapeutic networking. There are many ways in which astrology is appropriate for this task.

The life process as described by the sequence of twelve houses and their integrated signs shows the ages at which particular qualities are in operation and when each element is dominant. We all go through phases in our lives when physical values are dominant, and others when emotional satisfaction is most important.

The Advantages and Limitations of Medical Astrology

Medical astrology is the diagnosis of disease or the tendency to disease using the horoscope, but it is by no means complete or foolproof. It is important to understand its limitations as well as its benefits.

Although most medieval doctors were astrologers, this was a time when medicine was very primitive indeed. The range of diseases identified and the possible substances used for treatment were limited. In the last few centuries, especially since the development of man-made chemical drugs, there has been a profusion of substances, and with the rapid pollution of the environment and the foods we eat the entire process of diagnosis has become extremely complex. The complexity is exaggerated by the medical treatment people receive during their lives.

Since astrology has been excluded from the universities, astrologers must approach medical astrology as sensitive, intuitive and skilful amateurs rather than as medical professionals. Some doctors are practising astrologers, but they are few and far between. Why then, would someone consult an astrologer about medical issues?

The answer is contained in the context of astrology. In describing an individual's life from a psychological perspective or a traditional astrological viewpoint of personality analysis, it is inevitable that the correspondences between a person's psychological state and their physical state are made obvious.

There is a science of cycles which encompasses both the psychological and biological with the astrological – Ebertin's Cosmobiology. His *Combination of Stellar Influences* can be used as a textbook to determine astrological events for character analysis or prediction, and it is obvious that every characterological or psychological mechanism correlates with a biological mechanism. An example is the Venus/Saturn combination. Venus is hormonal balance and Saturn is restriction and the action of the anterior pituitary gland. When Venus and Saturn are in contact, Saturn restricts the hormonal balance of Venus, producing depression, difficult expression of sexuality and even glandular malfunctioning. The psychological qualities of Venus/Saturn are: soberness, a sense of duty, reserve, faithfulness, self-control, inhibited emotional expression, dissatisfaction, and an unhealthy expression of sexual urges. They often manifest as relations with older people or those who are emotionally repressed, difficulties in love relationships or separation from the mother, which is probably its deepest root. The glandular function parallels the psychological function.

Although when using traditional astrology it is possible to find the planetary mechanism responsible for an affliction and the symbolic pattern which activates illness, it is often difficult to determine which mechanism is the *cause* of the problem. When Venus or Saturn, or the Venus/Saturn midpoint are activated by the transits (actual passage of a body in the sky) of other planets, the mechanism operates on both emotional and biological levels. The implication is that our emotional reality is intimately connected to our physical health. Astrology is usually more useful after the fact than beforehand, although as you will see, this is changing.

Using medical astrology it is possible to identify health trends and behavioural patterns in the horoscope. Most doctors can identify symptoms but rarely know (or care) which aspect of the psychological mechanism was the cause. A psychotherapist could, after a number of therapy sessions, enable an individual to identify the emotional or mental issues or blockages behind personal problems, but typically cannot relate these to overt disease symptoms, nor determine even approximately when they are likely to recur. Astrology has the great advantage of being able to describe the individual's life on all these levels simultaneously, and as the planets move through the skies in predictable cycles, it is possible to determine exactly when a particular pattern is to be activated again.

Astrology can identify times of life when imbalances or problems which could manifest as disease will occur, although with traditional techniques this requires a great deal of time to work out accurately. The general type of affliction can be determined together with the time period involved. This information can be very valuable in altering habits and taking preventive measures. For instance, people with the Sun in Leo in difficult aspect to Mars are prone to heart attacks in middle age and beyond, therefore it is advisable for them to minimalise their consumption of fatty meats, dairy products, tobacco and alcohol. Many of the basic diagnoses of a medical astrologer are obvious and involve recognising which habits support good health and which habits undermine health for a particular problem.

Medical astrology, unless practised by individuals with therapeutic or medical training, cannot go beyond analysis. Astrology is not recognised as a therapy in itself, although great therapeutic value can result from an astrological reading. What astrology can provide is a context in which any other therapy may function and a symbolic language which will support other therapies. All medical astrological advice should be checked and supported by the appropriate therapist. Medical astrology cannot exist outside the context of other therapies, and indeed depends upon such connections for its effectiveness. Often the most valuable information an astrologer can give a client is in the form of recommendations of which therapies are appropriate for prevention and cure.

A fundamental problem of the current alternative therapy movement is that while many therapies appear to be holistic, in reality it is impossible for any therapy to be everything for even one person. Modern people are so complex that it is inevitable that multiple therapies are required just as multiple relationships are required. One drawback is that the counselling skills which are necessary in alternative therapy are often lacking, the same complaint often levelled at medical doctors. When a Rolfer does deep tissue massage it is common for quite powerful emotional contents to well up and even to be expressed through pain, crying, laughing, trauma and many other ways. While the best Rolfers are aware of and work with these phenomena, there are some who simply do not have the same level of skill or experience at counselling as they do with manipulation (and probably should not be expected to). The same is often the case with alternative therapists, although many take counselling or psychotherapeutic courses or training to enhance their skills. Most therapists today must have counselling and even psycho-therapeutic skills in order to understand the immensely valuable and important psychological material which is always associated with diagnosis and treatment, as well as the dynamics of the therapeutic process itself. As astrology is itself a counselling medium it is possible to integrate counselling with therapeutic advice.

Allopathic doctors often overlook their own health, or treat themselves with the same drug-based cures as their patients, but among alternative therapists it should be only occasionally that the therapist does not reflect and demonstrate the efficacy of his or her therapy. But that does not prevent the girl in the health food shop from having terrible skin problems.

While the notoriously high suicide rate for medical doctors is highly publicised, the incidence of 'burn-out' for alternative therapists is also quite high and probably just as great a problem. Astrology has the great merit of providing an exchange of information from the therapist to the patient and vice versa. Astrology as a language has been used for millennia and can express ideas and feelings which can only be otherwise expressed with great difficulty. In addition, through comparing the horo-scopes of the therapist and client, many realisations emerge which are mutually important.

Astrology and the Art of Healing is a unified approach to astrology and healing which are relevant to therapists and clients alike in this time of revolutionary changes.

3

The New Healing Paradigm

The Well is the symbol of that social structure which, evolved by humanity in meeting its most primitive needs, is independent of all political forms. There is one prerequisite for a satisfactory healing organization for humanity. We must go down to the very foundations of life. For any merely superficial ordering of life that leaves its deepest needs unsatisfied is as ineffectual as if no attempt at order had ever been made.[1]

Symptoms are the means by which the body-mind communicates and should not be regarded as annoying irritations. When this concept is understood, the entire idea of healing undergoes a profound change. When symptoms are summarily dismissed, their root causes simply return in more awkward and infinitely more painful forms, often in unrelated organs and organ systems. For true healing to result, it is necessary to discover and contact the root issues which have originally caused an affliction. In many instances, these are not merely the results of recent imbalances but of influences carried since childhood or even gestation. While some types of psychotherapy are very successful for locating and working with such material, few therapies acknowledge the existence of other approaches and most therapists do not have access to these other techniques. The dilemma is to integrate the physical and the psychological.

The discovery and elimination of root causes is at the core of the new healing paradigm. A very common example will illustrate this. As a result of the typical diet of dairy products, refined foods and meat, we gather and store toxins in our colon. Through time the colon wall becomes completely clogged with toxic waste material. From then on, even the best diet possible will not have its desired effect because the nutrients cannot be assimilated through the now impermeable colon wall. Even fasts do not have their desired effect because the toxic material will simply work in a more concentrated form to poison the system. In order for any dietary programme to work it is necessary first to cleanse the colon. The colon is a first cause of many diseases which are usually attributed to other sources. One of the primary techniques for detoxification is the practice of colonic irrigation, where the colon is cleansed with water until blockages have been rinsed away. At that point it becomes valuable to work on those afflictions which have originated in the impure colon. The process of cure must work from the deepest core outwards to the surface of the psyche or body. Likewise, homoeopathy cures by gradually bringing the irritations which lie within the body to the surface.

In modern psychotherapy the core issues are of critical importance, even though the most sophisticated psychotherapy cannot always approach the deepest traumas which are the source of modern illness. The reason is that the causes lie not only in childhood but also in gestation. We inherit many of our behavioural tendencies from our parents. In gestation we repeat the process of evolution and this collective unconscious contains myriad images and instincts which we all carry. In our lives we create a personal history but we also contain a much deeper and more powerful history embedded in the world of archetypes. In order to identify these influences astrology is essential. Using the Life★Time method of interpreting the horoscope, it is possible to create a healing profile which extends back to conception itself. To put Life★Time astrology in its proper perspective, a context for the connection of healing and astrology must be established.

The Microcosm and the Macrocosm

The medieval conception of the world was very different from our understanding today. For the medieval mind the world was created by and composed of a web of powerful and mysterious spiritual forces fathomed by the few. Most early doctors were also astrologers, and for very good reason, since the backbone of early medicine was herbalism and herbs were categorised and organised through astrological correspondences. According to the principle of correspondences, also called the doctrine of signatures, everything in the world is organised into categories or classes of phenomena which are in mutual relationship. To understand the relationships of bodies to each other, and humans to the cosmos within which they are born and die, is a critical aspect of their world view.

The Renaissance diagram (Figure 6) designed by Robert Fludd (1574–1637) illustrates the relationship between the microcosm (the little world) and macrocosm (the large world). In the centre a man is astride the concentric circles (the microcosm) of the planets known at the time, from the Sun to Saturn, surrounded by the fixed stars of the zodiac. Within the circles of planetary spheres lie the deeper and more symbolic levels of the elements. Surrounding the microcosmic man is another circular layer of concentric planetary spheres (the macrocosm) which reflects the inner layer exactly. This second ring is the macrocosm, within which the Sun and Moon are also shown. The inner world reflects and acts in accordance with the outer world, giving rise to medieval expressions like 'as above, so below' and 'the microcosm is the macrocosm'. Fludd believed that there was an archetypal world within which the movements and actions of the outer world were originated, formed and governed. The two worlds reflected each other and had a reciprocal relationship. The human being was the bridge between the two worlds, the mundane and the divine.

The most astonishing and revealing point about Fludd's diagram is easily missed as a detail. Enwrapping the two worlds is the triple winding of a spiral cord or rope which leads off into the skies, being pulled by an angel. It is my contention that this cord which binds the microcosm to the macrocosm is a symbolic

Figure 6 Cover from *Utriusque Cosmi . . . Historia*, by Robert Fludd

representation of the genetic code DNA, the spiralling heliacal pattern which creates organic form and governs growth, perceived by Fludd as the spiralling path of the planets through time. Although it sounds like an antique idea, the movements of the planets against the fixed stars have a direct bearing on life and provide an explanation for many important healing mechanisms. What has changed is that this relationship can be defined mathematically and is supported by modern physics, mathematics, astronomy and biology.

We are taught that the planets orbit around the Sun, which is a stationary star in space. This static image derives from the theories of the Greek Euclid and the astronomical theories of Galileo, and was the prevailing view of the Solar System until the time of Einstein. This view, however, bears only a passing resemblance to reality. The Sun travels through space, around the centre of the Milky Way galaxy at a rate of about 750,000 kilometres per day.

When the orbits of the planets are shown spiralling around the central filament of the Sun's path (Figure 7), the entire pattern functions as a huge step-down transformer of cosmic energies as it winds its way through space. The inner planets, Mercury and Venus, make tight spirals around the Sun, and the Earth makes its complete spiral in one year. The planets beyond Earth trace their patterns more gradually, and the asteroid belt presents itself as a hazy cylinder between Mars and Jupiter. The outermost planets take hundreds of years to make the entire journey around the Sun.

The Sun in turn makes its spiralling path around its sun, reputed to be the star Sirius, in an estimated 50 million years, which in turn revolves around the centre of the Milky Way galaxy. This system of spirals within spirals is responsible for the higher level order of our universe, which is reflected in all matter. The form and mathematics of the 'music of the spheres' is the source of all physical and metaphysical laws. What is not commonly realised is that the spiralling solar system is similar in form to the double helix of genetic code, DNA, which creates and regulates all living organisms on earth.

The way in which the spiral of the solar system communicates with the genetic code in each cell nucleus is through *resonance*. Resonance is a synchronised vibrational communication be-

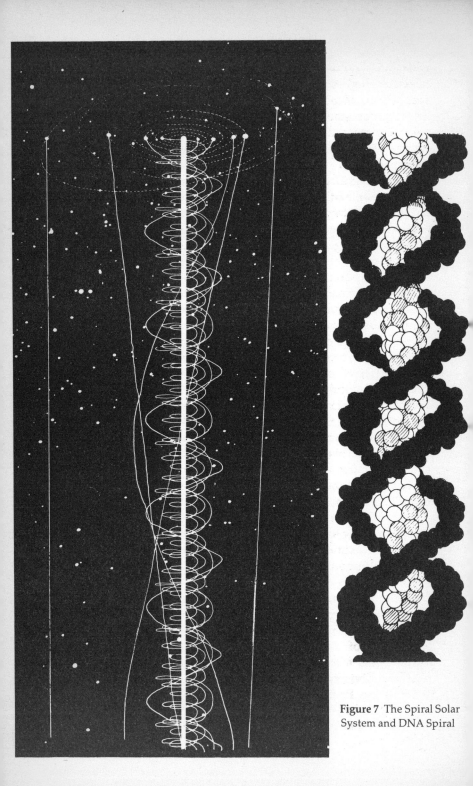

Figure 7 The Spiral Solar
System and DNA Spiral

tween any bodies which have similar patterns through time and space. Since all bodies in the universe are constantly moving, there is resonance everywhere. The DNA molecule within each cell resonates with the Solar System in the macrocosm and creates and partakes of a simultaneous two-way transmission of information.

The astrological horoscope is a slice through the spiralling Solar System, taken with the birthplace at the centre and disposed at an angle reflecting the time of the day and year of birth. All individual horoscopes are a succession of relative slices, disposed at varying angles. In a cosmic sense we all represent a series of relative viewpoints participating in the same cosmic mechanism. Astrology is the science and art of decoding the relative significance of these slices of time.

Although most astrologers only know the horoscope as a circle, when the spiral is diagrammed, it becomes quite clear that an individual lifetime is much more than just one slice, but rather a cylinder corresponding in length to the duration of a lifetime. While we often say that life 'begins' at birth, we are conceived about nine months earlier, and in the spiralling system this would spiral back before birth. The duration of life is a continuation of the cosmic pattern ahead in time. An entire life is a cylinder beginning with conception and ending at death, although even this is a simplification. In a very real sense, we are not created from nothing, nor does life just end at death. The causes brought into being at conception are a continuation and inheritance from our parents and ancestors, and the entire pattern of our energies in time cannot disappear at death. They certainly dissipate but never completely disappear. All patterns of all lives in time remain as parts of the continuing spiralling pattern of our solar system, available for decoding.

Astrology is a symbol system, usually used for describing character traits and predicting events from the movements of planets, but which in reality is a way to decode genetics. The similarities are powerful. The genetic code has four acid bases, each of which has three modes of operation, while astrology has four elements, each acting in three modes. The twelvefold division is common to both systems. Recent research by Professor Percy Seymour,[2] Maurice Cotterell[3] and others supports the hypothesis that astrology and biology are related systems in nature.

In early history the Egyptians, Indians, Chinese and many others recognised unconsciously that astrology was truly a *cosmic code*. An Egyptian stone carving (Figure 8) shows the 'twelve

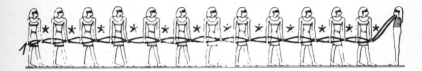

Figure 8 The Egyptian Double Cord

'Those who carry the intertwined double cord from which the stars come out.' Thus are designated the twelve persons who extract the double cord from the mouth of Aken. Knowing that at each hour a star is born, we can understand the rest of the text which says that at each new twist, an hour is born, then, after the passage of the Great Neter, Aken reswallows the cord (thus making time go backwards).
(*Book of Gates*, 5th division)

persons who extract the double cord from the mouth of Aken'.[4] As can be seen, the twelve figures alternating with stars hold an entwined cord originating in the mouth of the creator god Aken. This *chain* of causality, life and activity is the motivating force in life. Many more such images[5] are unmistakable representations of the genetic double helix within an astrological context. They symbolise the formative origin of life as coming from the stars. While many have taken this to mean that we were deposited here by visitors from another galaxy, the true implication is that the form of genetic code is derived from the movement of the planets around the Sun in time.

A relevant image is shown in *Hamlet's Mill*,[6] a book which investigates the origins of human knowledge and its transmission through myth. A central diagram shows the Egyptian gods Horus and Set in the act of drilling or churning. References are made to the Milky Way having been churned by the gods, but as can be clearly seen, Horus and Set are on either side of a spiralling tail which looks like the path of the solar system in time, and also, when the cartouche above is included in the image, human sperm. This is astonishing because sperm was only first seen in the nineteenth century – before then its structure was shrouded in mystery.

There are many representations of the human figure astride the world in medieval diagrams, which symbolised the use of correspondences by early doctors. They used astrology to determine which herbs would be useful for particular parts of the body. Such diagrams (Figure 9) show the human within a square, a circle, and an oval frame. In each case a correspondence is made between signs of the zodiac and parts and organs of the body. In the oval diagram, a complete range of body parts, diseases, herbs and other substances are shown.[7] Correspondences relate the physical world to energetic and spiritual worlds.

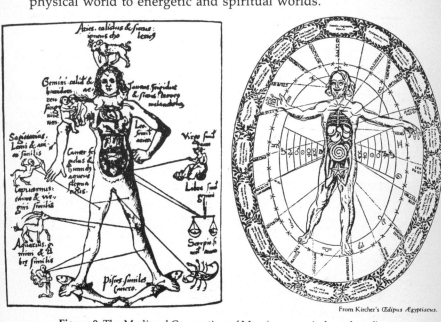

From Kircher's *Œdipus Ægyptiacus.*

Figure 9 The Medieval Conception of Man (square, circle and oval)

Bringing Past into Present

The speculations of Renaissance philosophers such as Fludd, John Dee and Giordano Bruno are very intriguing intimations of a cosmic science based on esoteric principles of correspondences. Unfortunately, the intolerance of the church ended the hopes for such a cosmic science. In recent years there has been renewed interest in these ideas which support ecology in the environment, vegetarian purification in diet, the campaign to eliminate additives in food, holism in medicine, peace in world affairs and the spiritual quest in the realm of religion. Embedded in this new movement is the concept of the *paradigm*. A paradigm is a 'constellation of beliefs, values, and techniques shared by the members of a given community'.[8] It is widely accepted at present that a shift of paradigm which will transform life on our planet is overdue. This is not only desired by a minority but is essential if our world is to survive into the twenty-first century. The change in attitude by people in the many different fields of finance, ecology, physics, psychotherapy, healing, astrology, spectrum consciousness and others is not one which ought to happen in some indeterminate future, but needs to occur in these areas now. Just as Freud transformed the prevailing attitude of the psyche and Einstein relativised the laws of physics, so a *humanistic paradigm shift* is coming into being.

The change requires the creation of an entirely new set of values which humanity can bring into the new century and which will stand up to the test of reality. As is very clear, in order for such a transformation to happen to the masses, it must originate with a few people changing their lives. At the moment, many therapists have difficulties manifesting their very positive views of human existence. Transformative therapists must demonstrate the new level of human relationships, and complementary healers must be healthy themselves. This is quite a challenge.

4
Life★Time Astrology

Biological Time

Astrology is 'knowledge of time', and a new way of under-standing time is emerging. In my books, *The Round Art: The Astrology of Time and Space* (1979) and *Life★Time Astrology* (1984), a system of astrology based upon the relativity of time was presented which integrated western scientific ideas with eastern philosophy.

In the early part of this century, Pierre Lecomte de Nouy investigated and formulated principles for *biological time*. Biological time is the mathematical correlation between the rate at which time is perceived by a living being and its respiration rate, metabolism, body weight, food consumption and age. By investigating the time wounds took to heal in soldiers of different ages, de Nouy discovered that there was a mathematical relationship between these factors. He proved the correlation in two ways, by measuring perception through the healing of wounds related to the age of the wounded, and by measuring the rate at which the eye receives images. The younger the person, the shorter the time it takes a wound to heal. The older one is, the slower the metabolism, the slower the respiration rate, the less rapidly the body consumes and processes oxygen, and the longer it takes for a wound to heal. What is surprising is that de Nouy's mathematical correlation was not arithmetic, but logarithmic. He estimated that the impression of the passage of time for a 20- and

50-year-old man would be four and six times faster than for a 5-year-old child.[1] The implications for healing are profound as it shows that the older one is when healing is required, the more slowly the body is able to recuperate.

Biological time is the relationship between metabolism and time perception. We perceive the passage of time in two very distinct ways which, nevertheless, are measured by the same mathematical proportions: one is biological, the other psychological.

Biologically, the passage of time is estimated by the number of images received by the brain in a given period of time. When metabolism increases, the rate at which images are received also increases. If in a normal state at a particular age one receives six images per second, this rate is the norm. When excited, the metabolic rate increases and nine images may be received each second. This would be interpreted by the brain as one and one-half seconds of duration instead of one second. Time would seem to move more slowly than normal. When metabolism decreases, only three images are received per second, but the brain will once again interpret it as only one-half of a second passing, and time would seem to pass very quickly. As metabolic rate slows down, time appears to pass faster.

The rate of metabolism is related primarily to age. At conception, when we are a microscopic single-celled fertilised ovum, the rate of metabolism is astonishingly rapid, at a 'molecular' level of change. As we develop within the womb, our body increases in size and the metabolic rate decreases until, finally, in later life it slows down so much that it stops altogether at death. This explains why time seems to pass very quickly, for example, when we are in school and a day seems to last forever, and certain, apparently insignificant, childhood perceptions are extremely vivid as though etched on our brain. As we age, our metabolism gradually slows down until towards the end of middle age we begin to notice it, yet our feelings about the passage of time continue to increase.

The change in metabolism is gradual with increasing age, but there are always local modulations. Excitement, stimulation and interest all increase metabolism, while boredom and depression decrease it. Our time sense is continually being altered by the food we eat, by the emotions we experience, by variation in sensory input, by our social life, sexuality, drugs, psychological states and physiological factors. What is always true is that the increase of metabolism is equivalent to youth, while its decrease is equivalent to old age. When we are stimulated we have the increase in energy like childhood and are engrossed by activities, but afterwards events seem to have passed extremely quickly. Days in childhood seem like years in middle age and decades in old age.

The psychological measurement of time acts according to the same mathematics and is embedded in our sense of memory. An entire lifetime of memories is built up from conception and added to continuously. Each perception in our life is naturally and instinctively compared to our memories of all other events to see if there are correlations. As each perception is added to the whole, we have a constantly increasing fund of memories. With every passing day more memories are added, so that as we age the total increases. Every day is complete in itself but it recapitulates all other days as well. If a mathematical logic were applied to this passage of time as measured by memory, on a day-by-day basis, the first day of life would be $\frac{1}{1}$ or 100 per cent of one's life. The second day is then $\frac{1}{2}$, the third day $\frac{1}{3}$, the seventh day $\frac{1}{7}$ and so on. Each day must be compared to the memory of all previous days. On the first birthday each day is $\frac{1}{365}$ of the whole, and at the age of about 30 each day is of the order of $\frac{1}{10,000}$ of the whole! The implication is that each day is a smaller and smaller proportion of the whole life. As a result, time seems to compact, to contract and to pass more quickly as we age.

The Three Bodies

The biological and psychological means of perceiving the passage of time are ascribed to the same mathematical correlation, that of a logarithmic progression. An arithmetic sequence 1, 2, 3 and 4 is equivalent to 1, 10, 100 and 1000 in a logarithmic progression (see Table 2). Rodney Collin related this base ten logarithmic sequence to the development of human life, by reasoning that the lifetime of the ovum is about one lunar month of twenty-eight days, while the lifetime of the cellular body is approximately 28,000 days or seventy-seven years. The intermediate divisions in life are at ten lunar months after conception, at birth, and at 100 lunar months after conception, the age of 7 years old at the end of childhood. This division creates three *octaves* in life from conception to death which increase in duration by factors of ten, but are equal perceptually.

Table 2 The Logarithmic Time Scale

Conception	Birth	End of Childhood	Death
1 LM	10 LM	100 LM	1000 LM
★	★	★	★
Gestation	**Childhood**	**Maturity**	
Physical Body	Emotional Body	Mental Body	

In *Gestation*, from conception to birth, the Physical Body is created within the mother. During this time we develop through the entire evolutionary process, with traces of brain and physical structures retained to carry influences within the final product. In the early stages we pass through what seem like reptilian, early vertebrate and other prehuman stages and retain the instincts associated with these evolutionary phases. The brain is created of spiralling germ layers and carries a record of our entire past encoded in its structure. During *Childhood*, from birth to about the age of 7 years old, we create an Emotional Body within the home and family system. We are exposed to emotionally patterned behaviour from parents, brothers and sisters, and either imitate or react against our family conditioning. The Personality is the emotional body, and we carry within our personality the traces of childhood emotional patterns encoded as behavioural mechanisms and conditioned responses, as distinct from the instinctual behaviour patterns of gestation. Therefore, it is implied that the emotional body is higher, finer, less dense and easier to change than the physical body, as indeed our experience would bear out. During *Maturity*, from the time when we begin forming relationships outside the family at school, at about 7 years old, until the end of life at death, we create a Mental Body within the world. Entrance into this developmental stage is contingent upon combining and integrating physical with emotional bodies to create a synthesis which we will express in the outside environment. The mental body contains all belief systems, ideas about the world, relationships, work and mar-

riage, and our intellectual structures. This third body is higher
and finer than the other two and also more flexible.

Each of these three bodies is created by every human in the
same sequence, but there is great variance regarding the relative
importance of each octave, and many other factors. As we age,
we create successively finer and higher bodies with which to
experience the world. At conception the entire whole is inherent
and through the life process we unfold our potential and create
being in life.

Life★Time Astrology

The image of the solar system spiralling through time, reverber-
ating with the genetic code double helix, leads to a more
profound understanding of the connection between the movement of the planets and genetics. The uniting principle between
the two is the perception of time and its correlation with
metabolic rate. The integration of Collin's general theory about
time with the specifics of astrology is critical.

Each person's life may be represented as a segment of the
spiralling movement of the solar system, like a cylinder beginning at conception and ending at death – corresponding to what
we consider to be the beginning and end of life. The astrological
horoscope is a slice through the spiralling circus of planets
(Figure 10) at a particular time, and can be decoded to describe
a present moment, although the accepted slice is that taken at
birth. The birth horoscope is a slice through the spiral path of the
solar system at an angle reflecting a specific time (along the
length of the spiral), a particular time of day (the orientation of
the Sun to the birth moment) and a specific place on Earth (the
latitude and longitude of the birthplace). The resultant plane
intersects at the birth moment.

Astrologers draw all manner of deductions and conclusions
from the horoscope of birth, assuming that the entire lifetime
is compacted into this one moment. Indeed, most astrologers
interpret a horoscope the same way whether the individual is 5
years old or 50. There is an acknowledgement that qualities
develop through life, but the conception of the birth horoscope is
the primary statement. This is a static view of the horoscope and

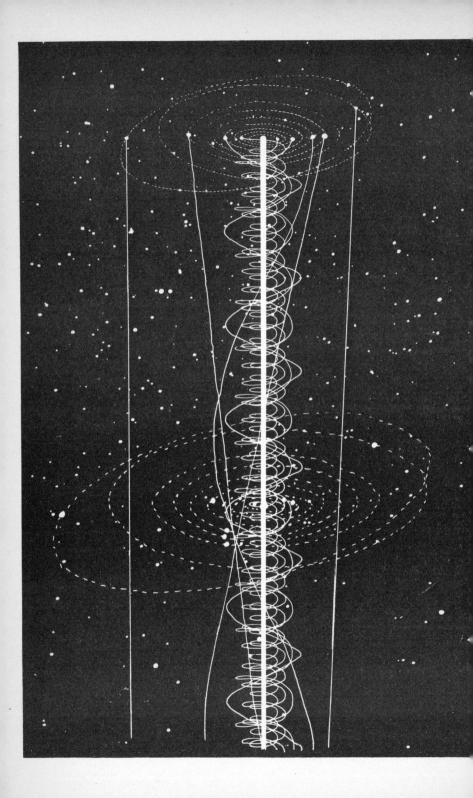

is a legacy from the prerelativistic era. The assumption is that the birth horoscope carries a pattern which is fully operational at birth. This hypothesis is central to science also; the idea that the universe is predictable, that effect follows cause, and that the rules which are in operation today will be in operation tomorrow.

A new perspective raised by Life★Time Astrology is that life is not static, two dimensional and flat, and that the reading of character from the horoscope is not enough, regardless of the level of sophistication of the psychology involved. Life is a *process in time*, beginning at conception and ending at death, and extending in influence both before and after these moments. It is the description of this process of life which is central to Life★Time Astrology.

When the three octave process of Gestation, Childhood and Maturity is superimposed on the birth horoscope, a unique and very valuable synthesis becomes evident. This synthesis is first of all a relationship between astrology and biology, and will be seen to be an integrating factor in psychology as well because it is artificial to separate the biological life from the psychological life.

There is universal agreement among astrologers (this is about the only astrological concept upon which there is such agreement) that the Ascendant (the eastern horizon point) is equivalent to the moment of birth. When the three octaves are aligned so that the Ascendant coincides with birth, the following diagram results (Figure 11).

The horoscope circle is a reference plane from which the cylindrical pattern above and below it can be construed. This issue raises an important new perspective on astrology that has many implications for astrology and healing. The life/cylinder does not originate from the void but begins with the uniting of sperm and ovum from the parents. In this sense the cylinder of life initially arises from the cylinder of the mother.

We inherit myriad impulses from our parents, their parents, *ad infinitum* all the way back to the first life, as well as influences

Figure 10 A Slice through the Spiralling Solar System

The logarithmically graded circle wraps around the horoscope so that the conception point is coincident to cusp of the 9th House. The end of childhood at about 7 years old corresponds to the cusp of the 5th House, and the end of life death-point coincides with the cusp of the 9th House again.

Figure 11 The Three Octaves and Life★Time Astrology Time Scale

from all humans.[2] Therefore, at the beginning of the cylinder, at conception, we do not start from scratch but inherit an entire genetic/astrological history. We enter the spiralling movement of the solar system at conception, and at that moment accept what the ancients called our *karma*, our inheritance of past lives, which we integrate with the human genetic code that we inherit. We enter the space-time continuum and are subject to the laws of the physical plane.

The pattern activated at conception is a spiritual legacy which finds form through the genetic code, affected by the common morphogenetic codes[3] which are shared by all humans. At this point, life is all potential and will ultimately unfold to fullness in time. The stages in development in life are transformations of potential into actual reality.

The logarithmic Life★Time scale superimposed on the horoscope is divided into three octaves, each of which is subdivided into four stages (Figure 11 and Table 2). The twelve houses of the horoscope describe the process of life from conception to death. The twelve signs of the zodiac are the archetypal significators of these twelve life stages. At each stage there are biological, physiological, psychological and outer events which must be taken into consideration and integrated before the next stage may be reached. The life energy is transformed and is graduated from level to higher level throughout life, either until a stage is reached when further progress is halted, forcing a regression to earlier levels, or the life is ended.

The integration of biological time with astrological houses creates a revolutionary picture of life in time, based on mathematically derived measurements. From the moment of conception, when father and mother make love and conception follows, the developmental stages of life are enacted against the influences from within in the form of genetic inheritance, embedded instincts and the spiritual legacy, and influences from without in the form of parents, family system, educational patterns and the life experience. The horoscope carries traces of all these levels of operation and the patterns are capable of being decoded.

Gestation is the creation of the physical body within the mother. During this time the entire evolutionary process is recapitulated, from one-celled organism to being fully human. The biological body is created in stages and the brain undergoes parallel programming. All events which register in gestation are qualified by the physical, emotional, mental and spiritual reality of the mother, and her circumstances, health and attitudes are crucial in the development of the body. All influences registered during gestation are stored within the body as either physical form, predispositions to certain physical behaviour patterns such as movement, or as basic instincts.

Childhood is the creation of an emotional body within the home and family system. At birth the personality, the vehicle of the emotional body, comes into independent existence in the world. In the following seven years the child must initially bond with the mother upon whom it is totally dependent for food and support, then experience and begin to accept the object-like character of the world, then walk and talk in communicating with others and finally perceive family relationships and the overall structure of the family. All this happens against the conditioning of the family's values, emotional attitudes, means and levels of expression, and many more factors. All the events of childhood are stored in emotional behaviour patterns within the personality. The important individuals in childhood are expressed as subpersonalities which have greater or lesser importance in the overall personality.

Maturity is the creation of a mental body within the outside world. At about the age of 7 years we begin to form relationships with others outside the immediate family structure. These relationships are made within or in reaction to school systems, racial, religious, cultural values and prevailing historical attitudes. We are educated, find a life work, make permanent relationships, produce family and live the remainder of our lives upholding a set of values which are our world view.

A fourth octave is available when there is a drive to live beyond the narrow confines of the physical life. Most people are conceived, born, mature and die, and they never attempt to extend their reality beyond their practical situation. Only in circumstances which threaten their lives do any people question their existence. Near death through battle, in accidents, in surgery, childbirth, emotional or physical shocks or similar events force one to consider what lies beyond. For the vast majority, life is a recirculation around the circle. They are locked into time. They may struggle early in life to find something indefinable, yet larger and more vivid, but give up the struggle before long. The two-dimensional life is like prison compared to freedom beyond the limitations of the body. The two-dimensional model of a mechanical lifetime is exactly like the common understanding of the form of the solar system as planets re-volving around a fixed sun. Life★Time Astrology is a way of looking at astrology and life which goes beyond the confines of life as we know it into the higher dimensions in which the cylindrical process of life in time parallels the cosmic movement.

The higher dimension is a *Transcendent* or *Transpersonal* octave which involves re-entering the gestation period on a higher level. Just as gestation started with an integration of male and female energies, so transcendence involves the conscious integration of animus and anima, our male and female essences. And, as in gestation, when our mother becomes aware that she is carrying a higher being within, so we recognise that our higher reality is within us. We must undergo a gestation to bring our higher nature to birth in the world after carrying it within.

Quite literally, we experience the events of our own gestation again as though they were happening within. The way in which we were created is a metaphor for the way in which we create our own higher reality in life. If we can reconstruct our own gestation, we are thereby enhancing creativity and reprogram-ming our higher being outside time. Problems during gestation reflect blockages on the archetypal planes of our life which may be preventing us from experiencing our transcendent Self. The events of gestation are a pattern which we enact in living our creative potential in life.

Gestation both begins and ends life in time, it completes and encloses the circle and provides us with an opportunity to go beyond the confines of the circle. In our lives the objective is to return to the beginning and to recognise it for the first time.

The Houses of Life

Every day, each significant event, each developmental stage, each life age is a stage of the transformation which is our life in time. The process of life begins at conception and extends until we die. The twelve houses of the horoscope describe this process in great detail.

At conception we are pure energy, spiritual energy which as yet has no form, but will rapidly attain a physical substance within which it operates. The pure energy at conception is gradually bound into matter in a physical body in more and more complex ways. As soon as the body is formed in prototype at birth, we begin creating an emotional body which is not tangible, but is probably more important. And upon reaching school age we begin creating our mental body composed of ideas and concepts. If we choose to advance beyond the three physical dimensions of life, the fourth transcendent level is the creation of a soul which will attain influence beyond the physical plane.

Life energy has been called by many names, including *prana, kundalini, libido, élan vital* or *pneuma, Reichenbach energy* or *orgone*. This energy must be transformed with each developmental stage of life into ever higher and finer forms. Freud identified that the total commitment to sucking for nutrition in early infancy is transferred to the oral function of speaking at a later age. When confronted with a difficulty in communication, a child will often regress to the earlier stage of sucking his thumb. Regression is a return to a previous level of expression together with its habits and mannerisms, a return to a time when energies were expressed more easily and comfortably. Our energies are transformed into more and more complex and demanding actions which express our nature more fully. The early stages happen in quick succession, while later in life the stages take longer and longer to fulfil and to move through.

For example, when marriage is problematic, a person will regress back to the adolescent 6th House of work, and a workaholic temperament is a result. When this stage is incomplete, one will regress back to the 5th House of primary school when creative activity, play and sport is the primary focus of energy – the sport-obsessed adult is the result. When even this expression is unsatisfactory, one regresses back into childhood, the state when one was mothered, protected by family from the nasty outside world and had no responsibilities. All of us are in the process of advancing our energy to the next higher level, but are always tempted, especially in crisis, to regress to earlier levels which were less stressful.

Due to the mathematics of the logarithmic time scale, each house in sequence, although equally weighted against the other houses before and after, is proportional in duration. The first houses are short, reflecting the compaction of developmental time in infancy and the speed of creation, while later houses get longer and longer, reflecting the greater amount of time required to meet their requirements. Houses in gestation last weeks, in childhood months and in maturity years or decades. Life is cumulative, and as we age we store memories from all earlier stages within our bodies, emotions and ideas. The entire sub-structure of our psychology and health lies in this pool of memory stored within psyche and body.

The mathematics of the time scale is such that each house developmental stage is approximately the same length as the entire preceding time from the beginning of the house back to conception. This implies that at each stage we have access to the experience of an entirely new unity, as we integrate new learned patterns to our fund of basic memories and behavioural patterns. The ages at which the houses begin and end vary from person to person due to the variation in house lengths caused by geographical location, and the time of the year or day of birth. We all develop through the same sequence but at different rates, and each developmental stage is signified by different astrological signs.

Table 3 shows the archetypal ages of the houses shown as a series of average ages.

Each house, while being an archetypal developmental stage, is different for everyone. There are many ways in which these differences may be identified and expressed, from major to minor. Most house division systems are unequal and 'time-based', and the duration of each house varies (Figure 12). Shorter houses indicate compacted developmental stages while longer houses show longer than average times for development. The further north or south of the equator the birthplace, the more distorted the houses become at certain times of the day.

Houses occupied by a planet are qualified by the nature of the planet working through the sign and at the age signified by the house. Saturn is serious, constricting and concentrated, therefore when Saturn is in the 7th House in Aries the self-assertive qualities of Aries would be doubly exaggerated by the serious-ness and concentration of the energy.

Planets occupying a house qualify its action, and they are in turn qualified by the planets that aspect them from other houses in the horoscope. For example, if the planet Saturn is in the 7th House governing the time from 23 to 42 when relationships are important, and it is opposite Venus in the 1st House soon after birth, relationships will always be in direct opposition to the need to be loved for oneself alone (opposition Venus in the 1st House). Aspects connect the times and qualities of other houses with the house of origin. This is like importing external qualities and influences from earlier ages to the present. In the medical context, the search for earlier causes of afflictions can be directed to following aspect links back towards the 9th house of conception.

Table 3 Archetypal Ages of the Houses

House	Archetypal ages	Degrees	Key words
	Gestation		
9th	Conc to +7wks Sagittarius	240–270	Mother's self-realisation Brain systems created
10th	+7wks to +12wks Capricorn	270–300	Recognition of conception Skeletal system created
11th	+12wks to +23wks Aquarius	300–330	Idealism and planning Nervous system created
12th	+23wks to Birth Pisces	330–360	Isolation and sacrifice Lymphatic system
	Childhood		
1st	Birth to 7mos Aries	0–30	Personality and assertion
2nd	7mos to 1yr 8mos Taurus	30–60	Physical–sensory reality
3rd	1yr 8mos to 3yr 6mos Gemini	60–90	Mobility and communication
4th	3yr 6mos to 7yr Cancer	90–120	Home and family emotions
	Maturity		
5th	7yr to 13yr Leo	120–150	Self-awareness and school
6th	13yr to 23yr 5mos Virgo	150–180	Higher education and health
7th	23yr 5mos to 42yr Libra	180–210	Partnership and business
8th	42yr to Death Scorpio	210–240	Separation and old age

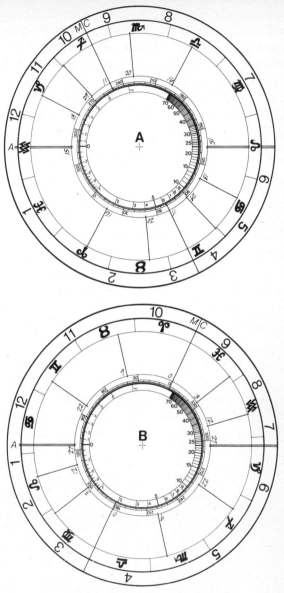

Figure 12 Unequal Houses

These two horoscopes are constructed for the same day, but seven and a half hours apart. In Horoscope A the 5th House Cusp registers at 9 years old, while in Horoscope B the 5th Cusp registers at less than 5 years old. The two horoscopes show differing rates of development.

The Process of Life

The process of life described by the houses begins at conception, uniquely among astrological systems, old or new. Even those ways of looking at astrology which are most contemporary in using timing scales, such as those of the Hubers[4] and Dane Rudhyar,[5] do not consider or even refer to this most critical formative time of life. It is equally lacking in the realm of psychology, particularly Freudian psychotherapy. As a result, a description of the events of gestation may seem foreign to most, but more comprehensible to women who have had children.

Each house is correlated, for the purpose of the archetypal descriptions, with an equivalent zodiac sign. The 1st House is correlated with the first sign, Aries, etc. This is standard procedure and in addition gives a further dimension of meaning to the houses, which are usually undervalued in current astrological thought. The primary reason for this is that most modern astrologers have not addressed issues about the nature of time, which would lead them to understand what the houses mean and how to use them.

In describing an archetypal yet individual 'historical process', we are entering the realm of personal mythology and an area in which stories are very relevant.

From the healing perspective, it is important to notice the biological stages of development which correspond to the sequence of houses so that correlations between biology and astrology may be understood in a new light.

The sequence of octaves will be described with the primary aim of showing briefly what happens at each stage on the astrological, biological and psychological levels. The traditional, astrological meanings of the houses remain, but are put in a more tangible and logical framework. A more complete listing of the houses and their healing significance follows in Chapter 5.

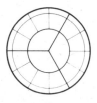

Octave of Gestation

Gestation is the time from conception to birth during which the physical body is created within the mother. The metamorphosis from one-celled fertilised ovum to fully developed human is complex and functions at many levels simultaneously. The primary levels on which Life★Time Astrology can describe events are as follows.

The *Spiritual Process* is the highest form of being, and conception is the bringing of a life spirit into physical being in a body. The spiritual body permeates and in a way organises all other, more dense bodies.

The *Biological–Physiological Process* is the creation of a physical body into which spirit can express its being in the world. At conception the genetic codes of father and mother combine and permute to form the physical vehicle. This pattern in time carries not only physical characteristics from both parents, but also a record of their lives up until the time of conception – indeed a record of all life back down the spiral staircase of DNA. Within the mother's womb the entire evolutionary process is recapitulated, not duplicated. We pass through stages which correspond to the earlier, subhuman forms of life on earth, with all the while the understanding that humanity, though carrying traces of those forms, are not those forms. We go through similar evolutionary stages as the primates, but we are not primates. We have a reptilian cortex in our brains which govern instinctive reactions, but we are not reptiles, nor have we ever been reptiles.

The stages of complex, multicelled beings, invertebrates, vertebrates, early reptiles, later mammals and primates are evident in our bodily structure and in our brain structure. Each stage leaves traces in our nature in the form of *instincts*. Instincts are ways of perceiving the world, of acting, behaving and responding. The cumulative process of creation, our biological history, is virtually identical in all humans. We call the study of the process embryology, and see it as a primarily physical process, although it has profound psychological implications which will be explored. Gestation is the *collective unconscious* described by Jung, a primal inheritance common to all humanity which forms the basic foundation of the individual psyche. The contents are undifferentiated instincts retained in our biological and psychological structure, which although within us are not necessarily a part of our conscious reality.

In the horoscope it is possible to see the outer and inner influences acting upon the mother during gestation, in the form of planets registering in the 9th–12th Houses.

CONCEPTION POINT – THE 9TH HOUSE CUSP

The conception point is extremely important, not only because without it we would not exist. In the horoscope the 9th cusp shows the nature of the sexual–emotional relationship between the parents at the time of conception as a metaphor for the connection between male and female energies. Conception is a process which is the prototype of one's creative process. It is symbolic of sexual communication and its quality.

THE MIDHEAVEN (MC)

Seven weeks after conception or thirty-three weeks before birth. (Ego-consciousness, life objectives, spiritual awareness, individuality, profession, honour, confidence, recognition.) The Midheaven registers about forty-nine days after conception. Hindus and Buddhist religions accept that the soul enters the physical matrix forty-nine days after conception, which is also the same period of time after the death in the previous incarnation. At the time when the soul enters, the new being accepts its *karma* (traces of past lives). Karma is an evocative term, but it can be defined as the genetic, astrological and spiritual pattern inherited by incarnation.

Astrologically the MC is the objectives, goals and aims of life, as well as the seat of ego-consciousness. In the timing scale the MC registers at the moment when the mother has confirmed the fact that she is pregnant.

Octave of Childhood

The Ascendant registers at the moment of the first breath at delivery. The birth process symbolises the way in which the personality acts, and individuals participating in birth are subpersonalities. Easy̆ birth promotes easy expression of the personality, while long labour can produce a restrained personality. The sign on the Ascendant is the environment into which a child is born, and the environment which will be attractive or created by the individual.

The octave of childhood extends from birth to about 7 years old. During this time we are born into the world, accept a personality related to the birth circumstances, and begin to develop our emotional body within the home and family system. The personality is a combination of our instinctive reactions to the world, the way in which we are brought into the world, our physical appearance and the way we come to see ourselves.

Octave of Maturity

By the age of about 7 years we have developed body and personality and must begin to project their combination out into the world, to gradually leave out parents and to create our own life and relationships in the world. Self-consciousness leads to alignment with life work, competition increases in emotional and material ways, and partners are sought and won. The mental body is created initially within the context of primary school (5th House), then channelled in secondary school and early work experiences (6th House), applied to the world in marriage and profession (7th House) and re-evaluated as old age is approached (8th House). The world view developed is the precursor of the soul, the whole being discovered through experience and work on oneself. A primary object of maturity is to transform personal models, integrate their projections and to gain access to the creative world of the transpersonal.

Octave of Transcendence

For the man or woman in the street, life begins at birth and ends at death. Most individuals are quite mechanical in that they limit themselves to the three octaves of gestation, childhood and maturity, if indeed they recognise the gestation period as being significant. They are unable to extend their perception beyond the tasks and 'reality' of the day-to-day life. But there is a fourth octave of transcendence available.

The Octave of Transcendence becomes available when an individual extends his or her reality beyond the immediate physical world. Access to this higher realm of existence is often through shocks which bring the very being into question, force a rapid reappraisal of life, or constitute a threat to existence. Accidents, operations, sudden realisations, religious conversion, the use of psychedelic drugs and many other methods can bring experience of the world beyond this one.

The genesis of the higher octave is in gestation. Women have a natural access to the transcendental reality through child-carrying and childbirth. When a woman becomes pregnant, her entire life changes, presuming it is her first pregnancy. She will never be the same again, and afterwards she will forever remember the events of this time. During gestation a woman is more deeply in touch with her core than at any other time in life, and the fact that it is possible to die in childbirth increases the power of the time.

The act of mother making love with father at conception is a metaphor for the integration of male and female aspects of one's own nature. The psychological integration of animus (masculine spirit) and anima (feminine soul) and the rites of initiation parallel each other, and are embodied in the creation of our own bodies and reality. When initiation is sought, the journey back to the source is required.

The importance of conception cannot be overestimated and understanding the messages it transmits is of vital importance in the process of attaining wholeness. Just as mother responded to inner changes which may have had physical or emotional form by looking within herself to discover the source of her deepest feelings, so we must look within ourselves and also back into our lives to discover the potential for unity we contain. The way in which mother discovered she was pregnant is symbolic of our path to self-understanding, and the people she chose to aid or assist her process are parts of our own nature upon which we must call in our own quest.

Since the transcendent octave is available beyond the 8th House of death, there is an element of sacrifice and death in its mechanism. It is believed that at the moment of death the images of the entire life pass through one's eyes instantly. This has also been reported in near death experiences by many people in all walks of life, all over the world. The vision of life at death is the *last judgement* of all major religions, a weighing of the soul before it is free to depart. This last judgement is an assessment of the meaning of life, a call for re-evaluation, and is believed to be the determining factor in subsequent incarnations. Symbolically it is the death of an obsolete reality which must die in order for a new and higher way of being to come into being. The existential qualities of death and rebirth are at the core of all mystical schools and ideas, and we enact the same mystery in our own life.

Within the image of the spiralling solar system, the life process is bounded by entrance to the space–time continuum at conception and an exit at death. When the pure spirit incarnates in a fertilised ovum, it becomes subject, for a period of eighty or so years, to the laws of physical bodies. At death, the spirit is released from its bounds. Esoteric lore describes this as being crucified on the cross of matter, a way of showing that our life is bounded by the horizontal and vertical axes of the horoscope. Our life in time is a profound limitation for the spiritual essence which is capable of being free of matter, and this paradox is at the core of all healing processes.

In recent years, stress has become identified as a major trigger for most of the critical diseases to which modern humanity has been subject. Stress is directly correlated with time sense – when stress is high, time becomes compacted and even more tense. Meditation, for one, is a conscious release from time, and it has been proved that it diminishes stress.

The transcendent reality is available through the death and conception point, the 9th House cusp, and also in the centre of the horoscope circle. The 9th cusp is activated when planets pass by as transits in real time and are directed according to predictive formulae, but the centre of the psyche is always available.

The four houses of gestation are metaphors for the four stages of the transpersonal or transcendent process.

Healing Zones

The three octaves of the horoscope and the overlapping fourth transpersonal octave can represent a model for healing. In Figure 13 is a series of concentric circles which radiate out from the centre of the horoscope. The centre of the circle is the *Centre of the Psyche*, and as such is timeless, beyond qualities or categories, and is the dynamic, energetic centre of the individual. In the truest sense, however, it is not individual but universal.

The sequence of zodiac signs from Aries to Pisces reflects times of the year, activities appropriate to those yearly times, and stages of development which affect all living beings. The signs are *divisions in space* as measured in the sky, and are ways in which we orient ourselves to the galaxy and to the universe. The ring of the houses rotates against the signs. The houses are *divisions in time* as they indicate the process of life around the horoscope. The progression of houses is not additive like the signs, but biological and logarithmic. As a result, each house in turn is successively denser as one moves around the circle. The gestation–physical body is most dense, the childhood–emotional body less dense, the maturity–mental body is less dense still. The transcendent–transpersonal body is without density at all as it is properly beyond or outside time.

The combination of signs and houses is the relativistic *space-time* context of life. The planets occupy the ring of houses measured against the backdrop of the signs. Planets combine

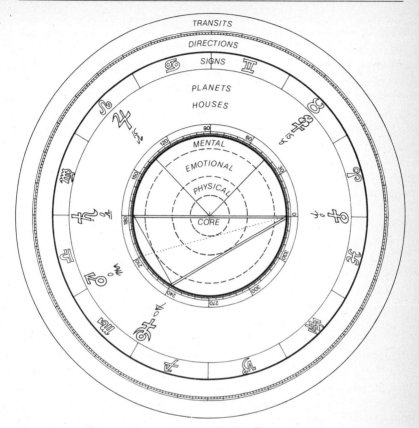

Figure 13 Aspect Healing Zones

sign and house information by combining qualities with times. The structuring planet Saturn, when located in Taurus and the 6th House from 12 to 23 years old, shows a very basic meat and dairy-based Taurean diet at the time of adolescence. This can indicate underactivity in the thyroid gland manifesting as difficulty in gaining weight, a tendency for restriction in voice, suffocation or excessive mucus, and a pessimistic nature prone to depression. The ability to locate any tendency to affliction at a particular age ties quality with timing and leads to a more correct diagnosis and treatment than would be the case when the timing is not known.

The sequence of planets occupying signs and houses around

the horoscope, from conception to old age and death is the process of life in time. The process from cause to effect around the circle is linear. The centre of the circle is, however, outside time and is the domain of the aspects, the *web of relationships* which connects various ages with each other, connects planetary qualities, glands, chakras, archetypes and subpersonalities. The aspect ring is the core of the psyche and shows the channels through which life energy travels and the overall pattern of energy which is central to the well-being of the individual.

The aspect ring is subdivided into a series of concentric circles which represent layers of the psyche. These rings are *healing zones* (see Figure 13). The types of aspect connections determine the healing zones.

The aspect considered by astrologers as the most powerful is the *conjunction*, the aspect of 0° and unity. Two planets within 7° of each other are considered to be conjunct and act together, blending their influences. They register at approximately the same time in life and whenever one is activated, the other will be also. The closer the conjunction between two planets, the more firmly bonded the qualities are to each other, until in exact conjunctions it is often impossible to differentiate the separate planets except by their sequence. The conjunction is bound to the periphery of the circle, and therefore into the sequence of cause and effect. The most peripheral zone is the surface of life around the edge of the circle. The 'inner' life of conjunct planets is only expressed through other planets to which they make aspect, which bring their influence beneath the surface and into the circle. Conjunct planets cannot act independently. For example, the conjunction of Venus and Saturn brings together the glandular secretions (Venus) and the principle of restriction (Saturn). The conjunction can express itself as a tendency to make loyal and faithful relationships with those older than oneself; restriction of love leading to depression; unhealthy expression of the sexual urge; duty dominating inclinations of the heart; or sacrificial relationships. When relationships take on the Venus/Saturn quality, the biological result will be malfunctioning of the internal glandular secretions; atrophy or enlargement of glands; and can result in pulmonary emphysema or goitre. The restricting quality will act either in inner or outer relationships, or both.

The sextile is a 60° aspect, one-sixth of circle and is a peripheral aspect, as it only enters the circle one-eighth of the way from the circumference. Sextiles skip signs, and therefore connect air with fire or fire with air, earth with water or water with earth, always positive sign to positive or negative to negative. Sextiles are slight movements forwards or backwards in time. The shape from which the sextile is derived is a hexagon inscribed in the circle. The sextile aspect defines the *Physical Zone* at the periphery of the circle, in which communication is brotherly and sisterly, not particularly deep or penetrating, but rather on the surface and often superficial.

The trine is a 120° aspect, one-third of the circle and enters exactly halfway to the centre, defining the *Emotional Zone*. Trines connect one sign of an element with the other signs of the same element in different octaves. A trine from a fire sign in childhood will either aspect a planet in gestation earlier or a planet in maturity later in life. As an aspect which describes balance, equilibrium, fluid communication and support, the trine is considered easy and static.

Within the trine aspect is the *Mental Zone*, in which life actions, world view, and psychic motivation act. It is the organisational centre of the energetic being. The aspects most often indicative of illness and imbalance are the *hard aspects* which penetrate into the central zone of the horoscope, these being the 90°, 135°, 150° and 180° aspects. Within the mental zone is the centre of the psyche and the timeless realm of the *Transpersonal Zone* which is beyond qualities, times or personality.

The square is a 90° aspect, one-fourth of the circle, which penetrates all the way to the centre of the circle and then takes a right angle before returning to the periphery. The square connects planets which tension or pressure the centre, are likely to produce change, but are capable of resolution. It is said that squares are either stumbling blocks or building blocks.[6] Sextiles and trines are peaceful and stable, but the square is quite highly motivated and potentially creative.

The opposition is a 180° aspect, halving the circle and showing two planets directly opposite each other around the circle. The opposition creates maximum tension and forces either resolution or polarisation. This aspect can signal the attraction that opposites exert upon each other, or it can represent irreconcilable differences within the psyche which can be highly antagonistic.

Energy travels from one pole to the other in an opposition, and it can take all the energy from the rest of the whole if not integrated. The opposition pushes through or just past the centre point of the circle, and as a result is very highly connected to the psyche and its mechanisms.

The hard aspect most often signalling illness is the inconjunct or quincunx of 150°. The inconjunct passes as close to the centre as possible without reaching it, which justifies its reputation as inflexible and frustrating. It is an extremely difficult and immovable combination for two planets. The energies entrapped by its aspects are hard to express, and can easily manifest as illness. On a nutritional level the inconjunct often shows a difficulty assimilating vitamins and nutriments as related to a difficulty expressing positive emotions.[7]

The sesquiquadrate is a 135° aspect which is halfway between a square and opposition. It carries a degree of tension as it does penetrate the central zone, but usually expresses itself as tension which does not reach the critical stage. The *semisquare* of 45° is a minor aspect halfway between the square and conjunction. It only touches the periphery of the emotional zone, so that its tension acts only on the emotional body as nervous irritation or disorientation.

The centre of the circle is the dynamic and powerful core of the psyche which is available at all times in life. When it is contacted at any time of life dramatic changes of state will be affected. The centre is particularly available in times of crisis.

The Cylinder of Life

When the cylinder of life is constructed from the two-dimensional circular horoscope, a true model of healing becomes evident (Figure 14). The cylinder of the life process begins with conception at the bottom and ends with the death time at the top, with the transcendental octave atop the whole. Within the cylinder travel the planets throughout a lifetime as they continue their dance through space and time. Since we are within our mother until birth, it is as though her cylinder is synchronous with ours, and certainly the father's cylinder also overlaps at the moment of conception. At birth we become free of the physical confinement

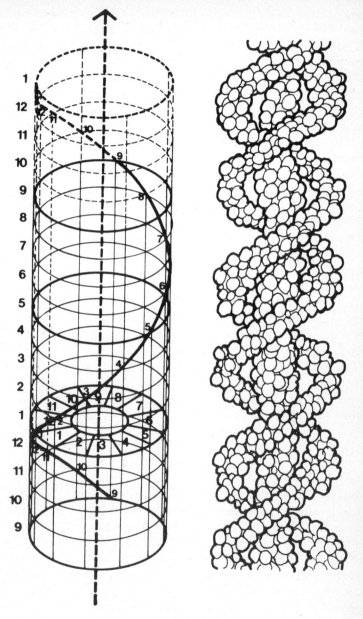

Figure 14 The Cylinder of Life

of the mother and graduate into the emotional life of the family. In childhood our relationships with parents are a gradual disentanglement from mother and father to create a life and personality of our own.

Relationships later in life start as tangent relationships between another's cylinder and our own, more intimate relationships imply an overlapping of cylinders, and when one lets another person into their centre they mutually intersect. At some stages of close relationships the contact seems like a complete synchronicity of two cylinders, but such connections are most often short-lived.

The bottom of the cylinder is conception, and as we age the cylinder fills up with memories and experiences, like filling up with water. The surface of the water at any age is the surface of consciousness at that time. The memories are stored as if in the layer appropriate to the time at which they occurred, but whenever its line on the periphery of the cylinder is passed by planets, the event is activated again.

Aspects within the cylinder move diagonally up and down through its central core. From a given age, some aspect events may reach back to gestation, implying physical issues, others back to childhood, implying emotional or family system matters, while others may even show premonitions of future events. We continually move back to certain life behaviour patterns in our 'present time'.

Horoscope 1 (Figure 15) is Neil Armstrong, the first man to walk on the Moon. When the Moon in Sagittarius (the sign of long journeys) registered (occurred in the time scale) in Armstrong's horoscope he was 37 years old, at the time when he went to the Moon. What is interesting is that aspects back into Armstrong's earlier life were activated at that time. The Moon is trine to the node (associations or cooperation) in Aries (assertion, being in control), which registered while Armstrong's mother was in the last stage of pregnancy, about twenty weeks before birth, when he was floating in a weightless state in the amniotic fluid, within a capsule like the ship which took him to the Moon. He must have been very active as a gestating child, and the lunar flight must have activated this deep memory.

The Moon also receives a trine aspect from the conjunction of Mercury and Neptune in Virgo in the 4th House of home and

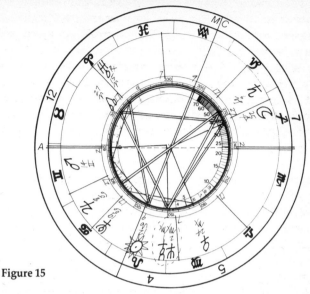

Figure 15

family, registering at the age of 3 years 6 months old. While on the mission, Armstrong had strong feelings which evoked his own childhood fantasies (indicated by the Moon/Mercury aspect), and also psychic experiences (Moon/Neptune). The aspect constellation also indicates extreme sensitivity after the event.

Planetary Complexes

The components of the horoscope are essential parts of the whole, but the entire picture must be grasped. Simple aspects link together to form *constellations* of varying degrees of complexity. Aspect constellations are very much like 'complexes' in psychology, that is, groups of characteristics which are linked together in the psyche. Some horoscopes are very straightforward, direct and clearly organised by aspects, while others can be so full of interconnections and complex linked chains of planets that it is nearly impossible to make any kind of order out of it.

Most often, a planet in the horoscope will have two, three or more aspects from other planets, either in the same or different developmental stages of life. The different aspects indicate the multiple possibilities available for utilising the energy of the planet. Some are easy channels for energy to pass through, while others are strained and blocked. As in the world around us, our own inner energy tends to follow the line of least resistance. When a constellation (Figure 16) is composed of planets in

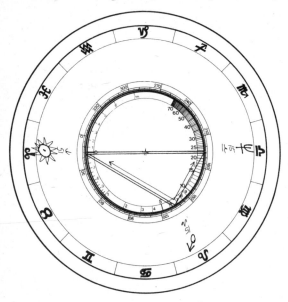

Figure 16 Planetary Constellation

opposition with a third planet mutually in aspect by trine and sextile, it will almost always be the case that the energy will avoid the opposition and travel the roundabout or superficial way rather than penetrate to the centre. The dynamic of the aspect configurations is usually more important in maintaining health than individual planetary positions. When the overall flow of energy within the individual and with outside sources is fluid, the support and immune systems are typically sound and able to deflect even major imbalances.

5

The Wheel of Therapies

The chapter in *The Round Art* (1979) which evoked the most powerful response was 'The Astrological Reading', particularly the diagram called *The Wheel of Psychology* (Figure 17). The wheel has since been extended to include other therapies (Figure 18).

Life★Time Astrology shows the development of the life process around the periphery of the horoscope circle from conception to death, and beyond to the transpersonal or transcendent domain. Therapists of all kinds are attracted to approaches to the psyche, life energy, body, emotions, mind and spirit which reflect their own inner history, needs and aspirations, as well as their astrology.[1] Jung believed that 'Every psychotherapist not only has his own method – he himself is that method.'[2]

The choice of which therapy is appropriate for any individual is a haphazard process, if indeed it can be called a process at all. The therapies are very different, and it is axiomatic that certain therapies suit certain people and not others. In the light of Life★Time Astrology, it is possible generally to evaluate therapies according to the time of life to which the therapy addresses itself. Each type of therapy can be related to particular times during the life process and therefore attributed to parts of the astrological wheel of houses. These attributions have proved to be very stimulating to therapists and helpful to those whose occupation requires that they recommend therapies to clients, based on case histories or horoscopes.

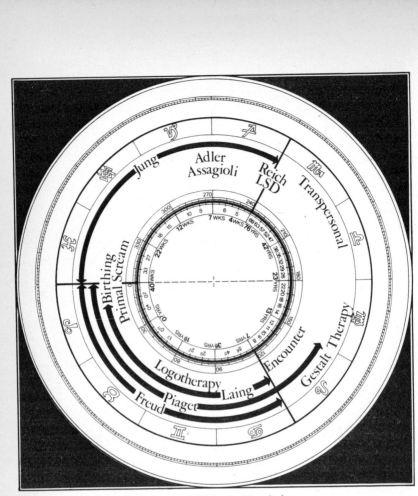

Figure 17 The Wheel of Psychology

Therapies need not be confined to a single sign or a particular slot in the lifetime, but the areas upon which a therapy is focused is usually clear. For example, the Primal Scream Therapy of Arthur Janov involves reliving the birth process and is intimately related to that time of life as a metaphor for the whole of life. Rebirthing has a similar approach to the birth process. The most interesting way to organise the wheel of therapies is with the astrological signs grouped by octaves, starting with gestation and the archetypal conception point, the 9th House cusp.

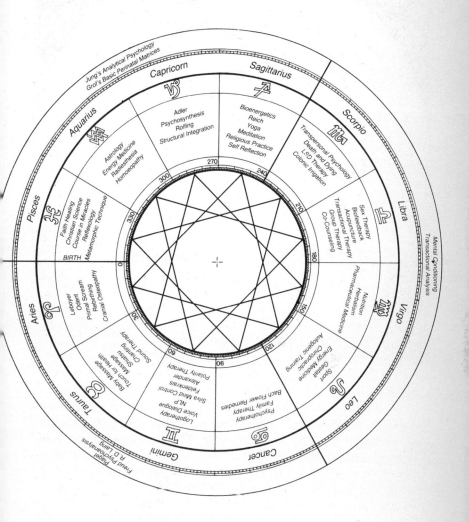

The outer ring, clockwise from top:

Jung's Analytical Psychology
Grof's Basic Perinatal Matrices

Mental Conditioning
Transactional Analysis

Freud Psychoanalysis
R. D. Laing
Piaget

Signs (clockwise from top): Capricorn, Sagittarius, Scorpio, Libra, Virgo, Leo, Cancer, Gemini, Taurus, Aries, Pisces, Aquarius

Capricorn
Adler
Psychosynthesis
Rolfing
Structural Integration

Sagittarius
Bioenergetics
Reich
Yoga
Meditation
Religious Practice
Self Reflection

Scorpio
Transpersonal Psychology
Death and Dying
LSD Therapy
Colonic Irrigation

Libra
Sex Therapy
Biofeedback
Acupuncture
Transactional Therapy
Group Therapy
Co-Counseling

Virgo
Nutrition
Herbalism
Pharmaceutical Medicine

Leo
Sport
Energy Medicine
Gestalt
Chiropractic
Autogenic Training

Cancer
Psychotherapy
Family Therapy
Bach Flower Remedies

Gemini
Logotherapy
Voice Dialogue
NLP
Silva Mind Control
Feldenkrais
Alexander
Polarity Therapy

Taurus
Baby Massage
Touch for Health
Massage
Chanting
Sound Therapy

Aries
Leboyer
Odent
Primal Scream
Rebirthing
Cranial Osteopathy

Pisces
Faith Healing
Christian Science
Course in Miracles
Reflexology
Metamorphic Technique

Aquarius
Astrology
Energy Medicine
Radiesthesia
Homoeopathy

BIRTH

Degrees marked: 0, 30, 60, 90, 120, 150, 180, 210, 240, 270, 300, 330

Figure 18 The Wheel of Therapies

Gestation Octave Therapies

The therapy most appropriate to the gestation octave is Carl Gustav Jung's *Analytical Psychology*. Jung's psychology is based on the concept of the 'collective unconscious', a substratum of the psyche, which is the common property of all humanity – a formative level of being transcending all cultural and individual differences from which all psychic processes originate. The archetypal collective unconscious is recreated during our gestation process, and lies both below and above the two 'conscious' octaves of childhood and maturity in the cylinder of life. Conscious life is the two central layers surrounded above and below by the form-generating archetypal world. 'Unconscious contents connect it *backwards* with physiological states on the one hand and archetypal data on the other. But it is extended *forward* by intuitions which are conditioned partly by archetypes and partly by subliminal perceptions depending on the relativity of time and space in the unconscious.'[3] Jung also recognised that archetypes are like potentised (homoeopathic) medicines which express themselves as plant, animal or mineral essences by their formal seed.[4] He also identified the idea of the first (octave of gestation) in unity with the fourth (octave of gestation as transcendence) as an alchemical axiom. Jung's psychology is the cornerstone of the gestation layer, and is highly effective for individuals with planets throughout this part of the horoscope.

Stan Grof's *Basic Perinatal Matrices*[5] originated from the stages of the birth process and describe a psychological architecture of emotional disorders which was discovered by extensive research with hallucinogens. The perinatal level of the unconscious is the intersection between the individual and collective unconscious, or between traditional psychology and mystical transpersonal psychology. These dynamic matrices are organising models operating on the emotional and physical bodies which affect us profoundly. The biographical events of life are structured unconsciously by systems of archetypes unfolding through outer events. The progression of four BPMs describe the process of leaving the original symbiotic unity and entering the world of multiplicity. Grof's ideas show that the events of gestation are the genesis and archetypes of life in maturity, psychologically and physiologically.

SAGITTARIUS AND THE 9TH HOUSE – MUTABLE FIRE SIGN

Conception until 7 weeks after conception.
(Higher mind, meditation, religion, law, long journeys, foreign influences, philosophy, psychology, initiation and self-realisation)

After the moment of conception when a sperm fertilises an ovum, a very rapid and complex process begins. The initial cell subdivides and differentiates gradually to form three spiral germ layers which are prototypes of the three main bodily systems. One layer will produce the brain, spinal cord, nerves and skin; the second will create the digestive system, liver and pancreas; and the third will make the skeleton, blood circulation system and musculature. This triple-octave system echoes the three octaves of the life process, and is a microcosm of the entire physical body.

Astrologically, the 9th House governs long journeys, life philosophy or psychology, religion and higher mind. The mother undergoes hormonal changes and throughout the time gradually comes to the realisation of her inner creative life. All her attitudes, beliefs, and particularly the way in which she discovers herself, store the metaphor of *self-discovery* so typical of this house and the sign Sagittarius.

The conception point at the 9th cusp of the horoscope is a metaphor for sexuality, creativity and the integration of male and female halves of the psyche. The core of the instincts are generated here and the long journey of the sperm to fertilise the ovum and the journey of the fertilised ovum to the uterus are encoded into the conception point.

The most striking psychotherapy of Sagittarius is *Reichian therapy* or *Bioenergetics*, originated by Wilhelm Reich, the student of Freud, who based his therapeutic work on the function and necessity of sexual and hence energetic release through orgasm. Quite naturally, since conception and death occupy the same position in the horoscope, Reich studied and formulated theories and methods of treatment which reflect the unity of the beginning and end of life. Orgasm is a striving to go beyond the self, beyond the confines of the phsysical body into a higher, more vital realm. Reichian therapy deals with sexuality as a way of releasing the armouring created as a defence mechanism to protect oneself from the convolutions and perversion of society. Reich also postulated the psyche as successive circular layers surrounding a core of healthy drives, a model strikingly like Life★Time Astrology.

Yoga is an oriental spiritual discipline which embodies a search for unity of mind/body through its experiences of itself via a wide range of techniques. Tuning the body to the highest degree of sensitivity and awareness leads to a state where disease is alien and ultimately is a preventive path beyond conscious suffering. Especially when breathing exercises are used, a state of total peace within and without can be attained and maintained, anxiety eliminated and drives balanced. At a deep level, yoga is a return to the state just after conception before the mind/body split has occurred.

Meditation encourages contact with unconscious matter deep within the psyche, below the surface of consciousness, and transforms it by bringing concentration to bear. Thoughts, images, magical journeys and pattern consciousness may cut through the spiritual materialism, lack of clarity or distraction created by everyday life. Breath is a central focus and simultaneously a healing power liberated through meditation, and can be directed to organs in need of renewal or regeneration. Meditation is rarely a healing mechanism itself, apart from its use in stress reduction, but can be used profitably in conjunction with virtually any other therapies, to ensure that the core of being is aligned with the outer forms of life and awareness.

Religious practices provide a path for awareness and represent a core, which once built, can be a foundation upon which the entire life may be constructed. These may be organised religion or Sufi, which espouse all religions and the synthesis of belief systems. Often religious practices include meditation, prayer, breathing, chanting and other pursuits which are usually practised without a religious structure.

Self-reflection is a way for understanding and potentially changing the context of self through which the life is perceived. The internalising of events and their organisation within the psyche provide a degree of objectivity which can restructure reality and provide an essential matrix for healing.

As the Sagittarian time is the earliest stage of biological evolution within the womb, it is also naturally the causal zone within which the biological code has broken down in some diseases. Some therapies can repair such deep disorders by instilling a new and higher reality. The path to realisation is central to all therapies here.

CAPRICORN AND THE 10TH HOUSE – CARDINAL EARTH SIGN

33 weeks to 28 weeks before birth.
(Perfected matter, concrete relationships, organisation, father, public affairs, fame and fortune, ambition, aspirations)

The first bone cells appear, the embryo becomes a foetus medically, sex is determined, all body components are formed and facial features are recognisable. Nerves and muscles, although weak, begin working together. Spontaneous movement ensues as arms and legs bend and total mobility comes. The foetus lives within the amniotic fluid, but the mother cannot yet feel its existence. Pancreatic digestive fluids are activated by ingesting amniotic fluid, and other vital functions such as urination and eating are tentatively attempted.

In the 10th House our parents are aware of the coming child, announce the fact to the outside world, come into contact with social pressures and exteriorise what was previously hidden within the mother. Decisions must be made about the procedure for gestation, the choices of techniques or doctors for delivery, diet, and all the other changes required by the time. Reality is confronted and the transition from inner to outer forms is complete. Capricorn and the 10th House begin with the MC, which is the moment when the soul enters the physical matrix to incarnate, when the embryo becomes a foetus, and when the mother realises for the first time that she is pregnant.

Alfred *Adler* broke with Freud by insisting that normality requires application of the power of the individual through conditioning to social adaptation. The power concept implied tends to minimalise the importance of the unconscious and yet is based upon a strengthening of the ego and will to survive.

After studying with Freud, Jung and Alice Bailey, Roberto *Assagioli* developed *Psychosynthesis* which was a dynamic framework for achieving synthesis through integrating the unconscious and reorganising its contents and attendant subpersonalities around the Transpersonal Self, which reigns at the head of an ovoid psychic field (Figure 19). The Transpersonal Self is an

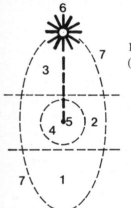

Figure 19 Psychosynthesis Egg Diagram
(after Assagioli, *The Act of Will*, p. 14)

1. The Lower Unconscious
2. The Middle Unconscious
3. The Higher Unconscious, or Superconscious
4. The Field of Consciousness
5. The Conscious Self, or 'I'
6. The Transpersonal Self
7. The Collective Unconscious

integration of love and will, as expressed in his book *The Act of Will*.[6] Psychosynthesis is particularly effective for creative people because Assagioli did not concentrate on the morbid symptoms of disorder, but rather worked to restructure the temporary imbalances of what he called 'healthy neurotics', i.e. most modern western individuals. Assagioli's teaching are an adaptation of the esoteric principles of Alice Bailey to transpersonal psychotherapy, with the addition of a spiritual dimension.

Capricorn is the skeletal system of the body formed in the womb and correlates with deep structural bodywork. *Rolfing* or *Structural Integration* developed by Dr Ida Rolf as a deep pressure massage for reforming the muscular facia in order to correct deformations which have been created by injuries, stress, and bad postural habits or traumatic events. The correction of the subsequent rigidity and lack of elasticity brings a more efficient use of energy and often a release of emotional pain, memories of past traumatic episodes and changes of behaviour.[7] Gestation memories are often evoked and intrauterine memories are common during and after treatment. Rolfing is more a preventive therapy than a correction for disorder.

AQUARIUS AND THE 11TH HOUSE – FIXED AIR SIGN

28 weeks to 17 weeks before birth.
(Altruism, selflessness, humanitarianism, idealism, planning, friends, groups relationships, social concerns, abstraction and detachment.)

The 11th House begins with the quickening, when the mother first feels movement within as the foetus rises above the hipbone. Swallowing is practised and the first respiration takes place, movements become more graceful and individual, inherited facial qualities are made manifest, and the entire neuromuscular system becomes active in accordance with the direction of the sympathetic nervous system. Towards the end of this period the reproductive organs are formed and primitive eggs and sperms are created.

Astrologically the child develops in a surrogate placental system within the mother, whose activities are conditioned by her new sensation of movement within. The mother is different from others, emotionally and physically separated by her condition from the outside world and her former self.

The internal communication system of the body is created with subtle interconnections between organs, glands and body parts. The developing foetus gradually becomes subject to astrological forces and therefore has taken on its esoteric forms of spirit, soul, astral and etheric bodies.

Astrology at its best provides a model showing the potential for integration of all levels of being. Astrology is a unique tool for recording and ordering associations in life, for attempting to understand and control the passage of time, for inquiring into the affinities of all things, and for the alchemical attempt to transform the self through conscious direction of the will. Many modern psychologists use astrology as a vital tool for working with personal experiences, and have used it as a valuable language for interpreting and applying archetypal levels of reality.

Cosmic occult sciences interact and overlap into *Energy Medicine*, which includes radiesthesia and radionics, which is diagnosis and treatment through the energy body. *Radiesthesia* is relatively modern, having originated within the last hundred years, but is based upon principles which seem simultaneously primitive[8] and highly sophisticated. Early researchers believed they had discovered and were working with a vital energetic force of nature (*prana, élan vital*, Reichenbach force, kundalini, psychic energy or orgone). Radiesthesia operates upon the 'subtle body', which is beyond the electromagnetic field of the body. The use of chakras, which are subtle energy centres without actual physical counterparts in the body, has proved very effective and is a step beyond traditional diagnosis and treatment. Chakras are altered and affected before the physical body shows symptoms and can be healed by receiving resonant healing patterns or thoughts. These approaches are representative of the spiritual approach to healing, and have recently been influenced by Alice Bailey's esoteric healing.[9]

Homoeopathy is based on the principle of 'like cures like'. Symptoms are recognised as behavioural expressions of disharmony, an indication that the body is fighting against illness or infection, and are seen as aspects of a whole pattern which includes all dispositions to ill health. Symptoms are valuable information, and are therefore to be encouraged in their expression rather than suppressed. Remedies are chosen to match the symptomatology and given in a highly diluted (potentised) form so that impurities and side-effects of the natural substances are eliminated and the potency increased. The production of such symptoms is accepted as an indication of a healthy organism seeking to restore balance.

PISCES AND THE 12TH HOUSE – MUTABLE WATER SIGN

17 weeks before birth until birth.
(Self-sacrifice, extreme receptivity, psychic activity, sensitivity, karma, destiny, escapism, institutions, isolation, drugs, loneliness)

From the beginning of the 12th House a child can be born and survive, although the breathing mechanism, liver and digestive systems are very immature. The child lives, breathes and moves around within the amnion, which is replaced every three hours. Much of mother's energy and psyche is focused inside, increasing her psychic contact with the child. While others may support her totally, she will eventually realise that at the moment of birth she is on her own, and it is a life and death situation. The acceptance and release of the deep instincts of birth finally come into play and coincide with the beginning of labour. Instinctive maternal responses and a trusting of the moods and hormonal modulations which lie beneath the surface are most valuable and ensure a healthy child.

During the last half of gestation the child establishes stronger psychic contact with the mother. The lymphatic system blossoms and the child is made ready for birth. This house is traditionally the domain of psychic phenomena, of ESP, of dreams and fantasies.

Faith Healing was originally performed by shamans who returned to the spirit world on behalf of the diseased. Shamanic practices were widespread in most early cultures including the American Indian, European, Celtic, Tibetan, Mongolian, Chinese, Japanese, Russian, Eskimo, African tribal and many others. Shamanic abilities may either be latent in one from birth or acquired in life. There are also 'scientific' approaches to spiritual healing which involve the direction and manifestation of will, such as *Science of Mind, Christian Science* or the *Course in Miracles*.

Prayer is directing the spiritual impulse towards a state of peace and balance.

Reflexology and *Metamorphic Technique* (formerly prenatal therapy) are methods of foot massage which assume that the entire structure of the physical, emotional, mental and spiritual bodies are reflected in the feet, and that an individual can learn to help themselves through working on their reflex points. Such work often evokes prenatal experiences which can then be integrated. Metamorphic technique is about touching, an intuitive process, which followed, leads within and can bring release from fixed programming and the creation of new patterns.

Childhood Octave Therapies

Childhood begins with the birth process, the experience which to most people and almost all therapists is the beginning of life, and extends until the age of 7 when relationships beyond the family are formed and the process of leaving home begins.

The primary therapy of the childhood time is undoubtedly Sigmund Freud's *Psychoanalysis*, which is based on free association and attributes the imbalanced development of the psyche to social and biological factors affected by infantile sexuality and relationships with the parents. Freud's unique contribution was the almost mathematical connection he made between the psyche and the energy economy of the body, giving rise to an understanding of psychosomatic illnesses. Some other characteristics of Freudian psychology include dream analysis, the detached relationship of therapist to client, the Oedipus and Electra complexes, and the creation of laws describing the realm of the human psyche which are largely held by the scientific world today.

Virtually all psychological disturbances appear to be related back to the childhood time, and Freud delighted in being the 'father' to all his patients, a paternal attitude which ultimately hindered his humanity. One of the most powerful of his concepts was that in our childhood development we recapitulate the evolution of all humanity, stage by stage, until when our energy reaches a barrier we regress to earlier stages when we were more comfortable. Freudian psychoanalysis covers the entire time of gestation. Interestingly, the numerous cases of incest reported by his female clients were ultimately invalidated, yet how could they have had such intimate knowledge, even on the fantasy level, of sexuality unless they had experiences in childhood? The earlier gestation octave and its astrological structure gives us the understanding that all humans have deeply carried sexual memories *of our parents making love at our own conception and possibly throughout gestation.* These traces are often essential information in Life★Time Astrology.

The psychologist *Piaget* formulated a theory of distinct developmental stages from birth through adolescence which, although not now entirely accepted, are valuable models for the evolution of children.

The psychiatrist R. D. *Laing* started by studying the family as the source of madness and/or sanity, and throughout his life has worked his way earlier and earlier into the life process until at present he is engaged in the power of the conception time and its implications. Laing's ideas and novel treatment centres liberated psychiatry from a self-imposed strait-jacket, and paved the way for family therapy and the need to put individual psychic reality into context.

ASCENDANT

Birth
(Personality, environment, birth circumstances, people present at birth, reactions to the world, the mask, ways of acting, personal attitudes)

It is almost universally acknowledged that birth traumas are responsible for many types of illnesses, both psychological and physical. The primary reason is that in the last century, with the rise and increase in power of the medical profession, childbirth has been transformed from a natural process to a pathological medical procedure. The dehumanisation of birth is seen by many to be the primary factor in the difficulties of our modern society.

The astrological correlation of the Ascendant/personality with birth is primary and very illuminating. When a baby is delivered surgically the planets Mars, Uranus, Pluto or Saturn are often in attendance, either conjunct or in aspect to the Ascendant indicating the delivering doctor or surgeon. Unfortunately, the same indicators also bring violence, discord and trauma to the personality of the child. Table 4 on page 128 shows the range of birth influences that relate to planets either on or in aspect to the Ascendant. Primal therapies related to birth attempt to reactivate the process with the intention of clearing the traumas, feelings of fear and pain, and the nearness of death. The women's movement has responded by developing alternative ways of birthing babies.

Janov's *Primal Scream* therapy recreates the sensations of birth, such as duplicating the pressure on the crown of the head experienced at birth, and by so doing liberates the experience of birth by the release of screaming. The catharsis can free energy trapped in the personality to allow fuller expression.

Leonard Orr's *Rebirthing* is a re-experiencing of the birth process achieved through breathing exercises, evocative visualisation or environmental keys, which can be very helpful in identifying and clearing birth traumas. Such a liberation through sound happens at stages of many therapies, accidentally or anticipated.

Cranial Osteopathy is a head massage technique which brings relief from childbirth traumas and can correct imbalances in energy flow.

ARIES AND THE 1ST HOUSE – CARDINAL FIRE SIGN

Birth until 7 months old.
(Self-assertion, personality development, shape and appearance of the physical body, early family environment, independence, bonding with the mother)

The newborn child bonds with the mother for nutrition, support, warmth and love. All needs must be met by the mother or her surrogates, and the child's energy is devoted to getting what is needed as quickly as possible. The child bonds with anyone close and does not distinguish its separateness yet. The thymus gland activates the heart and activities of growth, all of which are motivated by the ability to focus and receive light after the third month.

The primal therapies lap into the 1st House in treating the traumas associated with difficult delivery, first breathing and the pain of entering the world. Frederick *Leboyer* stressed the importance of establishing a strong bond between mother and child, which can be encouraged by birth in softly lit places, in congenial surroundings and with the maintenance of contact immediately after birth. And Michel *Odent* recommended birth in water as a way of creating a powerful mother–child bond which will be maintained continuously from gestation into the early childhood time.

TAURUS AND THE 2ND HOUSE – FIXED EARTH SIGN

Seven months until 1 year 8 months old.
(Physicality, undifferentiated matter, pure substance, the senses, passive perception, security and property)

The weaning from mother's milk onto digesting solid food signals the first separation from the mother and the independence of being an object in a world of other objects. The focus is on learning to use the senses to explore the physical world and develop possessive and sensual patterns. The parathyroid glands become active and lead to a stabilising, passive and steady life in harmony with the physical world. It is the time of crawling and the establishment of a relationship to the body and through it the physical world. The senses are investigated and applied to all experiences. Taurean therapies are physical, use touch, and are grounding.

Baby Massage and *Touch-for-Health* are ways of working with babies and young children to establish firm bonds and strong relationships with the mother.

Massage exists in a multitude of forms, the distinguishing issue being whether it is done for pleasure or therapy. Therapeutic massage is often painful yet pleasurable on a deeper level. Whatever the techniques, the massage stimulates skin and internal organs, unlocks tension from musculature and brings a sense of well-being. *Shiatsu* is a more sophisticated form of massage which uses the Chinese acupuncture points and is used to produce a wide range of cures.

Music Therapy, *Chanting* or *Sound* are types of therapy which are most often underestimated, although through sound it is possible to get in touch with the child on the many deeper levels of the psyche which are typically closed off from consciousness.

GEMINI AND THE 3RD HOUSE – MUTABLE AIR SIGN

1 year 8 months until 3 years 6 months old.
(Instinctive mind, communication, walking and talking, adaptability, mimicry, siblings, diversity, short journeys)

The application of energy in the physical world turns to walking, talking and other forms of communication. Fields of objects are perceived and the subject–object duality is characteristic as many objects seem to have their own life. People are copied and mimicked, while our identity fluctuates between outer and inner fantasy worlds. The adrenal glands promote flight and fight, anger and attachment and heighten sensitivity for self-preservation. The requirement that we communicate brings great pressure to bear on us to establish some form of contact.

Logotherapy was developed by Viktor Frankl and involves the mechanism of language as a matrix within which we store our basic feelings and attitudes to the world.

Voice Dialogue works with the subpersonalities which emerge throughout childhood, particularly when we learn to talk and mimic and identify with everyone in our environment. The learning process comes at the expense of great confusion of identity which requires sorting out in later life. By being able to identify and then disidentify from these parts of ourselves, we can initiate cure.

Neuro-Linguistic Programming (NLP) works with the way language is learned and used to express or not express feelings. Conditioned responses to words or means of expression can be understood, changed and used as freer channels.

Silva Mind Control uses visual cues to discover autohypnotic methods for improving memory, getting in touch with early emotional experiences and for understanding and working with the mechanism of the mind.

Feldenkrais Method is a form of body-centred learning procedure achieved through mastering new movement sequences which encourage learning. Based on children's movements in the early stages of childhood, Feldenkrais is a rediscovery of the possibility for graceful movement. Often stress release, the opening up of chronically tight musculature and the increase in freedom of movement are experienced.

Alexander Technique is a technique for postural reintegration and rebalancing through new movements and an increased consciousness of existing movement patterns.

Polarity Therapy likewise affects the entire organism by relearning to integrate and balance movements within the body.

CANCER AND THE 4TH HOUSE – CARDINAL WATER SIGN

3 years 6 months until 7 years old.
(Parents, mother identification, family system, feelings, home life, receptivity, heredity, intuition, the psychic world, personal feelings, belonging)

Emotional responses to the ability to communicate are conditioned by prevailing attitudes and the governance of parents, within the family system. A value system is created by reacting to feelings about parents, friends, family, religion and relatives. Relationships become more complex and the parents are differentiated. A growing sense of security or insecurity is generated by acceptance or rejection of one's feelings within the family.

When emotional structures first become defined and either excluded or integrated into the feeling patterns of the family, they are often determined by the relationship with mother and father. Cancerian therapies are emotional, family oriented and intensely personal.

Psychotherapies are emotional therapies in which the free expression of feelings is considered necessary to physical and mental well-being (see Figure 18 – the Wheel of Therapies).

Family Therapy is a method for treating individual psychological problems by investigating and influencing the processes of the group. Sessions include the entire family, and the focus of therapy is often upon family members other than those who appear at first glance to have psychological problems. Many psychological disorders arise from the family, and are perpetuated by its moral positions, attitudes, religious beliefs and behavioural patterns. Much of the early thinking which led to the family therapy model came from general systems theory, a primary concept in the mathematical sciences.

Bach Flower Remedies and *California Flower Remedies* are the diluted essences of flowers which can be used to modulate emotional behavioural patterns by introducing healthy patterning and re-establishing contact between soul and mind.

Maturity Octave Therapies

The octave of maturity covers the development of the mental body, our way of understanding and relating to the world, and is brought into practice throughout our life after childhood. The four stages of maturity are in themselves very different and important as our energy evolves and transmutes to ever higher forms. The maturity octave occurs when virtually all people reach the extent of their energy focus and is therefore the most likely place for regression.

LEO AND THE
5TH HOUSE – FIXED FIRE SIGN

7 years until 13 years old.
(Self-consciousness, creativity, game-playing, competition, pride, affections, love of self and others, acting, confidence, education, publication, speculation)

At primary school we learn the rules of the game of our society, religion and the world, while through games we learn to make contact with and forge relationships through others so that we express ourselves fully. Personal relations follow on from broadening game contexts and we find role-models in all walks of life on whom to pattern our fantasy lives. Self-consciousness is rife, and acceptance is the goal of much energy beyond the great expansion of growth, activated by the posterior pituitary gland.

Sport is a primary therapy and people of all ages benefit from the appropriate sport which will exercise them, and provide a channel for aggressive or team energies which are lacking in modern life. This is often a stage which is regressed back into in later life as armchair athletes re-enact their childhood victories and honours vicariously.

Gestalt was created by Fritz Perls as an interactive way to act out our personality processes and participate in them in a dynamic way. The role-playing of gestalt can be very helpful in allowing a deeper level of observation and participation in our own being. Changes in acting produce character alteration and can lead to biological change.

All forms of *Energy Medicine* are based on the creative play of the physical and emotional bodies and the outside world. Energies which flowed during a protected childhood often run into blockages everywhere when confronted with the realities of the world.

Andrew Still developed *Chiropractic* as a form of diagnosis and treatment of muscular–skeletal disorders which also cause aches, pains and psychological imbalances from the structure of the spine and body joints. Manipulation is used to correct structure and adjustments are carried out to increase movement or flexibility in the required places.

Autogenic Training is a form of self-hypnosis which has as its task the release from the fight-or-flight adrenal impulses, and the elimination of the dependency of client to therapist, a position which is not encouraged by many therapies. The freedom of choice and physical parts which correspond to either openings or blockages can be optimalised by linking mind with matter. Being the time when we begin to leave home, it is appropriate that the liberation from parental figures is central here.

VIRGO AND
THE 6TH HOUSE – MUTABLE EARTH SIGN

13 to 23 years 5 months old.
(Distillation, discrimination, naïvete, puberty, diet habits and health, secondary education, work, service)

As the adolescent grows, sexuality enters the equation, and is the primary drive at this time when the application of natural abilities leads to choices about how our body relates to the world and we to it. Games become serious, winners do win, and we must begin to take responsibility for our actions. The outer demands of life are exaggerated and ideals clash with reality, class barriers, mobility and the real world. Flexibility is needed where specialisation is encouraged, and experimentation in all areas, especially relationships, is flaunted. Criticism can be projected outward or accepted within, while self-organisation is learned to prepare for the world.

This is one of the most important times for health because many dietary and behavioural habits are created and set in the process of leaving home. The amount and variety of exercise is chosen, particularly after secondary school. The relationship to the body is formed at and after puberty when sexual experimentation begins, relationship mechanisms extended and the first steps towards independence are attempted.

Nutrition is one of the very most important therapies because it affects everyone. The diet of most people is unhealthy either due to the quality of food chosen, or because of the widespread use of hormones, additives, radiation, processing and other poisoning. Recent studies attribute a majority of all illness, whether mental, emotional or physical, to a faulty diet. Correct nutrition is a diet which includes the correct nutriments and eliminates substances which produce imbalance, and includes the use of vitamin and mineral supplements. Because of the way food is grown, stored and packaged, it is often difficult to receive proper nutriments even with a balanced diet. Diet may initially be therapeutic, but once balance has been achieved diet may be liberalised and the intention then becomes that of retaining balance.

The art of *Medical Herbalism* is the use of plant substances and extracts to relieve symptoms and support health. The whole plant remedies are often mixed with others to produce individual influences which encourage natural healing.

Pharmaceutical Medicine, while at the core of the problems created by allopathic medicine, is essential because some illnesses require drugs. Sometimes antibiotics are required, but the resultant wholesale destruction of intestinal micro-organisms will produce a need for intestinal bacteria to be reintroduced to restore balance. When chemical therapy is required for cancer or leukaemia, the immune system must be restored using diet, vitamin supplements and energy medicine treatments.

LIBRA AND THE 7TH HOUSE – CARDINAL AIR SIGN

23 years 5 months until 42 years old.
(Sublimation, balance, partnership, marriage and family, the public, obligations, justice, communal, social and business relationships)

With the 7th House cusp, one enters the upper, conscious half of the horoscope. Objectivity comes through relationships with oneself, one's partners and the outside world. The balance is achieved through sublimation of one's own personality in favour of a larger whole. The type of equilibrium we seek is reflected in the people, ideas and organisations with which we choose to associate. The balance between inner and outer worlds is also created through either projecting qualities outwards onto others or taking responsibility for them ourselves. The synthesis entails blending positive and negative qualities, and transforming our unconscious family inheritance into workable and loving relationships in the world.

As the 7th House is the highest level which most people will attain, it is very common for relationships to provide the ultimate blockages after a lifetime of sustained progress. When relationships are difficult to resolve, regression occurs into the unconsciousness associated with the first six houses.

As the time of partnership and business, much of the stress-activated illness of life erupts during the 7th House. As an airy house the focus is on mentally created afflictions and relationship difficulties. This is the time when psychotherapy is required for many people and the attempt at achieving balance in life is paramount.

Counselling and therapeutic *Sex Therapy* is an important

adjunct to many forms of physical and psychological therapy. The function and significance of orgasm and sexual release play a major part in Reichian therapy and the sexual component of other therapies is primary.

Biofeedback is the use of devices which measure heart rate, temperature, muscle tension or brain waves, and feed the information back to the client through sensory signals so that one can eventually learn to monitor and change these basic rates of function. Control can be exercised to lessen or eliminate stress and its corresponding physiological indicators such as cardiac disease or epilepsy. The training which goes along with biofeedback is meditation, creative visualisation, mandala painting or free association, writing poetry and many others.

Acupuncture and *Acupressure Massage* are Chinese techniques for maintaining balance in the organism at all levels by stimulating the channels of energy which run through the body. Chinese medicine has a sophisticated diagnostic system which uses many pulses and other techniques for determining the state of health on an energetic level, sometimes before any outward manifestations are apparent. The philosophy of yin and yang is central to acupuncture, and holds that the primary cause of disease is an imbalance of masculine and feminine energies, that it is essential to find the original distortion, that diet is critical in maintaining balance once achieved and that extremes are the primary causes of disease. Acupuncture uses fine needles, massage or moxibustion (burning herbs) to restore the flow of *chi*. Western news was made by acupuncture being used as an anaesthetic.

Shiatsu Massage is a Japanese form of acupuncture and is often used in conjunction with it. It has qualities similar to Rolfing which change deep tissue responses and create new patterns.

Group Therapy is a type of psychotherapy which works with group energies and creates a new context in which life and its essential relationships may work.

Co-counselling is a method of psychotherapy through which people may help each other without intervention from psychotherapists. This usually involves counsellor and client changing places in an even interchange which can lead to freedom of emotions.

SCORPIO AND THE 8TH HOUSE – FIXED WATER SIGN

42 years until death.
(Midlife and old age, life processes, karma, separation, the metaphysical, occultism, shared resources, legacies, perversity, death)

From the onset of the midlife crisis in one's forties, there is a gradual separation from the world, a falling inward upon one's own direction and needs and a tendency to ponder the nature of the world, ultimately leading to the prospect of death.

The senses developed in the opposite 2nd House are successively weakened and finally lost, bad habits of a lifetime come back to haunt or torture us and we must make our peace with the world. This can mean isolation, karmic repercussions of past misdeeds or a graceful exit from the stage of life. Towards the end of life the sense of the passage of time accelerates increasingly until it seems to fly by. Senility can often be the result of the distortion of time sense.

The search for meaning, the revival or restructuring of marital relationships after children have left home, and the need to search for higher and more central values in life is of primary importance. The transpersonal psychotherapies have reign here.

Transpersonal Psychologies focus on integration of the psyche after the mundane matters of life have been handled and the quest then becomes the next stage. This can take the form of creative work, collective activities or esoteric studies, as well as Buddhism, Taoism or other religious pursuits.

Colonic Irrigation Therapy cleanses the colon where toxins collect due to processed foods, meat and dairy products, and generally faulty diet. Often lactobacilli are replaced to counteract weaknesses in the intestinal flora caused by antibiotics. Colonics are often done in conjunction with detoxification programmes.

Death and Dying Therapies were first founded by Elisabeth Kubler-Ross and involve work with those mortally ill with cancer, leukaemia and old age. *LSD Therapy* is the clinical use of hallucinogens with the elderly or terminally ill to aid them in their journey beyond.

Transpersonal Octave Therapies

The ultimate octave of being is resonant with gestation, and the therapies of gestation are simultaneously of a transpersonal or transcendent nature. Most therapies of this level are concerned with initiating the individual to extend reality beyond the narrow physical domain.

Tibetan Buddhism is a multilayered theology which extends beyond the confines of the western ideas of life. Even those western mystical models which recognise a transpersonal reality only touch on the beginning of the Buddhist psychology which extends to many higher and finer realms. Many mainstream psychotherapists are highly influenced by Tibetan Buddhism.

Esoteric Psychology also maps realms beyond the physical, emotional and mental, and, based on the teachings of Alice Bailey, extends to the domain of the planetary consciousness.

Gurdiieff–Ouspensky work takes the view that the affairs of the individual life and physical realm are unimportant and mechanical, and that The Work begins with the recognition that group effort and transpersonal realities lie ahead on the higher levels of being.

Families of Therapies

Although this is a quite comprehensive survey of alternative and complementary therapies, many have not been included. The general feeling and quality of each zodiac sign and equivalent house should enable the reader to include any additional therapies, psychotherapies, religious systems, etc., to the list on the wheel.

The correlations of therapies with zodiacal signs is not intended to be absolute. Many therapies belong to more than one sign, and most incorporate elements of other therapeutic techniques. The attributions are therefore intended to be a starting point for further investigation rather than a rigid system. Every individual is different and the complexity of the modern time makes any system of absolute attribution too restricting and general.

Keeping the cylinder of life in mind, it is clear that the progress of disease is usually from 'above' to 'below'. Illness is separation from the path of full spiritual awareness and an entrance into a domain of imbalance. Alice Bailey described disease as 'a distorted reflection of divine possibilities'.[10] When the overall spiritual approach to life is distorted, its effects are most easily seen on the energetic level as a lack of energy or difficulties finding one's centre. The spiritual imbalance communicates itself rapidly to mental levels which, if not secure, manifest as distorted ideas, a lack of understanding or difficulty in communicating. The mental imbalance is transferred to emotional levels (childhood octave) when relationships break down and become unhealthy and when feelings cannot find adequate channels of expression. Only finally in the scale do symptoms begin to appear on the physical plane. Also, by implication, when physical symptoms have appeared, it is clear that the disease has a firm foothold on the emotional, mental and spiritual levels.

Many therapies which appear to be holistic are inadequate when seen in the context of the layered model of the psychophysical organism, because when physical symptoms indicating deeper (and higher) imbalances are suppressed or eliminated, it becomes virtually impossible to correct them and restore balance unless *every* level is shaken up profoundly, which is the case in chronic or life-threatening diseases. It is essential to select therapies knowing that often a series will be required, unless the therapy chosen contains the necessary perspectives.

Open Confidence

A primary issue in holistic, complementary healing is the nature of the relationship (transference) between therapist and client. Freud's doctrine stated that the therapist should retain an 'objective' stance outside, and occasionally above the client in order to prevent transference or identification with the therapist. While the holistic movement does accept that closer contact is essential, there remains a crucial area in which the communication is sabotaged. In the therapeutic context, there is assumed to be a *confidentiality* between therapist and client, which means that neither is open to talk about the results of sessions. What this confidentiality has led to is an overt denial of communication.

Often people have more than one therapist who do not know each other, or experience multiple therapies which are so different that they are seen to act on different parts of the individual. The confusion and mixing of signals which this situation can generate is very common, and very similar to the mixed messages known to encourage schizophrenia. This situation happens again and again, and is due to a lack of communication between therapist and client and between therapists themselves. At least in the medical profession the case history passes along with referrals.

A mechanism which would eliminate many of the difficulties of mixed therapeutic signals could be called *Open Confidence*. This is the conscious sharing of previously privileged information, both physiological and psychological, among all therapists working with an individual. At best, it would involve therapists sharing insights and information with each other to arrive at an approach to treatment which is fulfilling for each person. Such openness would dispel the primary problem which confidentiality creates, namely, that until personal insights and dilemmas become known to oneself as well as those in one's environment, they remain blockages.

In practice, the concept of open confidence means an acknowledgement that no single therapist, no matter how profound or effective, is able to be all things to his or her client. Many therapists and many therapies make claims that they are 'holistic', meaning that they can treat all people effectively, but this begins to border on the megalomaniac, and is often a defensive stance or a reflection of competition with other therapies. The reality behind this aspect of complementary therapies is that there is still a job insecurity for many, and the lack of acknowledgement from the orthodox medical profession exaggerates the insecurity. The taking on of holistic practice when the limits are stretched is a problem that requires solution in the short term.

The admission that the therapist cannot do everything takes a great pressure off both therapist and client. In the present therapeutic environment of complementary medicine or alternative therapy (and the confusion over names is symbolic of the problem of what the new movement really is), there is a very real danger of recreating the same maze of specialisation without the overview to integrate the therapies. A possible solution to this impasse is to institute open confidence in the process.

Ideally each person needs a series of therapies, each of which facilitates the acceptance of responsibility for parts of the whole. Therapies convey experiential techniques which allow us to create our own feedback loops and begin to heal ourselves. The taking of control back from doctors, whether medical or therapeutic, is a crucial test of the alternative vision of health and healing. Healing is not done by someone else to one, but rather is the regaining of harmony by one's own actions.

Too many therapists today treat their therapies as ends in themselves. They encourage their clients to enter training programmes to become therapists also, rather than allowing that psychotherapeutic techniques are tools. While the training programmes are essential in teaching techniques for self-help, the drive to become therapists with therapy as the whole world is a problem. The tools are needed, but the tools should not be confused with the territory.

Many therapists are beginning to recognise that they need the back-up of other therapies in order to perform their tasks effectively. Rolfers become aware that their clients begin to express emotions of anger or frustration, yet unless they have psychotherapeutic skills, which most do not, they cannot really take them in that direction. To work successfully with clients it would be necessary for the Rolfer to have training in psychotherapy (which many do). A useful option would be if they could refer them to a psychotherapist who is aware of the aims and goals of Rolfing and can interface with the process of bodywork to the mutual profit of both.

The same is true the other way. Psychotherapists identify the need for further body work to ground emotional experiences, yet often lack the requisite training. Here again the matter of referral is *not* a matter of passing a client on to someone more highly trained, but to allow *integration* with other therapeutic techniques at the right time. It is in this area that astrology is profoundly valuable. It is possible to see which levels, and hence which therapies, are likely to be needed by an individual at the start of their journey. In addition, the timing of changes of phase often coincides with astrologically defined phrases in life.[11]

Finding the Root Cause of Disease

The traditional form of medical astrology is a process of diagnosis and referral which takes little notice of timing. When a horoscope shows the tendency to a particular affliction, the issue of when that affliction could manifest is often left open. The systems by which such timings may be discovered are overlays on top of the birth horoscope, which itself does not have an inherent time scale, unlike Life★Time Astrology.

The two major systems are transits and directions. *Transits* are the present locations of planets in the sky compared to the birth positions (Horoscope 3 *see* Figure 21). When the disruptive planet Uranus transits opposite the stabilising Saturn in the birth horoscope, irritation, tension and movement are inevitable. The dissolving influence of Uranus will not alter the quality of Saturn, but will add tension. Transits qualify natal planets and can transform them when the transit event is consciously worked with. Typically, transits are used by astrologers to determine the timings of events in life rather than the quality of the event.

Directions are formulae by which the natal planets are advanced through the horoscope with the intention of finding the years in which changes may be anticipated. The most usual are Solar Arc directions, which advance each planet one degree for each year of life. At the age of 32 every planet has moved 32° along the zodiac, and when a directed planet makes an aspect with a natal planet, the base quality is reactivated.

It is important to understand the birth horoscope to use directions or transits, and this underpinning is often unsatisfactory in modern astrology. The Life★Time scale allows a base timing to be understood before any direction system is activated.

When the Saturn shown in Horoscope 2 is resident in the 2nd House and registered at the age of 1 year 3 months, when as a young child one clung to grandmother for security, when Saturn is opposed by Uranus, it could be that grandmotherly figures rebel or disappear, leaving the individual feeling abandoned. While an understanding will not recreate grandmother, it can allow the individual to create a grandmother within who will not only provide the necessary security but will always be there when needed. The attachment of a planet with its appropriate age of initial registration is essential in finding the initial cause of disease. Often the lack of ease can be traced back directly to the earlier registration of planets which created the imbalance, and the imbalance can be healed naturally without intervention.

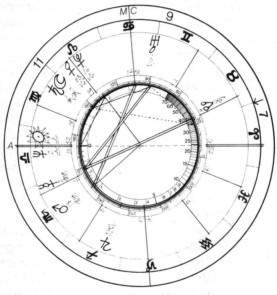

Figure 20

The approach for finding the 'root cause' of disease involves looking at the aspect pattern of the horoscope. The starting point is the age when a person first recognises the symptoms. In Horoscope 2 (Figure 20), a young man of 35 experienced what he considered to be 'demonic possession' as a result of a difficult drug experience and the accidental death of his lover. While the cause of his state was clearly attributable to drug usage, the underlying cause existed much earlier in his life. At 34 years old, there was a sensitive trine from the Moon and at 34 years 9 months from Saturn in Virgo in the 11th House, both following his entrance into the sign Taurus at 34 years old. As Moon/Saturn is particularly identified with 'psychic diseases or depressions; hereditary diseases; inhibited, lonely and sad people; the lonely woman or mother; anxiety, mood changes; estrangement from the wife or mother',[12] it is clear that the primary cause relates back to eighteen weeks before birth. His mother was clearly lonely, felt abandoned, and could possibly have been suffering from chronic disturbances of her body, which is often created by overindulgence of drugs or alcohol. The even earlier sensitive sextile aspect of Uranus in the 9th House just after conception, brings an even deeper tendency to 'inherited schizophrenia; an interest in the metaphysical sciences and realms; the tendency to exaggerate things; fanaticism; and overstrain of the nerves; contacts with nervous, restless or ambitious women'.[13] The afflictions inherited from his mother affected her while she was carrying him, and were reactivated by the combination of drug usage and an affair with a nervous woman much like his mother. The unconscious fear and anxiety created by the situation was thus shown to be an inheritance from his mother, and for him the correct therapy was through astrology, the therapy of the 11th House, which yielded information that clarified the problem from his standpoint.

The history of an affliction is most often traced along the aspect lines from a current age back into childhood and gestation. There may be two different and equally powerful strains, each producing its own set of conditions, indicated by separate constellations. In Horoscope 3 (Figure 21) a woman who had a series of abortions, stillborn children and suicide attempts had two distinct aspect constellations and also two distinct personalities, one mousy and overweight, the other a glamorous and highly sexual blonde. She had been suspected of having TB or meningitis in early youth. Both constellations led back into gestation and the registration of Moon sextile Sun. While this is a very good aspect in itself, the fact that the connecting aspects are sesquiquadrates to Saturn (anxiety, estrangement, hereditary diseases) and Neptune (disturbed consciousness, worry, self-deception, instability) from the Moon and an inconjunct Jupiter (weak re-

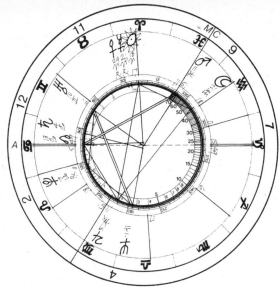

Figure 21

generative functions) and square Node (dysfunctions of the autonomic nervous system, separations from men) from the Sun show that there is a congenital weakness inherited from both her father and mother. Tracing her dilemma back to its earliest planets and allowing her to identify with the positive sides of the planets involved was a revelation to her, in the light of her life of pain. Both sides needed attention from her partner but as that was not forthcoming she ended up, after two unsuccessful marriages, living with three adopted children, who represented the parts of herself which could not be integrated previously.

Choosing Therapies from the Horoscope

One of the greatest virtues of astrology in association with alternative therapies is that it is often possible to determine from the horoscope the most effective therapies for a person. This may entail the choice of a single therapy or a series of therapies which interlock and provide a healing impetus on many levels. While it would be easy to generalise about the therapies which are most appropriate for each octave or element in the horoscope, the reality is that most people have planets in all three octaves and all four elements and, as a result, will require more than one therapy in life. If one continues to grow, there is a great likelihood that a succession of therapies will be essential.

The process of life determines to a large extent which therapy is required at a given time, once it has been determined which planet or constellation of planets is responsible for a particular life stage. The fact that we change in life supports this way of understanding therapy. While our essence may remain generally the same throughout life, due to the imprint at conception, the outer forms of our life, the rate at which we grow and the quality of our realisation about life can vary wildly, and must be taken into consideration. Most therapies treat their function as permanent, in that they all represent the end of the line, the ultimate source of understanding. This may be underplayed or be unconsciously transmitted, but it is there. Few therapies acknowledge that they are only tools helpful for part of the journey. The craving for the ultimate is deeply imbedded in us and is difficult to dislodge.

The first introduction to therapy is often miraculous, but with time comes the recognition that the 'answer' is an answer only for a present set of circumstances, rarely an equation which holds true forever. And, once discovering that the problems of life can be worked with, it becomes clear that work must be done on all levels.

The structure of the horoscope shows the *potential* for disease. Each of the planets represent the organ systems, glands and body parts with which they resonate. Only when the planet is activated in a negative way or blocked in its activity does disease occur. It is therefore necessary to discover which planets are the source of the problem.

The planets considered *malefic* are Mars, Saturn, Uranus, Neptune and Pluto – all except Mars are the outer planets which move very slowly through the signs. The signs inhabited by these malefics are often the weakest psychological stages of life and most vulnerable parts of the body. This is especially true when more than one are together in any sign.

Conjunctions of malefics are especially difficult, partially because they tend to compound the dilemma, and partially because it is difficult to separate the effects of the two or more

planets involved. Their actions become confused and inter-
mingled until clarity is very difficult. Certain combinations are
antagonistic to each other. In Horoscope 4 (Figure 22) Mars and
Uranus are both conjunct the ASC, showing that their principle
of 'sudden application of effort; operations; the urge for freedom
and independence; strains and stresses; or fighting spirit'[14]
caused by the surgical delivery, is attached to his personality.

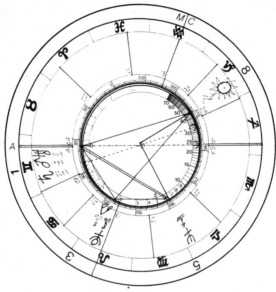

Figure 22

The delivery was induced, indicated by the exact trine from
Neptune, and highly traumatic, shown by the sextile from Pluto
and the Node. The constellation attached to the Ascendant/
Personality is particularly difficult because every time he expresses himself, all the tension of the birth comes into play.

The fact that the Ascendant, Mars and Uranus are all in the sign
Gemini indicate that the lungs are particularly stressed when the
constellation is activated. Both planets bring high stress and
imply a great danger from any lung afflictions. The difficulty of
expressing himself will gravitate to the lungs.

Because Mars, Uranus, Pluto and the Node near birth are in the
childhood octave, the experiences and tension are attached to the
emotional body. All are below the horizon, the surface of con-

sciousness, and he is likely to be unconscious of the problem, and will in any event not become aware that anything is wrong until the opposition point to the Ascendant at about 24 years old at the earliest. The individual in question began Freudian psychoanalysis at the opposite point to Saturn in the 1st House (concentration on the personality), but after five years of analysis felt a need for a more open context for his therapy. As a creative individual the qualities were indicated by the sign Sagittarius, through which he passed from 21 to 38 years 4 months old, provided therapeutic possibilities inherent in yoga, meditation and transpersonal psychology.

It can be that the therapy most appropriate is determined by a constellation in the horoscope which is not activated at the time of recognition of a problem. This is the case when the work required needs a firm basis in earlier material in order to be profitable.

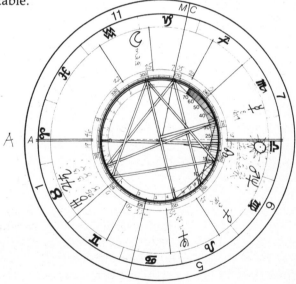

Figure 23

In the case of John Lennon (Horoscope 5; Figure 23), it is well known from his relationship with Yoko Ono and the lyrics of several of his songs, notably 'Mother' which decried his separation from his mother, that the primary focus of his psychological life was women, and by extension, mother issues. When Lennon entered the Scorpio time at 28 years 6 months old, it signalled a break-up of his relationships with the Beatles and his first wife, and the entrance into relationship with Yoko Ono. Lennon also began working with Janov, doing Primal Scream Therapy. The difficulty is directed to the personality, as can be seen from the position of the Ascendant in Aries. Aries Ascendant itself indicates trauma at birth, while the opposition from the Sun, showing that his father was not present at birth, exaggerates this fact. The separation at birth and subsequent rebellion against the masculine principle was a central theme throughout his life and he never got over it. As Primal Scream is a therapy particularly appropriate to traumatic births, he made the correct choice for the first phase of his psychotherapeutic work. He sought out men who answered his Libra Sun opposition Aries Ascendant, such as Brian Epstein, George Martin, Maharishi Mahesh Yogi and finally Janov, who ended his search for the missing father.

The registration of Mercury together with the sensitive square from Pluto produces a tendency to be highly affected by publicity and propaganda. The therapists to whom Lennon was attracted were propagandists of the highest order, fulfilling his own needs in that area.

In addition to the signs tenanted by malefics, the same signs when occupied by planets not usually considered malefics can indicate clues to therapeutic requirements. Horoscope 6 (Figure 24) was a young man afflicted with lung cancer at the age of 20. The condition was traced back to the same constellation as in the previous example, the Uranus/Pluto conjunction in Virgo, and he had a large part of his intestines removed surgically when just over 4, at their registration. The cause lies in the other conjunction of Moon/Venus registering just before the Uranus/Pluto but also in Virgo. His mother withdrew love from her child in his moment of need, which led to the coldness and disease indicated by a sesquiquadrate to Saturn back in gestation. The bottom line is that he was not wanted or loved. When the Moon/Venus conjunction was reactivated by square sensitive point at 0° and 1° of Sagittarius, at the age of 19 years 2 months, his mother remarried and was totally beyond contact. At this point he became mortally ill. The Sagittarian sign of residence indicates that Buddhist philosophy, yoga or meditation is required to understand and detach from the situation. As the afflictions are

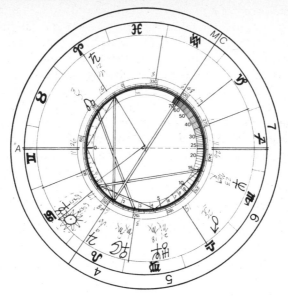

Figure 24

in mutable signs, the entire cross of mutables is activated.

Another rule of thumb is that often the opposite sign is reciprocally affected. The inability to adopt a more philosophical attitude (the way shown by Sagittarius) sparked off the affliction in the lungs, indicated naturally by the Gemini Ascendant.

Diseases can also be produced by an exaggeration in the activation and operation of a planet. Jupiter acting in its exalted sign Cancer can produce obesity, and a wonderfully placed Mercury in Virgo can indicate mental identification as a substitute for experiencing the world.

Integration of Therapies

It is usual that more than one therapy is required to act on more than one level simultaneously. Horoscope 7 (Figure 25) suffered from Khron's disease, indicated by the conjunction of Uranus and Pluto (changes in rhythm in biological processes) in Virgo (the colon) in sextile to the Ascendant (affecting the personality) and in opposition to the MC (endangered will to live), and

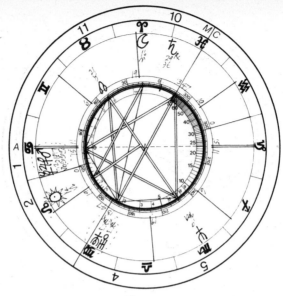

Figure 25

inconjunct to the Moon (inherent schizophrenia in mother/child relationship). Uranus/Pluto stressed the colon (Virgo) and gave rise to such problems that twenty inches of the colon had to be removed in a surgical operation. While the problem is overtly due to diet and stress by way of the aspects to the Ascendant, it has other ramifications. The sextile to Venus and Mars on the Ascendant bring sexuality into play, specifically competition with her older brother. Since the entire constellation except for the Moon is in childhood, competitiveness between sexes at that time is largely responsible for the severity of the problem. It was essential for her to become ill in order to receive as much attention as her brother.

The Cancer Ascendant constellation shows the need for motherly nurturing, and the need to express anger at her mother for frustrating this need for love. The solution was in a woman colonic practitioner who provided not only therapeutic support in detoxification but psychological assistance, providing simultaneous therapy on the childhood/emotional and gestation/physical levels. The improvement was rapid and spontaneous.

Horoscope 8 (Figure 26) was adopted immediately after birth

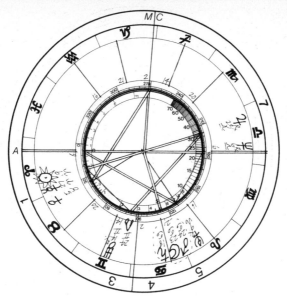

Figure 26

when the Sun registered in the 1st House at over 2 months old. The obvious psychological dilemmas began surfacing when Neptune (insecurity) in the 7th House (partnerships) registered at 23 years 8 months old, when a relationship created such anger that violence ensued. As the subject is very powerful and athletic, this was a dangerous situation. He was almost institutionalised but managed through psychiatric help to remain in touch. When Jupiter registered he went into therapy, working on the feelings around his adoption. At this point the birth time was inexact, but life events allowed a correction of the Ascendant (see Appendix 5). Jupiter registered and activated the opposition Aries Sun in childhood and the square from Saturn, Moon and Mars in the 5th House. The degree of game-playing from the 5th House involvement was astonishing, as every psychological exercise was seen as a competition. The problem was confined to the time during childhood to early maturity and the therapies suggested were Zen Buddhist meditation, Primal Scream, Cranial Osteopathy and stretching, as well as a regime of tennis and as much sport as possible to allow a channel through which his aggressiveness could be freed.

Afflictions in *Gestation* indicate hereditary diseases, diseases or afflictions derived from diet, imbalance or accidents to the mother during gestation, very deep feelings of insecurity or other archetypal angst, all of which are stored in the *physical body*. Often the genetic code itself stores the imbalance and energy medicine is required to communicate with this internal equilibrator. If these afflictions are not evident at birth, and few of them are, they are activated when the person passes a hard aspect of them in childhood or maturity. Diet during gestation and drugs taken at that time can prevent the immune system from coming into being and will result in later problems. All difficulties shown here require bodywork, deep touch such as Rolfing, Shiatsu or biodynamic massage, osteopathy or chiropractic, and energy medicine to affect the stored energy contained within for so long.

Afflictions in *Childhood* have their primary effect on the *emotional body*. A great number of such problems stem from the methods of delivery which have been common since the Second World War. Brutality, accidents, improper surgery, clumsy forceps, unnecessary anaesthetics, inducement and irresponsible care in the early years can damage the emotional body of personality. Often such afflictions do not surface until hard aspects manifest, mainly beginning in the late twenties and after. The later such afflictions occur, the more difficult they are to right as the requisite energy is lacking. Childhood diseases are much more critical than they seem as they are the foundation of the operation of the immune system. The child who never experiences the classic childhood illnesses such as chickenpox, measles, mumps or tonsil inflammation is less well prepared to accept minor or major afflictions later in life, because the immune system is not operable to the same degree and the emotional equipment to accept crisis is not there.

Afflictions during *Maturity* have their major effect on the *mental body* as their matrix, although as can be surmised, a majority of them are pre-existent, having been brought into being during gestation or childhood. While it seems that illnesses just happen during maturity because a majority of the serious ones occur there for the first time, it does not mean that they do not exist before.

The recognition of the earlier causes of physical symptoms

constitutes a primary difference of Life★Time Astrology from other astrological systems. Psychosomatic afflictions, nervous disturbances, stress-related diseases, deterioration of heart, lungs or other organ systems, and others are certainly activated by bad habits, but their seeds have been already sown. Resistance to disease requires regaining the resilience of childhood without the emotional immaturity of the child. Most people begin to harden and crystallise in their views past the Saturn cycle at 29 years of age, and their ability to express themselves in the world diminishes and comes to reflect their state of health. Afflicted sight is related to an imbalance of masculine or feminine sides of one's nature. Cancers are the lack of adequate outlets for anger or love. Due to the extension of perceptual time in maturity, illnesses take longer to form and also to be cured, until in later life they cannot ever really be cured, only their effects lessened.

Afflictions of *Transcendence* are conditioned by the status of gestation issues. Access to transcendence or the transpersonal is contingent upon utilising all levels of the constitution as a whole. The fact of good or poor health is not a barrier, just the willingness to utilise all experiences of the universe. Acceptance of one's entire range of strengths and weaknesses distinguishes the true artist and centred individual. The individual constitution must be integrated to the collective whole, and the body seen as a vehicle for higher perception rather than as a lead weight retarding progress.

It is a requirement that before or during death one experiences the entire range of affects created in a lifetime, and an inability to coordinate the parts or to want certain parts to disappear can produce a reliance upon just those parts. All traumas and afflictions from youth come back again with a vengeance and must be confronted consciously.

The quality of death is a necessary and just compensation for the quality of life lived approaching its portals. Old age brings wisdom and a lack of strength to resist anymore, hopefully to disengage gracefully and be received to the higher unity awaiting us all.

6

Astrological Diagnosis

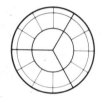

The sequence from conception to death in Life★Time Astrology is the primary context for diagnosing disease from the horoscope. Just as particular therapies are related to times in life, diseases can often be correlated to times in life when they originated, in distinction to the times when their symptoms appear. The sections and subsections of this chapter will describe the four octaves and the critical points of conception, birth, puberty and death which define their duration. In each section many example horoscopes will be shown to illustrate the principles of diagnosis. When therapies have been selected and worked or not worked, this information is included as well.

BEFORE CONCEPTION

As described fully in *Life★Time Astrology*,[1] the logarithmic time scale begins at the end of the first lunar month, by which time the fertilised ovum has attached itself to the uterus wall and the development of the cellular body has begun. The 9th House cusp is the conception point, a compaction of the events of the preceding lunar month cycle, which includes the time from the end of the mother's last menstrual cycle to fertilisation and then to the beginning of the creation of the cellular body (Figure 27). The twenty-eight day lifetime of the ovum carries the same pattern as the entire natal chart, compacted one thousand times.

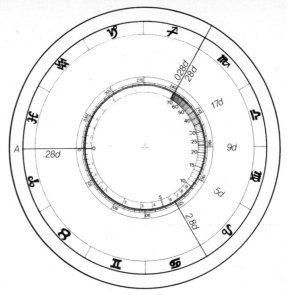

Figure 27 The Life★Time of the Ovum

The ovum carries a microcosmic record of the subsequent development of the cellular body.

Since the lifetime of the ovum contains a memory of the sexual act of conception, it can be seen in the horoscope what the relationship between the parents was before, during and after conception. The circumstances of the parents, their mutual relationship, the nature of their sexuality, and their tendencies to act at the time are highly significant as they are part of the first cause of life itself. Without the inspiration to mate, none of us would be here now. Although it is not something very many people have investigated, preconception events have a profound bearing on later life.

At the early stage of horoscope diagnosis, one must only be concerned with the Sun and Moon and those planets which conjunct them. The basic qualifying influences for the two luminaries are the quadrants they occupy, their sign and house, and their mutual aspect if there is one.

Moving backwards in a clockwise direction from the 9th cusp conception point, the first luminary to occur is the parent responsible for the initial impulse to conceive a child (Figure 28).

Figure 28 Back from Conception

This in itself can be a deep cause of unrest and a resultant tendency to disease. Traditionally, the 8th house is associated with deep, painful, intense and hidden pressures and pains, emotional insecurity, great but distorted intensity and reincarnation. This is because the 8th House just precedes conception. In nature the 8th sign, Scorpio, governs the life of the seed and the ruthless fight for survival, which is undergone by the sperm and ovum as they struggle to prepare to meet, fertilise and survive the journey up the Fallopian tube to the uterus.

Horoscope 9 (Figure 29) is Louise Brown, the first test-tube baby, and shows an interesting picture. Going backwards (clockwise) into the horoscope from the conception point at the 9th cusp, the first luminary is the 5th House Leo Sun, showing that the father was very interested in proving his own creativity despite weakness (sesquiquadrate from 8th House Neptune). This is coupled with the lack of any supportive aspects from the Moon (Louise's mother), and its trine from Neptune also. Neptune aspects both luminaries and is the common link between them as there is no mutual aspect. Neptune is the significator for the preconception time, and lies just before

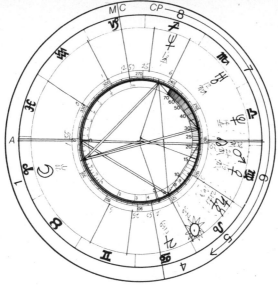

Figure 29

the conception point. The primary cause for the problem of conceiving would be Neptune's square to Venus showing a difficulty in expressing love. The sextile Pluto is the gradual commencement of a therapy, the trine to the Moon shows the mother as moody, immediately responsive to new influences and unusual experiences. Pluto is the doctor who performed the test-tube insemination, in direct opposition to the Moon (mother), implying an intervention. It is unfortunate that the horoscopes of the father and mother are not known.

Hereditary diseases are often indicated in the 8th House as being in existence before conception. Horoscope 10 (Figure 30) is Czarevitch Prince Alexis of Russia who inherited haemophilia, the inability of the blood to clot. His 8th House Neptune in Cancer (weakness through family inheritance) registers just before conception in square with Jupiter, which rules the blood. That it affects his destiny is shown by the sextile to the MC.

Recent studies[2] have shown that alcohol consumption before pregnancy can affect the genetics of the child. Astrologically, inherited alcoholism can be spotted by Neptune registering near conception point. Horoscope 11 (Figure 31) is one child of an

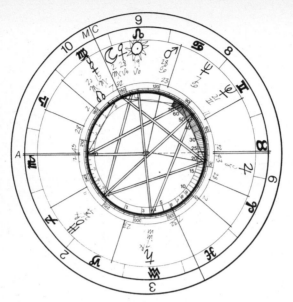

Figure 30

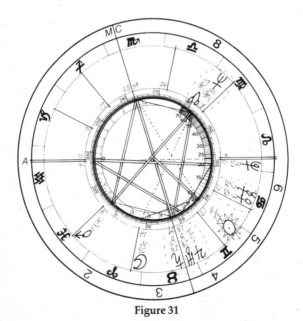

Figure 31

alcoholic mother who produced a succession of badly debilitated children. This child had leukaemia, and two were mentally retarded. The classic indicator of leukaemia is Neptune in the 8th House, as well as being a signal for alcoholism. Neptune is in afflicted opposition Mars (paralysis, toxic systems, alcoholism), square the Sun (hereditary weakness and alcoholism from the father) and inconjunct Moon (physical and mental defects from the mother). Mars/Neptune opposition is particularly implicated by Nauman[3] as an indicator of lymph-related ailments that can result in a high white cell count. As Saturn is restriction, it makes the problem very resistant to treatment. The Ascendant in Aquarius (bad circulation and weak heart) and Pluto opposed Ascendant (threat to vitality) are also both leukaemia indicators. The Neptunian influence of weakness, particularly to drugs and alcohol was pronounced, and leukaemia from a very early age was the result, its first signs appearing at the age of 5 when Saturn and Uranus registered in the 3rd and 4th Houses, and fully blown when the Pluto registered at 21 years old in the 6th House, the time when health afflictions tend to become known.

The Gestation Octave

The French psychologist and researcher Michel Gauquelin investigated astrological hereditary links from generation to generation in addition to his better known research into the correlations of the positions of certain planets and professions of famous athletes, doctors and artists. The 9th House occupies one of the so-called Gauquelin 'plus zones' (Figure 32) around the MC of the horoscope. Gauquelin found that this area and a similar zone from 20° before the ASC to 10° after the ASC are most critical in hereditary qualities which determine profession and tendencies to illness. While of little consequence in the practice of traditional astrology, in Life★Time Astrology the two areas are essential in the diagnosis of tendencies to disease. The area around the MC

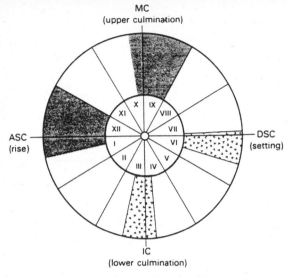

Figure 32 Gauquelin 'Plus Zones'

being critical for inherited afflictions, and the area around birth affecting the prebirth development, birth itself and the post-birth months.

President Franklin D. Roosevelt (Horoscope 12; Figure 33) was crippled for life by polio at 39 years of age, yet the tendency to such a difficult affliction was in existence from early gestation. The configuration is more informative because the Saturn/Neptune conjunction straddles the 9th House conception point, with Neptune registering in early gestation and Saturn in late life. Saturn/Neptune is the 'chronic and unhampered progress of a malady; organic decomposition' and by its semisquare ahead to Mars, 'infectious diseases; activity paralysed; the wasting away of muscles; susceptibility to epidemic infections; the consequences of an infection'.[4] Although Roosevelt was not struck by polio until a relatively late age, the indication is that his mother was exposed to an infection soon after his conception which left him with an inherited sensitivity to infections. Subsequently, when he was exposed to polio, he was a ripe target and succumbed immediately. That he was struck down suddenly and apparently at random is shown by the sensitive inconjunct from Uranus in the 1st House which had been followed by a sensitive

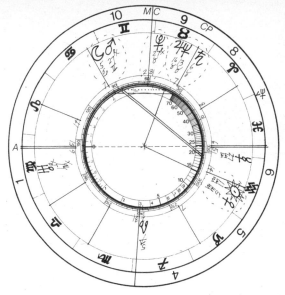

Figure 33

point semisquare from Neptune at 35 years and 5 months old during the First World War. Tendencies inherent during early gestation can manifest with a vengeance in later life, but it is equally possible to determine such tendencies very early, before they have had an opportunity to manifest in severe form.

Horoscope 13 (Figure 34) is another example of the potency of Neptune as an indicator of alcohol or drug abuse during gestation. In this case there are two indicators for the deformed hand discovered at birth. Neptune is conjunct the MC and at the midpoint of (halfway between) the Ascendant and Pluto, showing the shock and trauma attached to the deformity. The Neptunian position, being at the MC when the soul incarnates in the physical body, shows that there is a karmic significance to the malformation, which indeed is the case as the individual in question became a highly proficient surgeon and acupuncturist. The inconjunct between Mars and Saturn is also often in play when severe disturbances affect the physique. Saturn, registering in the 8th House just before conception, is opposite Venus, showing that the mother felt unloved and transmitted her anger (inconjunct Mars) on to the child within her.

Figure 34

The two glands responsible for growth are usually activated when a malfunction of growth occurs. In Horoscope 14 (Figure 35), a young woman was born a dwarf in a family with perfectly formed parents and another sister, although she did not realise that she was in any way different from other children until she was about 7 years old. The classic indicators are afflictions to Mercury as ruler of the thyroid gland and of Saturn as ruler of the anterior pituitary gland. In this case, they are conjunct at the age when she discovered that she was different, and also square to Neptune and trine to the Moon, showing strongly the cause was in a weakness passed down through the mother's side of the family (Moon just after conception inconjunct Neptune). Despite this she has a very strong and even powerful horoscope, and once past the hurdle of confronting others when she passed the Sun at 12 years old (opposite Pluto in the 11th as differences from friends), she went on to a successful career in the public eye.

In a case of Down's Syndrome, Horoscope 15 (Figure 36) can point to a reason why mongolism occurred. The mother was 39 when she conceived and had had a miscarriage immediately before the conception, as shown by the registration of Saturn in

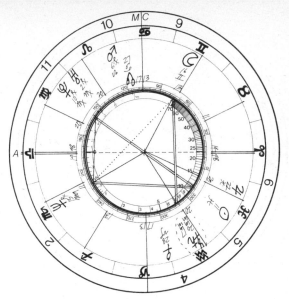

Figure 35

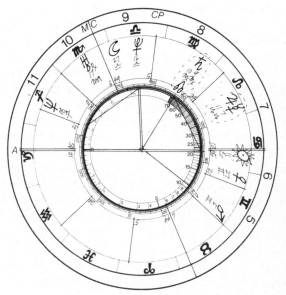

Figure 36

the 8th House just before the conception point. Saturn is in hard square from Mars, the death axis, and also in sextile to the Sun and Moon, implying hereditary weakness from both father's and mother's sides of the family. Further, the t-square of Ascendant square Pluto square Sun is an indicator of hypothyroidism and mongolism. The Sun is also the heart, and this unfortunate baby was also born with a hole in his heart which almost killed him in his first week. And as he was one month premature, the problems were compounded. There could have been parental violence during the first weeks after conception (Pluto in the 9th House), which could have exaggerated the inviability of the infant.

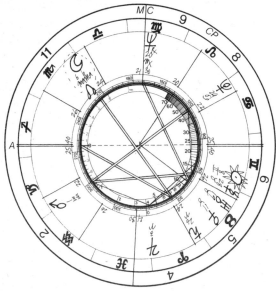

Figure 37

Near abortions are a more common problem than one would anticipate, and the indicators for this are the planets Mars, Uranus or Pluto in prominent positions around the MC, i.e. the moment when a mother realises that she is pregnant. Horoscope 16 (Figure 37) is the child of a single woman who was idealistic and naïve about sexuality, was seduced by a lover on the spur of the moment (square from Uranus to the 9th cusp) and became pregnant. Her reaction was to ignore it, as is often the case with Neptune just before the MC, and in any event the father had gone away (Sun aspected only to Mars and Jupiter). By the time the implications dawned on her, she decided that she did not want the child. The 11th House Scorpio Moon, fifteen weeks after conception, is dangerous, especially when in square to both Mars and Pluto, and during gestation often indicates an attempted abortion. As Moon conjunct Node is great powers of self-defence, the developing foetus was miraculously saved and obviously survived. Just before birth the father, who was a foreigner, heard that his love was ill with the attempted abortion and returned and married her. Subsequently, the child was raised as a 'love-child' and adored from birth, a symbol of the fertility and happiness of the relationship. Unfortunately, the young woman grew up having an overwhelming unconscious fear of women, including the woman in herself. This tipped the balance away from natural relationships and generated a score of psychological problems. At the time when the reading was done she had reached her wit's end (sextile sensitive points to Neptune and Uranus) and was about to journey home to see her mother, who was suffering from cancer. In a cathartic period of time the early threat of the near-fatal abortion came out into the open, producing a phenomenal change in the young woman and a

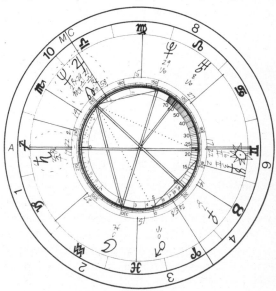

Figure 38

remission in her mother, who was finally able to release her pain and the great secret. It is often the case that very basic truths are available by retelling the life story and opening up areas of the psyche to therapy.

As a medical quirk, Horoscope 17 (Figure 38) belongs to a man born with two penises and two sets of kidneys, one set smaller than the other. Once again Neptune is implicated by its position in Scorpio in gestation at sixteen weeks after conception, and its sesquiquadrate to the Sun shows that the father is the genetic partner from whom the disability arose. Although a speculation, the fact that Neptune is conjunct the Node, sesquiquadrate Sun and semisquare the Ascendant all in double signs may be the indicator of the duplication of sex organs and kidneys, especially as the kidneys are the domain of Libra. That the problem will affect his sex life, which it did, as shown by the opposition to Venus from Neptune and the trine to the Pisces Moon, indicating isolation and loneliness. In this case a surgical solution is to be desired.

BIRTH

Birth is probably the most critical time in life, from an astrological and medical viewpoint. The entrance into the world is fraught with pain, the possibility of difficulties, and a necessary pressure. The description of the process of birth is a microcosm of the personality, which is also a mechanism that is subject to the laws and dynamics of processes. Stan Grof's work with perinatal matrices bears this out.[5]

The astrological birth constellation includes everything which happens before, during and after the actual delivery as metaphors for the preparation, actualisation and after effects of expressing oneself in the world. Generally, the planets in contact with the Ascendant show subpersonalities attached to the personality itself, as shown by the Ascendant sign, and they qualify the basic personality in a number of respects. Planets conjunct the Ascendant are people who were physically present at the delivery and are integral components of the personality. For example, when Mars is conjunct the Ascendant it indicates surgery, and also a subpersonality related to the surgeon.

Planets in aspect to the Ascendant are influences which are a part of the overall personality but which are capable of detachment. Planets in aspect to the Ascendant which are above the horizon are subpersonalities of which the individual is likely to be conscious, while those below the horizon are subpersonalities of which the individual is likely to be unconscious. The distribution of planets is an indicator of whether the personality is primarily conscious and unconscious. The following two tables show the interpretative factors at birth with a focus on the medical and psychological parallels. In the case of the aspects to the Ascendant from planets, both the possible basis of the subpersonalities and the possible adverse effects at birth are shown. Problematic birth almost invariably leads to difficulty lodged in the personality or in the health in a direct way.

The most critical indicators at birth are: Saturn when there is a difficult labour creating constriction, tension and nervousness; Mars, indicating the likelihood of a doctor delivery with the possibility of forceps, surgery, episiotomy or Caesarian section; Pluto, which shows the use of force and pressure, and can also show Caesarian section; Uranus which shows accidents, the use of technology, mechanical induction, drips, machines, monitors, or unexpected incidents; and Neptune, the primary indicator for anaesthetics, induction, the use of drugs, effects of smoking or alcohol by the mother, incubators, watery births or malformations. The Moon is typically the mother herself, anaesthetics, alkaloids, drugs, induction or watery births.

The determining factor in describing the birth when series of planets are in various aspects to the Ascendant is a blend of the *type* of aspect, the *closeness* of exactitude and the *sequence* of positions in degrees. A case history will illustrate the manner in which the Ascendant and its medical and psychological effects may be interpreted from horoscopes.

Horoscope 18 (Figure 39) is the middle child of a triple birth where the first male child died. The third baby, the sister, followed the individual by about four minutes and the first brother was six minutes before. The births happened in a very short space of time due to a Caesarean section performed in a

Table 4 Ascendant Birth Interpretation

Aries	= Restless; energetic; self-assertive; rash; aggressive; selfish; impatient; and from Mars ruling, surgery and surgeons; aggressive doctors or midwives; impatient people; forceps injuries; hospitals.
Taurus	= Stability, quiet; secure; domestic; sensual; beautiful; attractive; homely; and from Venus ruling, women; midwives; attractive people; artists; loving, attentive people; children.
Gemini	= Changeable; ambiguous; adaptable; superficial; mobile; talkative; observative; dualistic; nervous; and from Mercury ruling; children; crowds; thinkers; gossips; hurriers; talkers; conversationalists.
Cancer	= Moodiness; homeliness; simplicity; maternity; passivity; warmth; conservatism; reliance on others; sensitivity; and from the Moon ruling, feeling people; the instinctive; midwives; women; mothers; nurses; breast feeders; feminists.
Leo	= Authoritative; confident; open-minded; joyous; self-confident; open; active; proud; prominent; game-playing; and from Sun ruling, warm; domineering; purposeful; boldness; extrovert.
Virgo	= Naïve; virginal; stable; critical; nervous; hospitals; reserve; clean; hygienic; sterile; cautious; attentive; pedantic; and from Mercury ruling, intellectual; medical students; doctors; nurses; observers; critics; digestive problems; collaborations; teams.
Libra	= Balanced; harmonious; homely; lively; authoritarian; easy; vain; attentive; chatty; moody; obliging; social; and from Venus ruling, youths; women; nurses; midwives; woman doctors; beauties; friends.
Scorpio	= Disharmonious; humid; hotheaded; cautious; industrious; passionate; separative; violent; surgical; impulsive; dangerous; brutal; forceful; and from Mars, surviving; surgeons and surgery; Caesareans; technicians; forceps; brutality; danger; force; and from Pluto ruling, tragic events; endurance; large hospitals; forceful deliveries; violent public events; circumcision.
Sagittarius	= Enthusiastic; athletic; joyous; good humoured; expansive; foreign; natural; scattered; social; messy; lively; adventurous; talkative; religious; and from Jupiter ruling, expansive; doctors; grandparents and relatives; religious hospitals; nuns; nurses; foreign hospitals and countries; tolerance.
Capricorn	= Concentration; seriousness; practicality; long labour; inhibition; hard work; goals; reserve; pragmatism; anxiety; physicality; and from Saturn ruling, will; restraint; doctors and surgeons; older people; strictness; paternalism; masculinity; slowness; methodicality repression; unemotional; materialistic; expensive.
Aquarius	= Communal; abstract; friendly; detached; sociable; progressive; sympathetic; inventive; eccentric; idealistic; utopian; planned; and from Saturn ruling, realised plans; seriousness; older doctors or grandparents; and from Uranus ruling, inventive, technological, instrumentative; original; unorthodox; mechanical; rebellious; scientific; changeable; rhythmic.
Pisces	= Self-sacrificial; lacking confidence; externally influenced; anaesthetic; depressed; vague; lazy; comfortable; peculiar; passive; asleep; weak; drugged; induced; gentle; simple; and from Jupiter ruling, institutional; isolated; contented; visionary; wasteful; religious; and from Neptune ruling, psychic; dreamy, drugged; idealistic; utopian reserved; sensitive; mystical; escapist; overemotional; vague.

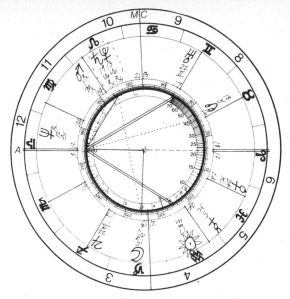

Figure 39

university operating amphitheatre. The sequence of aspects around the Ascendant indicates the sequence of events before, during and after the birth, as shown in the accompanying print-out (Figure 40). Pluto 5° before the ASC shows the presence of a specialist, the fact that many people were present, the alarm registered and the realisation that the birth was quite special. The square from the Moon shows the discomfort of the mother, her crisis and the difficulty which led up to the birth, necessitating the use of a general anaesthetic. The semisquare Mars is the consulting doctor who actually performed the birth and also the death of the first boy. The trine Sun is the father's energy given to the mother just before the birth and his relief in knowing that the remaining children were all right. The inconjunct Node just after delivery is the confusion and frustration of nurses and doctors at the difficulties presented by the births and the living boy's pairing with his sister. The sextile Saturn shows the sorrowful aftermath of the delivery.

Some of the elements of this birth have manifested as health difficulties for the individual. He suffers from a constant and irritating eczema over much of his body, which is often an after

Table 5 ASC/Planet Interpretation

Aspect	Personifications
Sun/ASC	Father, men, doctor, grandfather
Moon/ASC	Mother, grandmother, midwife, nurse, women
Mercury/ASC	Friends, talkers, nurses, young children, gossips
Venus/ASC	Women, sisters, nurses, girls, attractive people, lovers, midwife
Mars/ASC	Surgeon, doctor, midwife, men, fighters, aggressors, male children
Jupiter/ASC	Doctor, midwife, uncle, aunt, grandparents, team, positivists, priests
Saturn/ASC	Doctor, hospital staff, grandparents, serious people, inhibitors, lonely people
Uranus/ASC	Excitable people, innovators, originals, technicians, orderlies
Neptune/ASC	Anaesthetists, nurses, psychics, sensitives, druggists, mediums
Pluto/ASC	Doctors, staff, powerful people, authorities, fascinating people, those in control
Node/ASC	Family, friends, nurses, colleagues, follows, social workers

Relationships to men, recognition, popularity, personal attitudes to others, self-confidence, physical relations, the public, masculinity

Personal feelings about others, feminine influence, maternity, protection, breast feeding, sensitivity, receptivity, adaptability (alkaloids, induction, anaesthetics, drugs, watery birth)

Thoughts at birth, definition, talking, changing views, ideas, criticism (sense stimuli, nerves)

Harmonious personality, loving atmosphere, art, adornment, beautiful surroundings, easy birth, pleasure, even tempered (good complexion, general appearance, proportions)

Fighting, teamwork, forceful success, physical strength, restlessness, decision (surgery, force, circumcision, violence, episiotomy, forceps, facial scar, accidents, Caesareans, birth apparatus)

Easy birth, pleasant experiences, agreeable manner, compromise, generosity, correct acts, successful operations (large baby, jaundice, difficult breast feeding)

Isolation, restriction, inhibition, seriousness, experience, hindrance, depression, seclusion (separation, isolation, long labour, birth apparatus, skin trouble, blockages, tension, amputation, sensory disfunction, facial mark, premature birth, stillbirth, lack of attention)

Excitement, originality, scientific birth, movement, rhythmic, incidents, disquiet, sudden events, unexpected circumstances (quick birth, short labour induction, machines, monitors, headaches, forceps, accidents, sensitive skin, responsive nervous system, circumcision)

Impressionable, sensitive, insecure, peculiar contacts, disillusionment, sympathetic, exploitation (inducement, anaesthetics, alcohol, drugs, peculiar birth, dreaming, watery birth, sensory deception, malformations, incubators)

Fascinating personality, ambition, psychic forces, unusual influences, readjustment, dramatic changes, radical alterations (force, Caesarean, forceps, brutal birth, forced birth, physical transformation, surgery, accidents, circumcision)

Collective contacts, personal relations, family influences, social contact, teamwork, relating (respiration, metabolism, hospital birth, anti-social behaviour)

0	MARS	AUG	1947	01.58	VIR...............................
45	ASCENDANT	AUG	1947	03.06	VIR...............................
180	MERCURY	SEP	1947	05.08	VIR...............................
90	URANUS	OCT	1947	22.20	VIR...............................
90	JUPITER	OCT	1947	22.26	VIR...............................
0	CUSP 12	OCT	1947	23.42	VIR...............................
180	VENUS	OCT	1947	24.25	VIR...............................
45	PLUTO	NOV	1947	28.42	VIR...............................
0	LIBRA	NOV	1947	00.00	LIB...............................
30	MARS	NOV	1947	01.58	LIB...............................
135	SUN	NOV	1947	02.17	LIB...............................
0	NEPTUNE	JAN	1948	12.51	LIB...............................
60	PLUTO	JAN	1948	13.42	LIB...............................
90	MOON	JAN	1948	15.03	LIB...............................
45	MARS	FEB	1948	16.58	LIB...............................
120	SUN	FEB	1948	17.17	LIB...............................
0	ASCENDANT	FEB	1948	18.06	LIB...............................
150	NODE	FEB	1948	18.51	LIB...............................
60	SATURN	FEB	1948	19.24	LIB...............................
150	VENUS	MAR	1948	24.25	LIB...............................
0	SCORPIO	APR	1948	00.00	SCO...............................
60	MARS	MAY	1948	01.58	SCO...............................
120	MERCURY	MAY	1948	05.08	SCO...............................
90	PLUTO	AUG	1948	13.42	SCO...............................
60	MOON	AUG	1948	15.03	SCO...............................
0	CUSP 2	AUG	1948	15.31	SCO...............................
90	SUN	SEP	1948	17.17	SCO...............................
30	ASCENDANT	SEP	1948	18.06	SCO...............................
120	VENUS	NOV	1948	24.25	SCO...............................
45	NEPTUNE	DEC	1948	27.51	SCO...............................
0	SAGITTAR	JAN	1949	00.00	SAG...............................
45	MOON	JAN	1949	00.03	SAG...............................
90	MARS	FEB	1949	01.58	SAG...............................

Figure 40 The Elkus Print-out

effect of anaesthetic at delivery, and is indicated by the Moon square in the sign of Capricorn, governing the skin. Moon square ASC is also anaesthetic. The Libra Ascendant can indicate the inability to expel poisons through the kidneys and colon, a primary deep cause of eczema. A cure that would work wonders is colonic irrigation which would decongest the walls of the colon. Another is rebirthing or Primal Scream to re-enact the trauma. As the ASC is in Libra, the psychological effects of the birth are enacted primarily in relationships. The individual has an uncanny knack of associating with women who are distant or unavailable (Saturn and Pluto in contact with the Moon by inconjunct, all three aspecting the ASC), a choice which corresponds to the quality of his sister. His sister has the conjunction in the 12th House and is as introvert as he is extrovert and lives as a virtual recluse.

There are often many planets present on the ASC in multiple

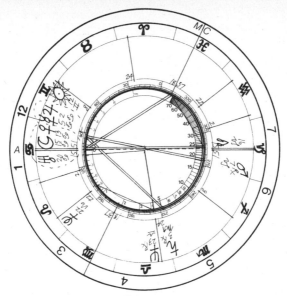

Figure 41

births. Horoscope 19 (Figure 41) was the firstborn of twin girls and has Uranus in the 1st House, whereas her identical sister has Uranus in the 12th House. The difference is profound as she is a patron of the arts and her sister is a heroin addict. The explosive and irrational qualities of Uranus are manifested as an unorthodox and eccentric personality for one and as a medical problem which is potentially life-endangering for the other. The constellation of planets in the 12th House do show a great susceptibility to outer influences and the Moon and Jupiter there in the sign of Cancer indicate the tendency for overindulgence. In this case psychotherapy is the indicated therapy.

The Childhood Octave

From birth until about the age of 7 the childhood time shows the development of the personality within the structure of home and family. The influence of parents is primary and the family system forms and causes a whole range of positive personality influences, as well as traumas and difficulties, all of which are stored in the personality. The influences here stem from the quality of bond with the mother during the 1st House, the nature of the weaning process from breast feeding or lack of breast feeding, early diet, toilet training and the process towards walking and talking, leading to enough independence at the end of the time to be able to go off to school and begin to become independent.

Horoscope 20 (Figure 42) has Pluto just after the ASC, not close enough to make a conjunction and effect the birth itself, but near enough to cause a severe disruption within the mechanism of the personality, particularly the ability for self-assertion which is inherent in the 1st House. The semisquare from Uranus in Cancer shows that the problem is dietary and the digestive problems stem from the mother feeling restrained from being free during the latter stages of pregnancy, indicated by the trine to the Moon and Mars in the 5th House. The mother was not free of her unwanted child until he went off to school at the time of the 5th House. He needed this severe health problem in order

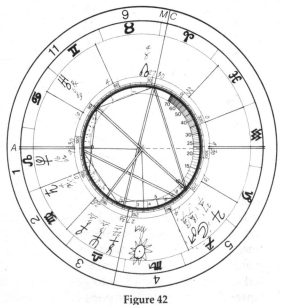

Figure 42

to attract her attention. The problem recurred at the opposite time in the 7th House at 27 years old, when issues of sexual identity surfaced and he was again subject to stomach irritations, ulcers and constriction. The fact that Saturn and Uranus are combined shows that the problems are stress-activated and that the therapies required are psychotherapy for the emotional problem with mother, biofeedback for stress and dietary or nutritional counselling for Saturn in Virgo.

ANOREXIA AND BULIMIA NERVOSA

Two cases of anorexia nervosa and one of bulimia nervosa will serve to illustrate a theory for the origin of this modern affliction. Horoscope 21 (Figure 43) is a young woman who

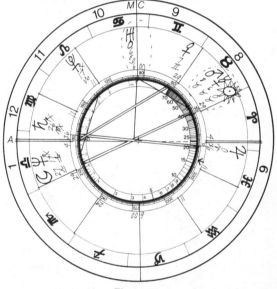

Figure 43

became anorexic at the age of about 16, at the sensitive point of 17° Pisces. Her 1st House Neptune in Libra showed that she had a very sensitive digestive tract from soon after birth and that she was weaned from breast feeding prematurely. The fact that Neptune only aspects to Pluto makes a psychological and energetic closed circuit leading back into gestation. In this case, her mother wanted to be free of the responsibility of looking after her child as she was initially wanted by the father (the Sun is the first planet back from the 9th House cusp conception point in opposition to the Moon), but not by the mother. This difference of view about having the child is characteristic of anorexia horoscopes.

During the 1st House, which is archetypally the first 7 months of life, a child cries for food and for anything else she wants, particularly affection. When a child is being breast fed, the cry elicits both feeding and warmth of cuddling. The two feelings and their resultant satisfaction are inextricably welded together forever and both associated with self-assertion and strength of personality. The natural time for weaning is the end of the 1st House, but often either the nature of the weaning itself or extenuating circumstances can create problems which lead to anorexia. The presence of Neptune implies that the breast feeding is interrupted, possibly by emotional insecurity or uncertainty on the part of the mother, and creates a similar uncertainty about being loved. In this case it could have come into being by force of outer circumstances (through Pluto). Sometimes colic is the result, which at its root is the child picking up emotionally discordant energies through the mother's milk. What remains is that when the child cries for love and touching, the response is to supply a bottle or food. In order to be cuddled or picked up, or to get the same amount of attention as previously *it is necessary to reject the food!* Thus anorexia is primarily a Neptunian affliction caused by the mistaken or illusory association made between affection and food. In this case the anorexia originated at the sensitive inconjunct from Neptune. The solution in her case was through an interest in astrology and a recognition that the responsibility to produce children is not inherently in her best interests, so as not to be trapped as her mother was.

Horoscope 22 (Figure 44) is a young woman with anorexia, caused when Neptune in Scorpio was activated by the detachment of her mother, indicated by the square from the Moon and her placement in the care of an older grandmother, shown by the sextile from Saturn. In her case, the detachment and abstraction of her mother was severe and gave her the message that losing contact with the possibility of touching through food meant possible separation and death. She responded by coming into contact with her father at almost 2 years old, and yet the father

Figure 44

also left to travel abroad (Sun conjunct Jupiter in Sagittarius). Again, Saturn represents her grandmother looking after her in the absence of both parents. Subsequently, when the sensitive inconjunct to Neptune registered at 7° Pisces, at the age of 13, the anorexia nervosa had begun. Contact with doctors followed (sensitive square Sun and Mars) and the problem was exaggerated. The solution was transpersonal psychology and gestalt, combined with regular bodywork to ground her in her sensation function.

Anorexia can also happen when the mother detaches from the infant, indicated by the Aquarian Moon, among other indicators. Horoscope 23 (Figure 45) is a young woman suffering from bulimia nervosa and alcoholism into her thirties. Neptune is implicated in the 2nd House and exaggerated by the distance from the father she adored, indicated by the square to Sun/Uranus in the 10th House. Neptune/Sun contacts incline to alcoholism, drug abuse and an abnormal psychic sensitivity, all of which she experienced in her early twenties, just before the Descendant from 23° to 26° of Aquarius, when the Sun/Uranus was inconjunct, Neptune in trine, Pluto in opposition and Mars in sextile. The combination produced a progression from severe dietary restrictions to extreme overindulgence fol-

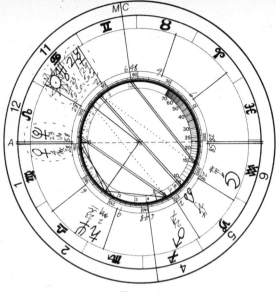

Figure 45

lowed by vomiting. The only help possible was Alcoholics Anonymous, a classic Piscean organisation with a powerful spiritual component satisfactory to the Neptunian energy.

The Maturity Octave

The primary function of the octave of maturity is to combine and integrate the physical body developed in gestation with the personality created during childhood, and project the resultant combination out into the world to work out its various possibilities. Gradually the influence of the parents is put behind and the school years bring a direction in life. The ability to create a soul is contingent upon understanding life as a whole in time. This period also sees the beginning of the rapid acceleration of time sense as consciousness increases. Much tension and stress is produced by an irrational attitude to time and its passage. Larry Dossey's *Space, Time and Medicine*[6] is an excellent book about recent theories and practice to heal such time-related illnesses so endemic to our age.

Most often maturity problems relate backwards to childhood and gestation, and therefore the source of solutions often involve work on earlier principles in which one has been enmeshed.

Horoscope 24 (Figure 46) is a classic case of an idealistic young

Figure 46

woman who clashes with the hard realities of the world upon leaving home. An obsession with ballet in youth (Jupiter in Aquarius) ended with terror at the concept of men, registering at Mars in Taurus square Pluto. An attachment to an older man at the registration of Venus at 19 years old, square Saturn and opposite Moon, led to a secret abortion (Scorpio/Moon in the 12th House). The result of the tension was to produce chronic lung trouble at the registration of Mercury in Gemini (sign of the lungs) at her inability to communicate her anger and rage at men and the world. As Mercury is trine Neptune, the insecurity lies in her fear of exposure if and when she has to produce children. The unconscious message was that her mother was prevented from pursuing a creative career by her own conception twenty-three years earlier. She entered psychotherapeutic training at 25, with the registration of Mercury as well. The symptoms began to subside and a transformation ensued (Pluto sextile Mercury), but she found the initial sessions slightly superficial. Her real turnaround happened when Uranus registered at 34 years old.

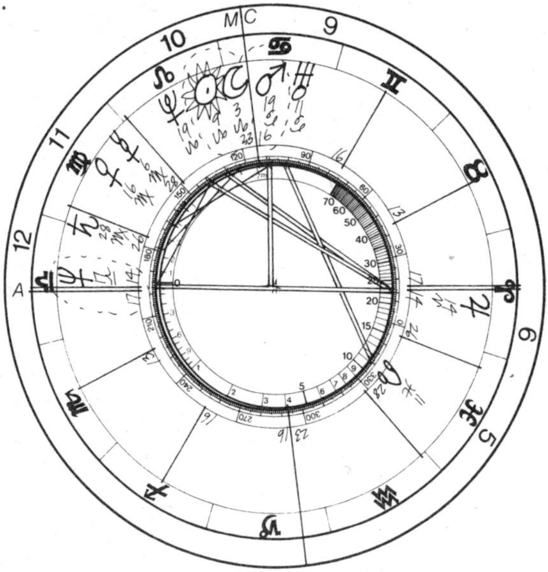

Figure 47

Horoscope 25 (Figure 47) is unique in pointing to an astrological answer to a seemingly insoluble dilemma. A young woman, lush and in the bloom of health, upon being married discovered that she was incapable of having sex because of an affliction called vaginitis which made her so tense and tight that sexual relations were impossible no matter what her attitude. This persisted for eight years of marriage and frustrated both her and her patient husband. The conjunction between Sun and Moon in the strong sign Leo and the 10th House shows powerful creative ability, but therein lies the flaw. The cause is not medical, but simply that her mother, on realising that she was pregnant, categorically refused to grant her husband sexual contact from that point on. The only other aspect to the Leo Moon in the 10th House (control) is the sextile to Mercury in the 11th

House, showing the propensity to lie. The lack of other aspects means that the mother disallowed any show of emotions except those related to her 'problem', and even that only with friends. The one recourse the father had was his work (Sun only aspecting Jupiter in the 6th House). Thus her parents were bound to each other despite the tragic and difficult circumstances. As the problem relates back to parental scenes, the gestalt therapy indicated by Leo is required to break through the history of resistance dating back to Old Testament times.

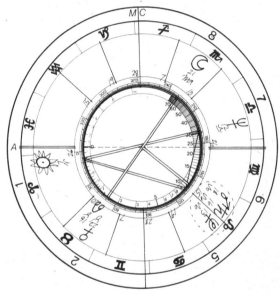

Figure 48

Horoscope 26 (Figure 48) is a young woman diagnosed as diabetic at the time of the registration of her 7th House Neptune in Libra at 31 years and 6 months old. Although the outward cause was the break-up of a relationship (Neptune opposite Sun), the deeper reason related back to the sudden death of her mother in childbirth when she, the eldest daughter, was 12 years old. The shock and resultant grief was deep and was to become a trauma that was not easily cured. In this case gestalt therapy with a particularly acute therapist would work with the anger trapped by her abandonment and its following insecurity. The diabetes prevented her from experiencing the fear of childbirth by requiring her to abandon any hopes of having children herself.

Horoscope 27 (Figure 49) was a woman diagnosed as having terminal cancer of the throat at the sensitive square from Pluto and the Mars/Saturn midpoint[7] at 39 years old. When counselled astrologically that she was due to change state so dramatically that she would virtually 'die to her old way of life', she responded so positively that within one year she had gone into remission, met and married the man of her dreams (inconjunct Venus from the 3rd) and despite a miscarriage immediately after, had regained her hold on life.

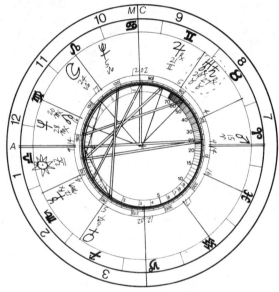

Figure 49

DEATH

Death is the most difficult diagnosis to make as there are many crisis times in the lives of people which could provide great tests. In many cases, the exact time of death is less an issue than the time when the fatal affliction took hold.

In the case of two AIDS victims the planet Uranus was implicated, although it would be irresponsible to suggest that Uranus is the only planet required to produce such a critical step, particularly as the planet Pluto is commonly accepted as being the governor of the immune system. In Horoscope 28 (Figure 50) the registration of Uranus in Taurus in the 8th House is the time of critical infection, although the illness was hidden from family and friends until the last possible moment. When it became too much to bear the subject shot himself at the exact square sensitive point from Jupiter in Aquarius at 48 years and 6 months old.

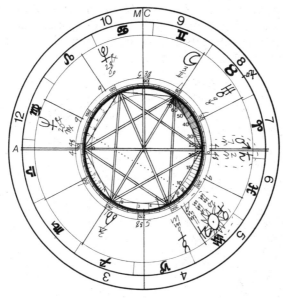

Figure 50

Horoscope 29 (Figure 51) died of AIDS at a sensitive sextile to Uranus at 40 years old after experiencing the sensitive inconjunct from Jupiter and Venus in Scorpio in the 3rd House, showing an interest in conceiving pleasure within sight of death. The tragedy occurred at the trine sensitive points from Saturn/Pluto in the 11th, indicating that the fatal infection came from many friends.

Transits are the continuing movements of planets at a given moment compared to their natal positions. They do not usually create events themselves, but act as a system for timing the activation of deeper natal configurations. At death the transits can show the nature of the last moments.

In Horoscope 30 (Figure 52), a man dying from leukaemia had experienced progressively more critical afflictions in the form of

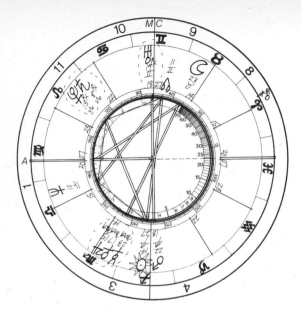

Figure 51

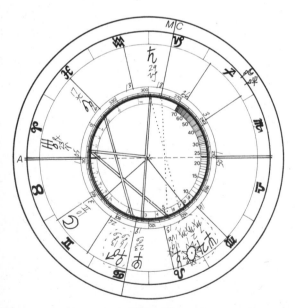

Figure 52

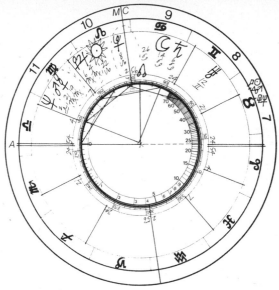

Figure 53

sesquiquadrate Uranus followed by sesquiquadrate Pluto followed by square Neptune. As the opposition Moon approached and was within orb, the transit from Uranus in square to the Sun (vitality and overall state of health) administered a *coup de grâce* and ended years of brave struggle.

After a history of years of flaunting death, Horoscope 31 (Figure 53) held off fate with only a partial stomach and intestines through sesquiquadrate Neptune, trine Mars after a succession of difficult aspect sensitive points. However, when the square Sun registered at 42 years and 5 months old, the vitality was gone and the end came accompanied by the semisquare Saturn, the hand of time itself.

The Transcendent Octave

It occasionally happens that a person goes beyond the end of the typical life into the fourth octave, usually as a result of a

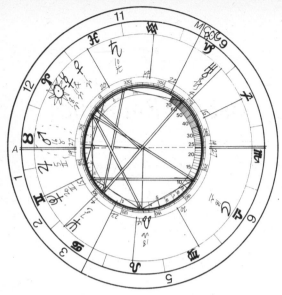

Figure 54

compaction of the 7th and 8th Houses. Horoscope 32 (Figure 54)
is a miraculous woman who dedicated her life to the quest for
freedom and spirituality while remaining real and earthy. She
knew more about nature than naturalists and more about mysticism than yogis. At the cusp of the 9th House, the archetypal
conception/death point, she took her first LSD trip in a London
park and went beyond that into her desired eccentricity. The
frustration of progressively worsening arthritis wore her down
(Uranus opposed Neptune sextile Saturn), but she fought on
until, upon reaching the MC, the higher objective reared its head
and she died suddenly after relinquishing her will at the apex of
the t-square involving the Sun and Moon.

The life and death process is sacred because its journeys and
routings are within and beyond our control. Often the only
consolation is that to understand the meaning of life does no
more than allow the hint of a smile as we leave the scene.

7

Astro★Radionics

Classical Radiesthesia

> The purpose of radionics is to teach the body to heal itself.
>   Malcolm Rae

Radionics is a technique for diagnosis and treatment at a distance through the energetic field of the individual, using the resident ESP faculty of the healer. Every being radiates fields which are continuously fed by and interact with the electro-magnetic fields of earth, and which constantly fluctuate by minute shifts of polarity and modulation. Energy fields form the physical body, and are altered first when any blockages or disruptions occur on the most subtle levels. When the energy field distorts to an extreme degree, illness manifests on spiritual, mental, emotional and physical levels of the organism.

Within everyone, the individual organs, glands, body parts and the diseases and imbalances which affect them all have characteristic vibrational rates and patterns which can be detected by some psychics or by dowsing with a pendulum. The art of such diagnosis is *radiesthesia,* a healing art which dates back hundreds of years. When imbalance or illness is detected, it is possible to heal through communicating to the subtle body a corrective vibrational rate using patterns, pyramidal devices, resonant circuits or direct thought.

The ultimate radiesthetic device is the human mind which is capable of creating action at a distance, which in turn activates the patterns to bring about the desired reaction.[1] Hundreds of types of patterns have been created and used for various functions. The treatment is the introduction of a healing pattern which may incorporate homoeopathic remedies, colours, shapes or names. When introduced to the patient by oral ingestion or simply by preparing a geometric pattern, with all other factors notwithstanding, it will support a return to health.

The brilliant work of Dr David V. Tansley has revolutionised radionic theory and practice in recent years because he has recognised that the mechanism of diagnosis and treatment by radionics, with its amplifier, magnets and black boxes, is really only amplifying the awareness and efficiency of the practitioner, which in turn would have the effect of increasing the potency and effectiveness of all remedies given, patterns activated and thought-forms energised. The healing impetus is provided by the healer rather than emanating from the device itself, as is often believed.

Radionics as a diagnostic and treatment system utilises homoeopathic techniques. Each homoeopathic remedy has an individual signature which is the sum total of effects it produces when given to a healthy individual. The *materia medica* as developed by the originator of homoeopathy, Samuel Hahnemann, describes these effects on the psychological, mental, emotional and physical body according to the Paracelsian principle of 'like cures like'. When an individual is ill, the range of symptoms expressed are matched as closely as possible with remedies in the materia medica and given until cure is effected. The remedies include animal, mineral, elemental, vegetable substances, colours, chakras, glands, potentised body parts and diseases (like vaccines, but even more diluted), and many others. A remedy is diluted so many times (in the millionths) that its physical substance no longer exists in measurable quantities, but its energy pattern remains in the crystalline structure of a medium such as distilled water with a trace of alcohol or milk sugar pilules.

Homoeopathy treats the whole person and by using a methodical technique of remedy selection, the correct one can be found and administered. The cure is the activation and removal of the symptoms in the reverse sequence in which they appeared, from the physical, emotional and mental bodies. The devices for amplification in radionics assist in finding and treating with the correct homoeopathic remedies.

As a result of fifteen years of treatment, observation and study with Dr Westlake and Dr Tansley, as well as other practitioners, I became acquainted with the theory and practice of radionics, dowsing with a pendulum, homoeopathy and radiesthesia. It seemed that there was a valuable link between astrology and radionics. What follows is a brief history of this connection and its ramifications.

Upon learning, in 1974, that the dowsing faculty can detect any pattern of energy in living or seemingly inanimate objects, it became natural to investigate whether the horoscope diagram (a cosmic signature) can be considered an energy pattern representing an individual and function as a witness. What became immediately apparent is that every horoscope, when oriented in an identical direction relative to the dowser, has a particular axis which is symbolic of that horoscope. When holding a pendulum over the centre of the horoscope, the pendulum swings along a particular axis, whatever the time or orientation. When a stack of horoscopes are superimposed on top of each other, at a mental command the pendulum can select the axis of the individual who is, for example, most dominant mentally, or who has specific qualities required.

The axis of the horoscope corresponds to what Edward Russell called the *Critical Rotational Pattern* or CRP possessed by every form of matter. Therefore, the horoscope as a pattern is immersed within all other patterns and beings in nature, and responses of the individual represented can be detected through the horoscope by the process of resonance.

It became clear that the rotational axis of horoscopes was most often along an astrological axis which contained either very important planets or significant oppositions. If an individual horoscope contains an opposition such as Sun opposed Pluto, one can almost expect that to be the major axis in the horoscope.

Dowsing the Circle

The difficulty of dowsing with a circle is that when the pendulum swings across the central point from 10° Aries to its opposite point 10° Libra, it is impossible to tell in which direction it is pointing. This problem has led to the use of fan-shaped dowsing and radionic diagrams so there is no confusion. But there is a way to use the entire circle for dowsing with astrology.

In Figure 55, the central circle of the horoscope is filled with twelve concentric circles from centre to periphery. The most central circle corresponds to Sagittarius and its symbol is placed in the direction of the sign and its residence, the 9th House. The next circle out corresponds to Capricorn, the next to Aquarius, the next to Pisces, etc. The final circle at the periphery is the ring of Scorpio.

The first stage for using this astrological dowsing diagram in the book is to hold a pendulum, with elbow parallel to the ground, above the central dot. Then without consciously moving the pendulum or your arm, tell your unconscious mind, outwardly at first and then silently, to move the pendulum from Sagittarius to Gemini, but *within the innermost circle*. After a few moments the pendulum will swing infinitesimally within the circle. Next, instruct the pendulum to swing from Capricorn to Cancer and back within the second circle. Then instruct the pendulum to move within the third circle radius from Aquarius to Leo and back again. Repeat the operation until the pendulum is swinging from Scorpio to Taurus in the outermost ring.

It is obvious that there is a distinction between the pendulum swinging between Taurus and Scorpio. When it is moving towards Taurus it swings out to the sixth ring out, while towards Scorpio it swings out to the outermost twelfth ring. With practice, it is possible to instruct the pendulum to move within its programmed parameters from the tiniest circle to the largest and back again in the correct fashion. When the exercise is repeated indefinitely, it will, in time, become internalised so that you can simply swing a pendulum over any object and understand immediately to which astrological sign the pendulum is pointing. In this case the diagram is assumed to exist, within the mind, directly in front of one with the archetypal MC point straight ahead.

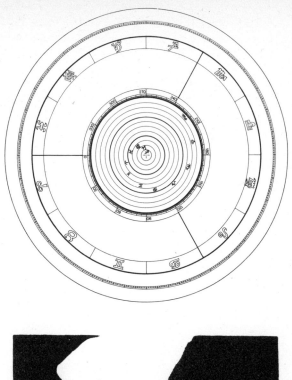

Figure 55 Dowsing the Circle

With this dowsing tool available, the astrologer is able to ask questions about the horoscope such as: which planets are directly responsible for the present affliction of (blank)?; in which time of his life did a traumatic emotional experience create such a powerful blockage?

Astrology and Radionic Cards

It seemed that astrology and radionics could profitably be used together because the horoscope functions as a witness. Astrology is an exceptional diagnostic system, particularly in its description of time cycles in one's individual life and its capacity to investigate the early causes of later afflictions. But there is no way that astrology can function as a treatment mechanism, apart from the therapeutic value of the horoscope reading, a topic discussed in Chapter 3.

Renaissance doctors such as Paracelsus used astrological talismans to treat illness. Although there are many examples extant,

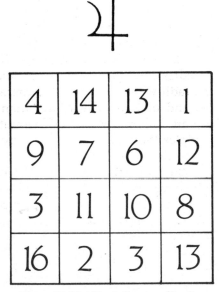

Figure 56 The Magic Square of Jupiter

few people understand exactly how they functioned and what benefit they could possibly bring. Recent developments in the new physics have cleared up this conundrum. The circle full of squiggles which is the form of most Renaissance medical talismans uses *magic squares* to determine the seemingly random pattern of lines and curves typical of talismanic magic. The magic squares were related to the numerology of the planets. As the number of Jupiter is four, a magic square of Jupiter is four by four equals sixteen (Figure 56). Within each square is a number and a letter, often in Hebrew or Greek. The name of the body part, the being responsible for the cure or the remedy was translated into the language of the square and linked together in sequence by straight and curved lines. What is fascinating is that they have a direct parallel today in the bubble chamber patterns created by subatomic particles accelerated by the ultra-modern synchrotrons of physicists. This parallel is represented in a cover I designed for a book by David Tansley, *Radionics: Science or Magic?*[2] (Figure 57). The illustration shows a human figure within a circle and triangle with hands on a bubble chamber diagram on the left and a magic sigil on the right. In both cases the energy contained in elementary particles is harnessed and used in the service of humanity.

When I first read the books of David Tansley[3] describing the radionics work of Malcolm Rae, I immediately recognised the connection between astrology and radionics. Rae discovered that homoeopathic remedies and other substances could be encoded on cards as partial radii within circles. Since there are 360 such points in a circle, and most remedies have from five to nine partial radii, there are billions of possible permutations. Typically, the more complex the substance encoded by the card, the more partial radii required.

Rae developed the *Magneto-Geometric Potency Simulator* (Figure 58) which impregnates the energy pattern of the appropriate remedy into a matrix, such as a moistened blank milk sugar pilule, and the crystalline structure of the medium entraps the energy of the remedy.

The transmission of the energy of a curative substance rather than its physical substance has proved to be effective through homoeopathic potentisation, and the detrimental side-effects of allopathic medicines are eliminated. Toxic substances can be

Figure 57 Radionics: Science or Magic?

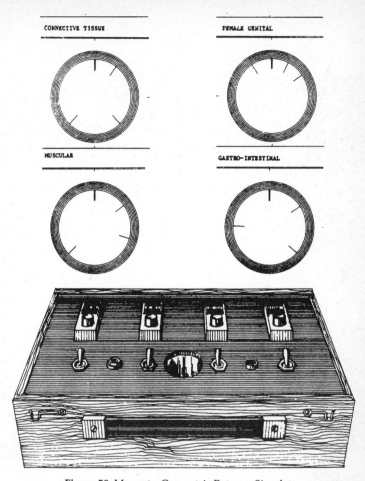

CONNECTIVE TISSUE

FEMALE GENITAL

MUSCULAR

GASTRO-INTESTINAL

Figure 58 Magneto-Geometric Potency Simulator

homoeopathically turned to healing usage, and environmental toxins do not permeate the remedy itself.

What is even more important, the Rae cards are like astrological horoscopes of the remedies. The Magneto-Geometric cards can be correlated to the zodiac degrees. They describe the cosmic signatures of homoeopathic remedies, elements, cell salts, animal, vegetable and mineral remedies, colours, chakras, and many others. And it is possible to correlate these remedies with individual horoscopes.

DEGREES AND BODY PARTS

In the Ebertins' *Anatomische Entsprechungen der Tierkreisgrade*, the 360° of the zodiac are correlated to body parts, glands, bones, nerves and musculature. While each sign correlates to body parts in a general sense, as has already been demonstrated, extensive researches provided a much more detailed version. The correlations of body parts to zodiac degrees are shown in Appendix 3.[4] Using this data it is possible to determine from the horoscope the body parts most likely to be afflicted in life and to work backwards from afflicted part to astrological cause.

There are many ways to use the degree attributions of Ebertin, particularly when a symptom location is given and the root cause is investigated. Headaches as Aries afflictions will show problems related to self-assertion or traditional 1st House matters. Likewise for the twelve signs and houses.

DECODING THE RADIONIC CARDS

It is possible to decode the Rae cards by interpreting their radii as corresponding to the body parts affected by a remedy. These body parts can be correlated with the entire disease picture as described in the *Materia Medica*.[5] Since all remedies produce many more effects than can be attributed to the partial radii of the card, it must be assumed that the code necessary to reproduce the remedy is simpler than the total effects of the remedy – much like the ten planets describing an entire life or four acid bases the entire genetic code. My research is therefore an attempt at the groundwork for a more detailed correlation.

Table 6 Analysis of *Aconitum Napellus*

Degree	Body part	Materia Medica
12° Ari	Tongue	Tongue swollen; tip of tongue tingles; red face; pressure in head; neuralgia.
21° Tau	Nasal artery	Pain at nose root; throbbing nostrils; haemorrhage of blood; tonsils swollen; throat dry, red and constricted; frenzied menses with nose bleed.
03° Leo	R coronary artery	Violent invasion; arterial tension; tachycardia; chest pain; vertigo; heart afflictions with pain; stiff painful spine.
13° Cap	L knee joint	Knees unsteady; weak and lax joint ligaments; pneumatic inflammation.

The following is a comparison of the symptoms of the common remedy *Aconitum Napellus* with the partial radii of the Aconitum card against its primary symptoms from the *Materia Medica* (Figure 59).

Aconitum Napellus

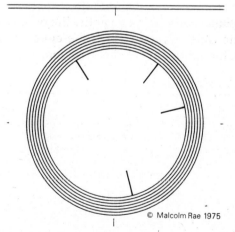

© Malcolm Rae 1975

Figure 59 Horoscope and *Aconitum Napellus* Card

The picture of *Aconitum Napellus* compares favourably with the radii in the Rae card for the same remedy. It obviously follows that when planets are situated at degrees covered by a particular remedy, that remedy should be thought of as a possible treatment.

The remedies *Arsenicum Iodatum* and *Arsenicum Album* have two radii in common. One of them is at 10° Scorpio, the sign of death and putrefaction, and the degree indicating neurasthenia. Under *Arsenicum Album* we see Scorpionic symptoms such as 'ptomaine poisoning; stings; tobacco; illness from decayed food or animal matter; putrid discharges; degenerative changes; septic infection'.[6] Scorpio activates certain symptomatology in relation to its opposite sign Taurus, governing nose, ears and throat. *Arsenicum Iodatum* indicates irritating and corrosive discharges with emphasis upon the nose and Eustachian tube and coughing complaints. The common point at 2° Capricorn produces afflictions in the opposite sign Cancer in the stomach. The *Arsenicum* remedies would therefore be useful for those with planets in the signs Scorpio and Taurus, Cancer and Capricorn.

Another example is the series of *Calcarea* remedies which share 21° Aquarius, indicating spinal disease. *Calc. arsenicum, calc. carbonate, calc. fluoridum* and *calc. phosphate* all produce afflictions of spinal origin. These include back weakness, spinal curvature, chronic lumbago, osseous tumours and lower back pains.

The originator of homoeopathy, Samuel Hahnemann, recognised that it was necessary to prove a remedy not only on the physical level but also on emotional and mental levels, so that an entire profile of the remedy could be made available. This model is consistent with the astrological model presented, in that the substances act on the same three levels at which symptoms are recognised. The dynamic plane of activity which permeates all organisms through electromagnetic fields is the origin of health and disease in the body. Astro★Radionics is a way to transmit the correct healing information through broadcasting a remedy which corresponds to the astrological pattern.

Since substances which effect cures resonate with the person to be cured, it follows that an astrological compatibility would be highly desirable. The issue then becomes: how to correlate the remedies in the homoeopathic materia medica with the zodiac signs and degree segments of Ebertin?

The resources to investigate such an important concept have not been available to date, so the necessary correlation has not been made, except for a few of the more commonly used remedies. The essential technique would involve computers in which the astrological radii (and their degrees) of all remedies were stored. Each horoscope can be analysed, the planets responsible for a particular affliction or blockage determined, and a series of remedies chosen which had as many partial radii as possible in contact. The resultant remedies would supply the correct homoeopathic remedy and also provide the resonance required to activate the healing communication for the whole organism.

Each remedy describes a constellated pattern of effects in the psychophysical organism, and the combinations clearly provide a total greater than the sum of the parts, just as the planets of a birth chart provide the information for a lifetime. In his wonderfully evocative book *Psyche and Substance*,[7] Edward Whitmont, a prominent Jungian analyst, describes how he understands the homoeopathic remedies as archetypes of behaviour. Like the planets, the remedies are symbols of psychic processes which are the outer images of inner functional dynamics. His approach throws homoeopathy open to psychological astrology as well.

Astro★Radionic Cards

In practice, the Astro★Radionic practitioner determines by traditional methods or with a pendulum which planets or angles in the natal horoscope are instrumental in a given situation. A Rae card can then be made to make a homoeopathic potency of the constellation which is the root cause and which is transmitting critical information on the inner levels. By reactivating the discordant energy it is possible to re-establish the flow and begin the healing process.

Horoscope 33 (Figure 60) presented a symptom of constant insomnia such that he had been unable to sleep at all for most nights of his adulthood. No amount of drug therapy, psychotherapy or subtle healing seemed to improve the situation. None of the practitioners consulted had discovered the cause. It is immediately apparent that the planet causing insomnia is

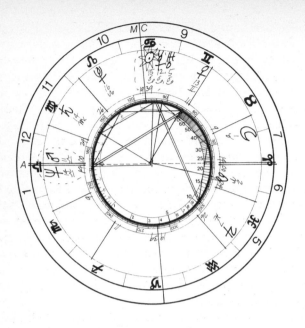

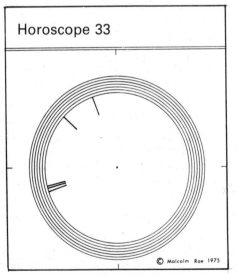

Horoscope 33

Figure 60

Neptune, which happens to be conjunct Mars and the Ascendant. Ebertin describes Mars/Neptune as: 'Activity paralyzed; self-destroying forces and agents; moodiness; irritability; feelings of inferiority.'[8] What is interesting and alarming is the square aspects from the Sun and Mercury, and the sextile from Pluto to the Ascendant. The Sun, as the carrier of the vitality and energy transmission, afflicts the vital power, leading to a 'weak physique, little vitality, the undermining of the health' and even, in extreme situations, 'dissolution of the body'. The square from Pluto can cause dissolution or death. The Mercury square creates an excess of nervous energy, weakness of mind, sensitive nerves and other such problems, which the client made manifest. What appears to be a critical theme, as Neptune is involved, is two-fold. One, that there is a constant implication that drugs were involved in the initial event causing the insomnia, and two, that an irresponsible (Neptune square Mercury) doctor or surgeon (Mars and square Sun) was involved at the time of birth. Upon presenting the material to the client it was discovered that when he was born the doctor administered an inducement by injection and gas as a general anaesthetic, despite the fact that his mother had had two previous children perfectly naturally. It was subsequently discovered that the doctor had acted irresponsibly.

The astrological factors in insomnia are Neptune/ASC and Mars/Neptune/ASC, all of which the client shows. The treatment was an Astro★Radionic card with the partial radii of the ASC, Neptune, Mars, the Sun and Pluto. When broadcast at a very high potency there was immediate positive reaction in the client, who began to experience nights of sound sleep. It was advised that Primal Scream or rebirthing would support the psychological trauma which was caused by the delivery. The combination of the understanding that the birth was primary in causing the problem rather than current anxieties and stresses, although the current situation was supportive of the problem, and the Astro★Radionic treatment brought satisfaction.

Horoscope 34 (Figure 61) is a young girl who manifested anorexia nervosa at the age of 14 years and 8 months. The sensitive points operative around the age in question are the sequence of sensitive semisquare Mars at 13 years old, sensitive sextile Sun and Jupiter, sensitive semisquare Saturn. The cause of the anorexia is not Neptune in the first or second houses,

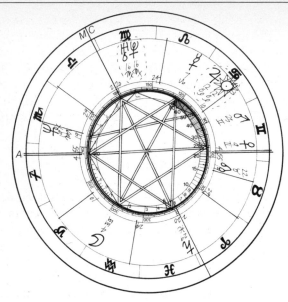

Figure 61

indicating problems of weaning from the breast-feeding which were the case in earlier examples, but involve the sensitive opposition to Neptune in the near future at 17 years and 4 months. The trigger in her case is the planets Mars and Saturn, considered by Ebertin to be the death axis, with the sensitive sextile Sun and Jupiter in between. This combination indicates 'weak vitality, the inability to meet all demands or master all situations, the necessity to overcome illness' and a 'fortunate separation'.[9] One can only assume that a separation from father was cause and also resolution to the anorexia. Indeed, the father was an elusive figure to her and his distance from her was the inner need which activated the illness and brought the desired attention.

The pendulum analysis indicated that the planets Neptune, Mars, Saturn and Sun were to be broadcast, as the path to resolution involved reconciliation with the real father and a passing out of childhood which was attended by them both. It is often the case that the parent is childlike when anorexia affects an adolescent.

The Astro★Radionic card serves the function of focusing the

mind of the healer upon the planetary issues activated by disease, whether psychological or physical. But the resultant cure, although possible in many cases, does not necessarily create unity in the individual. The branching off of parts of the whole being and then curing them is still artificial and temporary because the whole will eventually seek to take the healthy part into itself and imbalances will again permeate the part.

The Astro★Radionic Analyser

The history of radionics and energy medicine is documented by a series of patterns used for healing and as instruments of healing energies. Often the healing patterns perform diagnosis and treatment. Initially the horoscope diagram itself is a suitable pattern for medical astrology dowsing. But the need for more detailed patterns and dials upon which the strengths and weaknesses of planets, signs or other combinations of elements of the horoscope becomes apparent. The author designed a device which worked with the standard Magneto-Geometric Potency Simulator produced by Magneto-Geometric Applications.

The Astro★Radionic Analyser has two sections (Figure 62). The top wheels rotate against each other upon the base horoscope diagram, with a small knob above the central spindle large enough to support a small sample of hair or a blood spot between circular sticky labels. The horizontal axis of the Ascendant and Descendant remains the datum plane. The circle of astrological signs can be rotated so that the Ascendant sign and degree of the individual to be analysed can be set to the ASC at the left. This setting orients the zodiac to the same position as that at the birth of the individual. By referring to the individual's horoscope, it is possible to go through the planets and determine the health status of each in turn.

The third wheel in from the zodiac signs has a series of symbols in the upper half of the wheel on either side of the −/+ signs at the top. The range of values are from −6 to the left to +6 to the right. When the pointer is oriented to a particular planet, the pendulum is placed over the centre of the circle and asked 'What is the energy charge of the Sun?' The plus numbers indicate overactivity and the minus numbers indicate under-

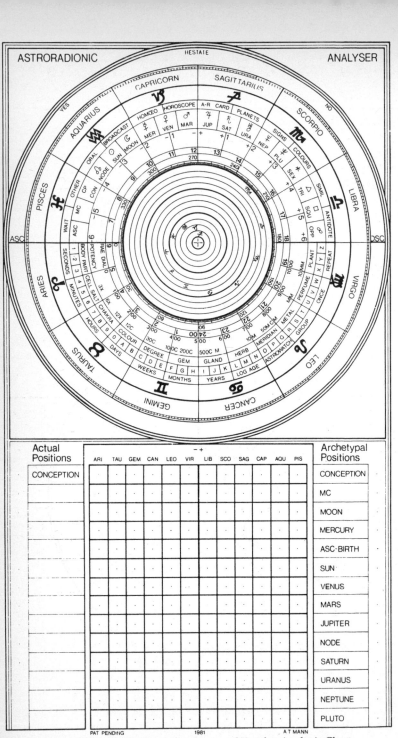

Figure 62 Astro★Radionic Analyser and Tansley Analysis Chart

Advanced Radionic Consultants

Dr. David V. Tansley, D.C.

38 South Street, Chichester, Sussex, England   Tel (0423) 775383

Vitality Index	
Physical Health Index Psychological Health Index	
Congestion	
Over-Stimulation	
Lack of Co-ordination	

Name	Date
Address	
Birth Date Day Month Year Place	
Symptoms	
Miasms Toxins	

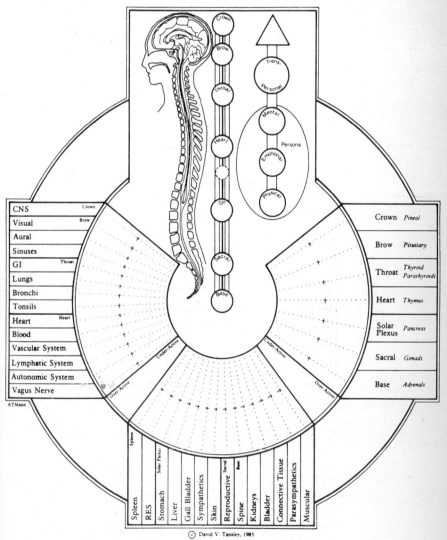

activity. The resultant profile shows clearly the status of all planets, allowing the astrologer to advise accordingly.

While astrologers have many very precise systems for prediction, there are not absolutes in such astrology. Often the correct diagnoses depend upon accurate intuitions, not so much in determining *what* has gone wrong, the *which* of the indicated qualities or astrological events is really responsible for the afflictions presenting symptoms? The Astro★Radionic Analyser can be used to determine which planets are active at a given time, against which to compare the results of more traditional techniques.

It is also possible to use the pendulum to ask which combination of planets is active in the horoscope at a certain time. The pendulum is placed over the centre of the circle and the requisite question asked. It may point in turn to one, two, three or more planets as being implicated. The resultant combinations can be checked against Ebertin. If, for example, the planets Mars, Uranus and Neptune are indicated, the permutations in Ebertin are:

Mars/Uranus = Neptune	Frenzy, fainting fits, car accident
Mars/Neptune = Uranus	Changing energy levels, suddenly emerging weakness, lack of energy, crisis caused by accident or injury
Uranus/Neptune = Mars	Misdirected energy, lameness, paralysis, lack of stamina

In this way a picture can be built up which includes the range of qualities in operation at the moment. As can be seen from the above example, when the first combination involves inner planets such as Sun, Moon, Mercury, Venus or Mars the indications are often causes, while the outer planets Jupiter through Pluto are more pathological states which result from earlier causes. In the example the trauma of paralysis can result from the shock of an accident in youth manifesting at a later age.

In Horoscope 35 (Figure 63), an accident occurred at 1 year 5 months old when the child was almost drowned in the bath by his older brother, indicated by the Saturn/Mars conjunction in Cancer. That the father was present but did not prevent the accident is shown by the opposition of the Sun and MC. What remained in the client was a very deep sense of threat so powerful that when confronted with authority figures (Sun/MC) such as employers, police or civil servants he would suddenly begin choking and throw himself on the ground. The resultant fits of strangulation happened regularly and became highly distressing to the client.

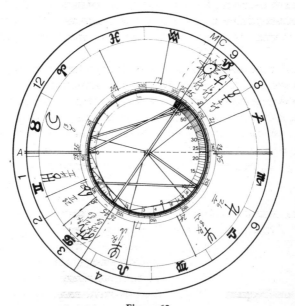

Figure 63

Psychotherapy had lessened the symptoms but not located the root cause. At the time of the consultation the client was 30 years old, at the exact registration of the trine sensitive point from Pluto, which is also in a tensioned sesquiquadrate (135°) from Saturn/Mars and a semisquare (45°) from the MC, i.e. at the exact reconciliation point hitting both ends of the opposition. The session itself was enough to dissipate the symptoms, which were gradually eliminated over the next year or so.

What was also astonishing about the previous example horoscope was that during the reading the client clutched his throat and began choking at the time of the reading when the childhood incident was described. Upon his recovery he needed to rest and recuperate, and was sent home. Within some six hours I received another telephone call from a friend whose lover was suffering from a similar choking sensation caused by a family argument. It transpired that she was born one day later and had virtually the same configuration except that it registered at the age of 6 years old, when she watched family violence. She had exhibited similar symptoms which, in her case, were activated by even the slightest hint of domestic arguments. In both cases, the constant trauma resulted from early childhood shocks which did not directly harm the individual, but were easily reactivated. While the therapeutic release of the reading was partially responsible for the cure, Astro★Radionic treatment was given in support of releasing the energy attached to the early event.

A great advantage of working with Astro★Radionic treatment is that early traumatic events can be acted upon and their trapped or blocked energies redirected in more profitable directions. The issue of 'free-will' in astrology involves this precise point. The blockage exists by the time one discovers it, and the issue is whether it is possible to flow through the difficult situation whenever it is reactivated or not. Freedom lies in discovering blockages and identifying the causes, and then following the initial identification with techniques or therapy which allow disidentification to clear the charge.

Often the combinations of planets are not connected by aspects, transits or directional systems, but are in mutual action none the less. The perspectives thus gained can be very useful in addressing unusual situations and catalysing cures.

Once the combination of planets is chosen there are optional ways to broadcast the requisite energy to the individual in need. An Astro★Radionic card can be made with only the partial radii of the planets required drawn. Another possibility is to use the set of astrological remedy cards made for use with the Rae devices. Examples of the planetary and sign cards are shown in Figure 64. The signs are defined by two partial radii defining the location of the signs' domain in time and space, while the planetary cards are marked by partial radii at the positions of the degrees associated with their rulerships and exaltations. It is therefore possible to treat a client with a very potent Mercury to stimulate thought processes, or a basic Neptune to increase sensitivity. The broadcast energy of the planets approach the techniques envisioned by the celestial magicians and healers of the renaissance.

While the Astro★Radionic Analyser is very useful for assistance in diagnosis with astrology, there is available a much more powerful way to use Astro★Radionics.

Patient Simulator Card

In the practice of homoeopathy a series of remedies are used over a period of months or years as a more and more complete picture of the overall complexity of the constitution is created. The ultimate remedy for each person is called the *simillimum*. The simillimum is the sum total of all physiological and psychological dispositions of an individual throughout his or her lifetime.

In astrology, the horoscope is equivalent to the simillimum in that it contains the total of all characteristics of the individual throughout life, if only they can be decoded. It occurred to me that the ultimate curative card would be an Astro★Radionic card of an individual's horoscope. The resultant cards have had very powerful results when tested by radionics practitioners. In a very real sense, such a card allows the possibility of restoring balance in even the most difficult cases.

The greatest problem of the twentieth century is that it becomes more and more difficult to assimilate ourselves. We get drawn further and further from our own centre and ultimately become disenfranchised and homeless. A constant phrase in depth psychology and psychotherapy is that an individual feels cut off from his or her true home. The Astro★Radionic card of the horoscope allows the practitioner to give the client a dose of a highly dilute and potentised version of themselves to assimilate. Through time the dosage can be built up until the client can take a good look and accept their own identity.

The cards have been particularly useful when therapy is started, when breakthroughs are imminent, and when intractable problems are evident and further growth seems impossible.

The use of Astro★Radionics, the planetary cards, the Analyser, and individual horoscope cards is in sympathy with the doctrine of signatures of Paracelsus, and extends the dictum of Malcolm Rae quoted at the beginning of this chapter.

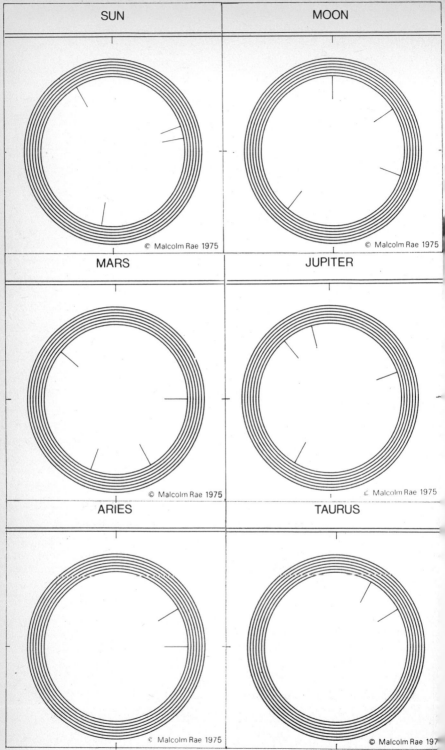

SUN	MOON
MARS	JUPITER
ARIES	TAURUS

© Malcolm Rae 1975

Figure 64 Astrological Radionic Cards – Planets and Signs

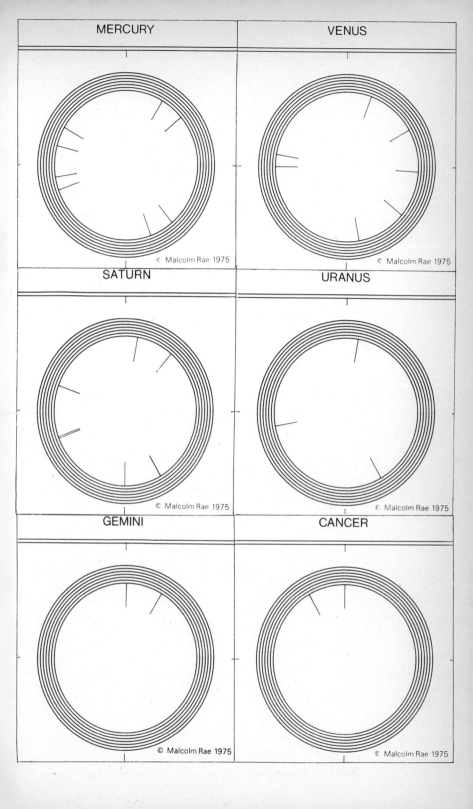

MERCURY	VENUS
SATURN	URANUS
GEMINI	CANCER

© Malcolm Rae 1975

Astro★Radionic cards and treatment devices are available to radionic practitioners although such tests have been severely limited in the past by the lack of individuals who have a working knowledge of both astrology and radionics. Hopefully this will change in the future. An intended result of my investigations is that astrologers will become healers again, and that radionic practitioners will investigate the space-time context of their marvellous healing arts. The integration of radionics and astrology involves no less than the nature of life and the universal unity itself. That the genetic code is similar to the movement of the planets around our Sun through time can be a key to unlocking new methods which are less interventive, bring the individual more into a position of responsibility in their own healing, and bring new meaning to life in our universe.

8

Healing the Future

In the future many developments unfolding at present will come into being and a planetary healing can and must happen. In order to survive on our little planet, it is essential that we heal our world and this can only occur when we learn to heal ourselves first. This starts with taking responsibility for our own body, emotions, mind and spiritual quest.

Many facts are becoming known which are affecting the quality and essence of our lives. The primary factor is diet. The extremely high level of additives, hormones, antibiotics and pesticides in our food makes us highly toxic, despite our careful attention. Even subtler, yet more dangerous practices of microwave cooking, which strips the energetic life field from food, and the irradiation food to increase its shelf life are also producing dangerous conditions.

The quality of the food we put into our bodies is so inferior and dangerous that it is essential either to live exclusively in the country and grow our own vegetables or to take vitamin supplements which can supply the nutritive agents lacking in food. Even organic gardening is tainted by the spectre of leaks from atomic plants, which cover large areas of the earth's surface with radiation that infiltrates every aspect of the ecosystem, including our bodies.

It seems that civilisation is making demands upon the individual to choose the manner of his or her life at the survival level, and taking steps to striate all humanity into the layers in which they belong. Many are becoming more and more sensitive to environmental issues but the vast majority ignore them and continue in their deathly ways to kill the earth. The increased sensitivity which comes from vegetarianism, healthy habits, restrained sexuality, avoidance of alcohol and drugs, and a peaceful attitude to world affairs is in many ways creating a vulnerability which is difficult to defend, yet it is the only way. Increasingly, it is necessary to utilise a new level of technology to the advantage of such individuals to stay alive and well. A primary tool of such awareness is vitamins.

When an individual is healthy, the resonance between his or her body and the solar system's movements is intact, information is transmitted, and responses to the resultant forces are appropriate, natural and healthy. By artificial habits, stress and other discordant practices of our age it is possible to subvert the resonant process. When this occurs, all subsequent messages are distorted, and this affects the life field of the mental body and the imbalance finds its way inexorably through the emotional body to the physical level. When the natural communication system breaks down, it is exactly like the collapse of the immune system, and the two may well be connected.

It is not coincidental that the planet Pluto governs the immune system in the body and also the large-scale transformations of mass consciousness. In support of the immune system there are a number of coherent steps which must be followed to restore natural communication within the body and ultimately with the moving solar system, the meta-system beyond.

Detoxification

First, it is essential to detoxify the system. Detoxification involves more than a change of diet, it demands a change in the very quality and habits of life. To even start the process it is necessary to clean out the colon. According to a score of eminent doctors, 'Death Starts in the Colon',[1] due to the use of food additives, refined sugar and grains, the consumption of alcohol and drugs, dairy products, meat and high stress. The walls of the colon become embedded with decaying food matter similar to the way in which the arteries leading to and from the heart can become blocked by cholesterol. Since the colon is the second largest eliminatory organ in the body after the skin, this secondary means for the body to pass toxins out of its system is lost. This process is known as alimentary toxaemia. As a result, the colon passes toxic waste into the body, causing a myriad of problems including ulcers, constipation, distention and dilation of the stomach and intestinal area, inflammations and cancer of the liver. Abdominal walls of the intestines atrophy, so that the passage of contents is hindered, and the resultant loss of peristaltic action creates further problems. Catarrh, foul gassiness, colitis, enteritis, appendicitis, distention of the abdomen, gastritis, gallstones, infection of the gums, tooth decay, ulcers, headaches and a score of other afflictions endemic to modern society are directly caused by such toxicity.

The symptoms which appear are usually attributed to other causes – when any causes seem to be evident – but the general malaise is compounded by the reluctance of medical doctors to acknowledge the importance of such cleansing of the colon.

It is a commonly accepted part of natural cancer cures to have colonic irrigation, the cleansing of the colon with warm water, which allows the body to begin assimilating more healthy food products which are another part of the cure. The danger of changes of diet without cleansing the colon are summed up as follows:

The colon is a sewage system, but by neglect and abuse it becomes a cesspool. When it is clean and normal we are well and happy; let it stagnate and it will distil the poisons of decay, fermentation and putrefaction into the blood, poisoning the brain and nervous system so that we become mentally depressed and irritable; it will poison the heart so that we are weak and listless; poisons the lungs so that the breath is foul; poisons the digestive organs so that we are distressed and bloated; and poisons the blood so that the skin is sallow and unhealthy. In short, every organ of the body is poisoned, and we age prematurely, look and feel old, the joints are stiff and painful, neuritis, dull eyes and a sluggish brain overtake us; the pleasure of living is gone.[2]

Replacing Intestinal Flora

Once the colon is cleansed, it is possible to recreate the strength of the immune system. The second issue to be addressed is the replacement of intestinal flora.

It has long been understood that the immune system improves when the intestinal tract is made more efficient. In turn, intestinal absorption as well as digestion and detoxification of the intestines are promoted by the presence and action of micro-organisms, principally *Lactobacillus Acidophilus*. This organism inhibits the growth of other harmful toxin-producing micro-organisms and detoxifies toxic and hazardous material found in the diet. It produces enzymes which help with the digestion of food and are needed for the breakdown of lactose (milk sugar). It also produces B vitamins that help in food digestion and are needed under stress and to cope with nervous disorders. It is thought that it may be helpful in increasing the body's natural immunity for fighting infections of viral, bacterial and fungal origin.

Many infants and children have an imbalance of intestinal bioculture, often because they were either not breast fed or not breast fed long enough. Up to the age of 7 years, *bifido* bacteria is the predominant strain of 'friendly' bacteria found naturally in the gastrointestinal tract of healthy breast fed infants. As breast fed infants are weaned, the bifido bacteria are gradually replaced by acidophilus. Since many infants are not breast fed, as adults they will need to start 'from the beginning', so to speak.

Poor nutrition, illness, chlorine and pesticide-laden tap water, the use of alcohol and drugs have historically produced fatal effects on acidophilus. In addition to this, in recent years the use of antibiotics and medicine, the unknown consumption of anti-biotics in dairy products, meats, poultry, etc, and the effects of industrial and chemical pollution in our food and atmosphere have had even more lethal results. Furthermore, the high stress in today's life, cigarette smoking, alcohol, and diets that are high in sugar, fats, and hidden food chemicals that are consumed daily, contribute to the eradication of the *acidophilus* in our intestines. Therefore, in the absence of *acidophilus*, the intestines become the fertile ground for growth of harmful putrefactive bacteria. This, in turn, leaves the intestines without any protection and thus open to numerous kinds of infection and digestive distress.

There are approximately 3.5 lb of living micro-organisms in the intestines. To create a significant impact upon such a population, billions of compatible *acidophilus* cells are required. Clinical and scientific research has established that large quantities of live organisms administered orally are essential for a healthy intestine and for preventing problems originating in the intestinal tract. *Acidophilus* is a living organism which must survive passage (if taken orally) through the stomach which normally destroys living organisms passing through it with its acid secretions. *L. acidophilus* culture, a powder containing billions of *acidophilus* micro-organisms per gram, is an excellent way to restore the correct culture to the intestine.[3] A large number of organisms per dose ensures that a sufficiently viable number arrive in the small intestine.

Most modern western people have had many antibiotic treatments in the course of their lives. What is not generally known about antibiotics is that their action is non-specific, which means that when one takes an antibiotic to cure a minor infection in a finger, the antibiotic attempts to kill all internal bacteria everywhere in the body. This primarily affects the intestinal flora, which must be replaced by taking *acidophilus*.

Vitamin Resonance

While it is acknowledged that, because of the problems of getting proper nutrition from food, vitamins are necessary, it is not generally known that they can go rancid like other natural products. This applies especially to the essential B-vitamins which will not only not work as they should, but will leach other essential nutriments out of the system. With rigorous testing with a pendulum, it is possible to see it demonstrated that many available vitamins and supplements are rancid and therefore ineffective.

The second problem essential to receiving benefit from vitamins is their degree of absorption (Table 7). There is a chain of chemical structures in which vitamins and minerals are contained, which ranges from those which are indigestible, at the bottom of the scale, to the amino acid chelates, which are extremely easy for the body to use, at the top of the scale.

Table 7   The Scale of Mineral Absorption

Amino acid chelates	most absorbable
Ascorbates	
Orotates	
Gluconates	
Carbonates	
Oxides	
Chlorides	
Sulphates	least absorbable

Pure vitamin and mineral substances can be evaluated according to this hierarchy of values. Naturally, the higher up the chain towards amino acid chelates, the more expensive they are to make, and the more sensitive to time and other conditions. What is interesting from the astrological viewpoint is that the amino acid chelates resonate with the genetic code in every cell, and therefore also resonate with the astrological pattern of the cosmos. The use of the highest quality vitamins can increase the contact on every level with the hierarchical information structures of our solar system. The next stage of healing is to institute a *vitamin resonance* so that we are all returned to contact with our higher information centres.

The Grounding of Psychology

The psychological world view distorted without much awareness of its distortion. The core of the problem is that those entering the therapeutic process tend to become embedded in the process rather than understanding it as a means to an end. The therapy itself becomes the goal, which produces a circular and ultimately very frustrating life. The necessity for transpersonal quests reflects the need to go beyond traditional psychotherapeutic ideals.

Similarly, the psychological schools of astrology blithely proceed by looking at individuals as though their bodies are insignificant, when the body is the vehicle through which the psyche acts. In eastern cultures it is known that the body is the *temple of the soul,* and as such must be worshipped just as the deity is worshipped. The necessary correlation of biological and psychological ideas is the next stage in the development of a suitable life on our planet. The two are inseparable and must be brought into practice in a workable manner, as outlined by the concept and practice of Life★Time Astrology. Psychology has its head in the skies and must be grounded.

A great virtue of astrology is its ability to take a physical fault, disease, accident, or difficulty in relationship, and discover the appropriate astrological configuration and, by extension, psychological expression of the root qualities involved, their duration and their meaning. The correspondences bring a greater depth and power to traditional psychological astrology, and even more weight to medical understanding. The direct correlation between diseases, psychological state and astrological pattern can bring profound benefits.[4]

The Future of Astrological Healing

The next stage in the creation of astrological healing is to pool information and synthesise it into an available form, so that therapists and astrologers can take advantage of the insights afforded, and provide a way in which to utilise feedback. The creation of feedback loops of information on medical and psychological astrology is paramount.

At the moment, most astrology, as well as computer-generated astrology, is a one-way process in that there is little regard paid to recirculating the resultant information fed back by the client. There has not been the mechanism to allow this to happen. What is needed in the near future is two distinct advances to facilitate the feedback of information.

An extensive and exhaustive index of astrological interpretative data is required, probably in the form of a computer database which is interactive. It is essential to correlate the interpretative information in the many valuable astrological works, from the myriad viewpoints of psychotherapy, medical astrology, traditional astrology, nutritional analysis and other areas. One source available to practitioners and researchers would make it possible not only to have the correct range of information available at a push of a button, but it would also be possible to test the data more rigorously than at present.

A database must also be created which stores the complete medical, psychological and therapeutic history of many individuals in such a form that their astrological life histories become available for correlation. Only when such a field of information is produced and accessed together with the next stage of processing will the true, ultimate healing art of astrology come into its own. It is anticipated that such developments will be forthcoming in the near future.

Healing the Life of Humanity

The healing process being embarked upon by countless individuals on Earth at the present time is mirrored by the larger healing of the planet which is also required. In order to realise the dream of planetary consciousness, recently called *Gaia*, it is necessary to eliminate the toxic aspects of our lifestyles. The emotional and intellectual pesticides must be banned as well as the outer poisons. Our planet has need of its higher levels being cleansed to complement its physical reconstruction.

Furthermore, beings on Earth can no longer disregard their neighbours, since all are required in the monumental task of rebuilding the planet and its spiritual self. Understanding and manifesting the whole being in ourselves is the necessary first stage in finding the way to transform our world.

> Man follows the earth.
> Earth follows heaven.
> Heaven follows the Tao.
> Tao follows what is natural.
>   *Tao Te Ching*, trans. Gia-Fu Feng and Jane English

Afterword

The Well Centre

The idea of The Well Centre, conceived in conjunction with my colleagues Lola de Gelabert and Dr Robert Jacobs, is a unique and original healing concept designed to respond to the needs of modern men, women and children at every level of their being. The basic idea is that every person coming to the centre would be provided with a programme of integrated assessment and treatment by a team of experienced nutritionists, bodyworkers, acupuncturists, homoeopaths, counsellors, family therapists, psychotherapists, energy medicine practitioners and astrologers to define and create a new *human ecology*.

Most modern alternative or complementary clinics are set up on the traditional model of a Harley Street practice, letting space to whichever therapists want to rent space there. What is required is a therapeutic overview which synthesises all the therapies and presents a model for doing so. The Well Centre is an experiment towards this aim. Its basic premise is that truly holistic assessment and treatment depends upon the cooperation of many practitioners working in unison on various levels with a client. The selection of treatments and the evaluation of the assessment would be done from an astrological context.

This new model for therapy involves an extension of existing therapeutic models in such a way that all therapies acknowledge their counterparts towards a total healing process.

The model of The Well Centre is more than just an idea for a particular clinic, it is also a model for therapeutic action on a planetary scale. This is partially the case because the primary pressure within the holistic clinic, based on the principles of true integration of therapies, is placed squarely on the shoulders of the therapists themselves. Each individual therapy will be forced to change so that it will continue to respect and act in coordination with those other techniques and therapies with which it has a resonance. And the therapists must expand their horizons to include the physical, emotional, mental and spiritual levels of action within each therapeutic exchange. The new kind of healing also places a focus on the need to recreate a healthy way of being with ourselves, our families and loved ones, and with our world.

Appendix 1:
Planets in Signs and Planetary Aspects

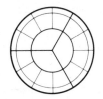

Sun

Principles	Spirit; mind; energy; wholeness; holism; ruling; individuality; life; vitality; organisation; consciousness; libido; kundalini; objectivity; conscious life; sympathy.

Sign	Interpretation
Aries Exalt	Assertion; energy; boldness; leading; warlike; impatient; sporty; enterprising; egotism; pride.
	Blood congestion; fainting; headaches; acne; insanity; hysteria.
Taurus	Perseverance; materialistic; practical; secure; physical; obstinate; possessive; jealous.
	Diphtheria; nose polyps; eye diseases (29°); sore throat; croup; venereal disease; melancholia; scrofula; enlarged thyroid.
Gemini	Dextrous; articulate; educable; dual; identity crises; nervous; glib; superficial; moody; changeable; vivacious.
	Pleurisy; tuberculosis; bronchitis; lung anaemia; pulmonary congestion; injured hands; defective lungs.
Cancer	Domesticity; shrewd; conservative; parental; comfortable; religious; psychological; feeling; deepness.
	Anaemia; dropsy; gastric fever; disordered stomach; dyspepsia; organic stomach defects; bloated stomach.
Leo Rule	Confident; domineering; assured; rising in life; publishing; protection; speculative; teaching; bossy; arrogant.
	Backache; heart palpitation; madness; afflictions of dorsal vertebrae; organic heart trouble; eye disease (6°).
Virgo	Efficient; detail oriented; orderly; attentive; critical; fault-finding; service; demanding; healer.
	Incorrect assimilation of nutriments; blocked colon; bowel diseases; typhoid fever; dysentery.

Sun

Personifications	Administration; ruler; governor; politician; leader; captain; speculation; public figures; father; grandparents; doctor; personalities in media; official; famous people.

House	Interpretation
1st	*Childhood* Attention; parental approval; strong will; vitality; awareness; recuperation; temper; selfishness; physical health; compulsive.
2nd	Endurance; humour; enjoyment; gentle; constant; sensual; secure; withholding; stubborn; solid; possessive; indulgent; parents protect.
3rd	Quick mind; verbal; curiosity; versatile; adaptable; learning; change; siblings; expression; inquisitive; charming.
4th	Secure family; emotional base; pride; parents; beautiful; possessive; domestic; natural; love of comfort; benevolent.
5th	*Maturity* Self-expression; self-conscious; boastful; domineering; leading; artistic; practical; fastidious; virginal; discriminating.
6th	Methodical; analytical; naïve; simple; critical; fussy; studious; verbal; practical; fastidious; virginal; discriminating.

Libra
Fall

Balancing; relaxed; consistent; sociable; political;
charming; amenable; unitary; unreliable; lazy;
dominated; loyal mate.

Skin eruption; Bright's disease; weak kidneys.

Scorpio

Passionate; dependent; moody; vindictive; jealous;
forceful; self-destructive; dynamic; tempered;
magnetic; imperturbable.

*Genito-urinary diseases; menstrual disorders; uterine
and ovarian afflictions.*

Sagittarius

Aspiring; free; sloppy; imaginative; success abroad;
undisciplined; open; realised; exploratory; hedonist;
split.

*Sciatica; paralysis of limbs; eye disease (8°); pulmonary
disease; leg ulcers; arthritis in hip and thigh.*

Capricorn

Goal conscious; egocentric; inhibited; dutiful; hard-
working; selfish; industrious; loyal; inflexible;
noble; material.

*Rheumatism; bone diseases; skin diseases; digestive
troubles; lame knees; sprains.*

Aquarius
Det

Abstract; humanitarian; knowledgeable; human
nature; understanding; social; methodical; help from
others; selfish.

*Sprained ankles; varicose veins; dropsy; heart
palpitations; poor circulation; blood disorders.*

Pisces

Compassionate; universal; loving; addictive;
empathetic; poetic; deceitful; absorptive; negligent;
restricted.

*Typhoid fever; intestinal troubles; colds; deformed feet;
lethargy; diseases of the lymphatic system; swimming
accidents.*

7th

Subliminative; partnership; adaptive; vain; worldly; constancy; associations important; popular; dependent; diplomatic; friendly.

8th

Separative; insular; intense; metaphysical; mysterious; secretive; obstinate; suspicious; esoteric; fanatical; fearless.

9th

Gestation (Transcendence)
Mobile; enthusiastic; changeable; dualistic; spiritual-religious; inspired; foreign; moral; positive; open; imaginative; unreliable.

10th

Pragmatic; paternal; practical; calculating; reserved; tight; depressed; self concentrated; reversals; tenacious; clinging; hardness.

11th

Idealistic; grouped; observative; detached; friendship; intuitive; planning; cranky; independent; reformative; erratic.

12th

Sympathetic; impressionable; secretive; retiring; solitary; estranged; institutional; drugged; sacrificial; passive; reserved; odd.

Moon·

Principles	The feminine; mother; feeling; emotion; home; family; reflection; rhythm; instinct; change; protective urges; catalytic action; child-raising; integration.

Sign	Interpretation
Aries	Volatile; restless; haste; rashness; powerlust; primal; lusty; rebellious; spontaneous feeling; impatient.
	Insomnia; headaches; lethargy; weak eyes; convulsions; rapid pulse.
Taurus Exalt	Constancy; art appreciation; enjoyment; firmness; caution; protection; stubborn; gardener; wealthy; lazy.
	Throat cancer; neck swellings; sore throat; disturbed menses; bronchitis; eye disorders (29°); genito-urinary problems; laryngitis; miscarriage; gluttony.
Gemini	Unpredictable; vacillation; talkative; multiple relations; sentimental; imitative; inconstant; instinctive.
	Lung catarrh; asthma; pneumonia; rheumatism of the arms and hands; lung cancer; weak arms; ulcers on hands; nervous diseases; swollen hands; allergies.
Cancer Rule	Related; secure; obsessional; clannish; indigestive; ulcerated; hypersensitive; restrained; inhibited; dissolute.
	Stomach cancer; dropsy; obesity; bloating; epilepsy; digestive disorders; convulsions; breast cancer; colic; over-developed breasts.
Leo	Gambler; fertile; childlike; amusing; luxurious; social; magnanimous; open; impressive; sporty; entertaining.
	Backache; bad circulation; convulsions; eye trouble (6°); scrofula; heartburn; heart dilations; palpitations.

Moon

Personifications	Mother; women in general; midwife; grandmother; aunt; wife; emotional people; gynaecologists; obstetricians; cook; collector; domestics; gardener.

House	Interpretation
1st	*Childhood* Self-awareness; influenced; impressionable; impulsive; strong personality; susceptible; maternal strength; corpulence; irritable.
2nd	Stable home; comfort; physical focus; food; deep emotional ties; beauty; firmness; stable; possessive; jealous; habitual; growth.
3rd	Manifold emotional expression; mobile; change in mother; fantasy; dreaming; curious; fond of siblings; restless; contradictory; superficial.
4th	Familial; affectionate; impressionable; depth of feeling; domestic; unconscious; mediumistic; attached; sensitive; smothered; withdrawn.
5th	*Maturity* Speculative feeling; intuitive; confident; passionate; vain; impressive; romantic; imaginative; hedonistic; warm; popular.

Virgo	Exacting; methodical; hard-working; neat; clean; retiring; emotionally critical; serving; perfectionist.
	Bowel disorders; constipation; abdominal tumours; dysentry; peritonitis; colon cancer; irregular bowels.
Libra	Reactive; close partnership; charm; elegance; need approval; public relations; dependent on others; social.
	Bright's disease; kidney disease; uricaemia; insomnia; disturbed renal functioning.
Scorpio *Fall*	Death wish; licentiousness; control; bias; seriousness; extreme jealousy; revenge; domination; subtlety.
	Disturbed menses; bladder infections; throat trouble; food poisoning; syphilis; miscarriages.
Sagittarius	Imaginative; foreign feelings; kind; hedonistic; jovial; lofty; traditional; travel; mobility; holier-than-thou.
	Blood infections; hip disease; broken legs; asthma; over-active stomach; lameness; gout; deformed thighs.
Capricorn *Det*	Austerity; unforthcoming; reserved; materialistic; ambitious; egotistic; personal bias; selfish; calculating.
	Articular rheumatism; skin eruptions; eczema; psoriasis; weak knees.
Aquarius	Unsolitary; civilised; humane; cold; inane; abstracted; detachment; political; frigid; unreliable.
	Varicose veins; leg ulcers; dropsy; fractured ankles; poor blood; blood-poisoning; lameness.
Pisces	Yielding; restless; seductive; poetic; secretive; occult; sympathetic; vulnerable; lonely; mysterious; too open.
	Alcoholism; drug addiction; lethargy; boils.

6th   Head rules heart; psychosomatic; practical; careful; correct; naïve; pedantic; coldness; reserved; modest; restrained; undemonstrative.

7th   Emotional dependence; compromising; evasive; irresponsible; fateful partners; vivid expression; sensitive; mother figure; fickle.

8th   Separation; destructive relations; intense; death of mother; possessive; reserved; deep; psychic sensitivity; resentful; dependent.

Gestation (Transcendence)
9th   Vivid inner life; moody; striving; idealistic; changes; fullness; frank; free; restless; alert; emotional attachment; careless; offhand.

10th   Recognition; paternalism; repressed; patient; dutiful; sobriety; ungratified; depressed; cautious; reserved; loyal; possessive.

11th   Friendly; little meaning; group activities; woman friends; idealism; influenced; opinionated; many plans; sympathetic; hoping; wishes.

12th   Moody; insular feelings; isolation; sacrifice; psychic; mediumistic; druggy; induced; easily hurt; hypnotic; reluctant; susceptible; dreamy.

Mercury

Principles	Mentality; intelligence; communication; understanding; mediation; neutrality; nervousness; balancing; business sense; criticism; scientific work; logic; self-expression; adaptable.

Sign	**Interpretation**
Aries	Quick thinking; repartee; creative; rash; mental overwork; decisive; argumentative; impulsive; temper; irritated.
	Brain disease; vertigo; spasms; nervous headaches; facial neuralgia.
Taurus	Logical; material; decisive; common sense; organised; businesslike; blind; secure; structured; obstinate; closed.
	Stuttering; speech defects; hoarseness; deafness; nervous genito-urinary disease; neck swellings.
Gemini Rule	Businesslike; contractual; writer; variety; changeable; inconstant; talented; alert; articulate; perfunctory.
	Gout in arms and shoulders; bronchitis; asthma; asphyxiation; pleurisy; arm diseases; paralysis of arms; neuralgia.
Cancer	Psychological; intuitive; capricious; sentimental; parental ideas; slow mind; conservative; profound.
	Nervous indigestion; dyspepsia; phlegm; catarrh; flatulence; alcoholism; gluttony.
Leo	Willed; fixed ideas; prudence; planned; foresight; dignified; expansive; broadminded; intellectual; self-centred.
	Back pains; fainting; palpitations; heart neuralgia.

Mercury

Personifications	Siblings; friend; intellects; thinkers; mediators; teacher; writer; artisan; architect.

House	Interpretation
1st	*Childhood* Mental activity; observation; quickness; nervous; precocious; noisy; assertive; enthusiasm; awake; over-active; self-expressive.
2nd	Patience; logic; possessive; deliberate; one-sided; talkative; ponderous; thick; sensible; slow; acquisitive; formal; endurance.
3rd	Versatile; conversant; active; adaptable; imitative; siblings; naughty; facile; clever; friendly; gossipy; fluent; superficial.
4th	Perceptive; familial; thinking feelings; memory; immersible; individual; homely; talk; disputative; irrational; retentive; narrow.
5th	*Maturity* Enthusiastic; creative; extrovert; talkative; bossy; critical; mental competition; games; teachers; conceit; organised; dogmatic; rude.

Virgo
Rule
Exalt

Unholistic; nervous; collaborative; shrewd; patient; organised; sedentary; precise; scientific; psychosomatic.

Flatulence; colic; short breath; nervous disorders; gas; nervous dyspepsia; neuralgic pains in the bowels.

Libra

Social; learns through others; vapid; eclectic; unoriginal; reasoned; boring; comparative.

Renal colic; kidney disorders; nervous disorders of the kidneys.

Scorpio

Critical; fanatical; practical; sceptical; cunning; crafty; profound; sharp; investigative; piercing; acid.

Bladder pains; genital pains; nervous menstrual trouble; PMT.

Sagittarius
Det

Frank; versatile; foresight; unstable; thinking deeply; manifold interests; philosophical; just; conflicting views.

Neuralgia in legs; coughs; weak legs.

Capricorn

Organised; practical mind; capable; material ideas; goals conscious; realistic; humourless; crafty; shrewd.

Rheumatism of knees; stiff joints; skin diseases; melancholy; neuralgia in legs or knees; knee pains.

Aquarius

Informed; collective; abstract; cold; inconstant; scattered; quick grasp; scientific; archetypal ideas; occult.

Shooting pains in legs; varicose veins; lameness.

Pisces
Det
Fall

Receptive to others; imaginative; plans without energy; irrational; unconscious; karmic; feeling; psychic.

Gout; cramped feet; distorted feet; corns; neuroses.

6th	Specialised; skills; methodical; patient; alert; superior intellect; analytical; critical; sarcastic; naïve; tidy; healthy.
7th	Subliminative; teamwork; just; balanced mind; thoughts of others; co-operative; public; intellectual; mediators; opinionated; charmed.
8th	Deep; occult; hidden; spiritualistic; deadly; intriguing; grudge holders; interest in the dead; penetrating; senile; suspicious.

9th	*Gestation (Transcendence)* Deep mind; higher mind; rebirth; ethics; moral; curiosity; knowledgeable; religious; gurus; prophetic; scattered; evasive; free; learning.
10th	Ambition; egotistic thoughts; prestige; power; planning; career thoughts; concentration; patience; reserve; rational; serious; exact.
11th	Interested; detached; progressive; groups; reform; invention; involved; Utopian; planning; inquisitive; eccentric; contrary; work alone.
12th	Influenced; sacrificial; reproductive; dreamy; imagination; retentive; mediumistic; poetic; impressionable; refined; influenced by others.

Venus

Principles	Relationship; harmony; love; aesthetics; physical affection; beauty; art; unity; integration; aberration; bad taste; sentimentality; indulgence; affection; affectation; illusion.

Sign	Interpretation
Aries Det	Aggressive love; outgoing; passion; ardent; creative powers; attractive personality; erotic; self-centred. *Catarrh; mucus; kidney congestion; lethargy; head disorders; facial swellings; head tumours.*
Taurus Rule	Love of luxury; taste; constancy; conservative; artistic; musical; loving; indolent; loyal; touching; innate value. *Occipital headaches; goitre; tonsillitis; genital inflammation; swollen throat glands; throat ulcers; enlarged neck veins.*
Gemini	Many loves; social; flirtatious; attractive; charming; accommodating; discuss ideas; superficial relations; romantic. *Dropsy; warts; pulmonary inefficiency; eruptions on hands.*
Cancer	Domestic; delicate; feminine; sentimental; indigestible; lush; tender; indulgent; exploited; affectionate; unselfish.
Leo	Premature relations; ardent; fixed affection; fiery relationships; garish taste; squandering; indulgent; pride. *Spinal disease; backache; enlarged heart; broken heart; heart dilation; palpitations due to excessive indulgence.*

Venus

Personifications Lovers; maidens; women; the beautiful; artists; musicians; entertainers; clothier.

House	Interpretation
	Childhood
1st	Beauty; personal grace; proportionate; happy; love; demonstrative; popular; love at first sight; social life; clothes; enhancement.
2nd	Physical beauty; objects; needing love; good taste; grasping; deep feelings; personal attraction; possessive; faithful; plodding.
3rd	Love of words; drawing; social; siblings; close relationships; variety; curiosity; friendly with everyone; flighty; fickle.
4th	Deep love; familial; appreciating home; love; dreamy; imaginative; possessive; loyal; tender; flattered; shy; deeply sensitive; stable.
	Maturity
5th	Love-relations; games; pleasure; amusing; hedonistic; vivacious; creative; proud; jealous; romantic; popular; warmth; social.

Virgo
Fall

Repressed feeling; fastidious; polite; perfectionist; indecisive; shared work; hypercritical; cold exterior; beauty.

Impeded peristaltic action; worms; tapeworm; dysentry; intestinal tumours; constipation.

Libra
Rule

Lively; crafty; companionable; engagements; artistic skill; important affections; bonding; beauty; money; conformist; social.

Uraemia; polyuria; headaches; gonorrhoea; flatulence.

Scorpio
Det

Intemperance; legacies; withholding love; deep feeling; immoral; secretive; serious relations; hatred; indifference; occult art.

Venereal diseases; female complaints; uterine prolapsis or tumours; painful menstruation.

Sagittarius

Spiritual love; frank; moodiness; many loves; demonstrative; objective relations; ethical; foreign aesthetics.

Hip tumours; gout; eruptions on legs.

Capricorn

Materialistic; distrusting; jealous; maturity; attached; experienced; over-controlled; separate; proud; reserved.

Gout in knees; skin diseases on legs.

Aquarius

Easy contact; free love; refined; amenable; indiscriminate; unconventional; gay; sponsorship; effervescent.

Varicose veins; swollen ankles; poor blood.

Pisces
Exalt

Longing for love; exploited; tender; gentility; sentimental; musical; romantic; religious; cosmic feeling; suffering.

Tender feet; chilblains; gout.

6th	Work love; critical affections; naïvete; friendly co-operation; moral; practical considerations; puritanical; refined; modest.
7th	Great love; affairs; infidelity; attractive; amorous; friendly; artistic; happy marriage; public; charming; gentle; lovable; frivolous.
8th	Strong attraction; love of separation; lust; fanatic love; passion; jealousy; wavering; licentious; sexual; magnetic; charming.

Gestation (Transcendence)

9th	Love of art, religion, philosophy; wishing; romantic; responsive; scattered emotions; idealistic; imaginings; unstable; cultural.
10th	Social ambition; good relations; legal; cold emotion; faithful; constant; control; formal sense; loyal; undemonstrative.
11th	Abstract love; frigidity; homosexuality; idealistic; progressive; social; kind friend; group activities; women's groups; protected.
12th	Secretive; solitary; masturbative; artistic; seductive; impressionable; sensitive; soft; psychic love; sexual restraint; charitable.

Mars

Principles	Energy; aggression; will; activity; desire for change; conflict; intervention; adventure; impulse; competition; sexual drive; initiatory force; passion; violence; ruthlessness.

Sign	**Interpretation**
Aries Rule	Fighting; spirit; ambition; temper; zeal; independent; irascible; brutal; headstrong; competitive; egotism.
	Fevers; violent headaches; sunstroke; congestion; brain tumours; delirium; head pains; insomnia; head wounds and scars; inflammations.
Taurus Det	Work capacity; practical; foresight; executive; acquisitive; industrious; material; skilled; aggressive; strong.
	Tonsillitis; mumps; suffocation; adenoids; diphtheria; nose bleed; infected larynx; excessive menses; prostate diseases and removal; scrofula; pains in neck; neck wounds and scars; surgery; surgical births.
Gemini	Mobility; communicative; sarcastic; versatile gifts; agile; lively; ready; mental; debater; journalistic; rude.
	Lung haemorrhages; nervous stress diseases; eczema; pulmonary emphysema; pneumonia; cough; fractured or sprained hands or collarbone; itching; fever; rashes caused by nerves; accidents to hands or arms.
Cancer Fall	Instinctive actions; temper; lacks persistence; irritable; sensuous; tenacious; frustration; ulcers.
Leo	Confident; possessive; ardour; frank; domineering; creative; willed; leading; competitive; strong belief; strength.
	Rheumatism of the back; enlarged heart; stress disease; heart pains; suffocation; heart damage; hardened arteries; arterial sclerosis.

Mars

Personifications	Fighters; soldiers; surgeons; athletes; mechanics; craftsmen; men in general; strong women; engineers; metalworkers; technicians; builders; police.

House	Interpretation
1st	*Childhood* Energetic; lively; self-willed; violence; muscular; robust; impulsive; strength of personality; action; impatience; injuries.
2nd	Endurance; practical ability; obstinate; intractable; possessive; purposeful; desiring; tenacious; sensuous; persistence; intense.
3rd	Witty; criticism; scattered; active mind; direct; writing; impulsive movement; anger; argumentative; nervous; talkative; hasty.
4th	Intense feelings; moody; impulsive; instinct; not persevering; domestic dominance; ecology; acquisitive; energetic; uncontrolled; working.
5th	*Maturity* Formative power; self assurance; enterprise; gambler; player; athlete; audacious; sexual; artist; speculation; egotism; dictatorial.

Virgo	Scientific; orderly; irritable; astute; criticism; skilled; medicine; practical action; perfectionist; fussy; nervous.
	Typhoid fever; worms; peritonitis; diarrhoea; ventral hernia; appendicitis; gastro-enteritis.
Libra Det	Social activities; public affairs; leading; teamwork; dependence on feeling; frank; ardent; idealistic; loving.
	Nephritis; excess urine; renal stones; kidney disease; pyelitis.
Scorpio Rule	Magnetic sex; strong emotions; forceful; selfish; critical; revengeful; occult; sex magic; courage; jealousy.
	Excessive menses; renal stones; enlarged prostate; inflammation of ovaries, uterus, vagina or urethra; cystitis.
Sagittarius	Explorational; enthusiastic; strong beliefs; religious; hedonistic; rude; unconventional; adventurous; spiritual.
	Fractures of the thighs or legs; accidents or injuries to hips and thighs; sciatica; leg pains; dislocations.
Capricorn Exalt	Authoritative; directed; independent; energetic; extremely materialistic; possessive; power mad; efficient; controlled.
	Smallpox; measles; chickenpox; pimples; inflammatory skin diseases; knee fractures; broken legs; ankylosis; gout.
Aquarius	Organised; inconstant; superficial; masculine groups; perverse; impatient; revolutionary; upsetting; methodical.
	Blood-poisoning; varicose veins; fractured leg or ankle; weak ankles.
Pisces	Addictive; silent work; uncontrolled; over-emotional; romantic; illusory men; seductive; vivid dreams; waiting.
	Deformed feet; bunions; corns; blisters; accidents to feet; drowning; bowel inflammation; diarrhoea; narcotic addiction.

6th	Detailed work; organising; tidy; endurance; methodical; critical; skill; energy in work; surgeons; precision; ingenious; frustrated.
7th	Associative; subliminative; cordial manner; work partnership; impulsive; aggressive affairs; joint finance; entangled; passion.
8th	Survival instinct; courageous; sensuous; dissipated; sadistic; craving power; active corporate desire; violent death; illegality.

9th	*Gestation (Transcendence)* Sport; convincing others; adventurous; brave; travel lust; social causes; reform; inspired; experienced; extravagant; rude; sloppy.
10th	Famous; ambitious; self-reliant; hard work; realistic; sober; defiant; obstinate; heroic; irritable; cold; unfeeling; reversals; power.
11th	Male friends; reforming; detached; asexual; deliberate; freedom; contradictory; revolutionary; superficial; progressive; perverse.
12th	Lacking energy; drug desire; alcoholic; secretive; hidden emotions; sensuous; hoping; unconscious; desire; institutions; isolation; unreliable.

Jupiter

Principles	Expansion; optimism; positivity; generous; enthusiastic; philosophical; religious; psychological; travel; wise; justice; harmony; aspirations; amoral; indulgent; sloppy.

Sign	Interpretation
Aries	Leading; travel urge; noble; positive; generous; free; spiritual; extravagant; frank; innovative; faithful; foolish.
	Cerebral congestion; inflammation; dizziness; sleepiness; fainting; mouth ulcers; strange dreams; obesity; sanguinary fevers; facial boils.
Taurus	Hedonist; good hearted; indulgent; exploitative; financial interests; stewardship; productive; beneficent.
	Obesity; apoplexy; ringworm; mouth ulcers; nasal catarrh; nose bleed; flatulence; excessive eating and drinking.
Gemini Det	Obliging others; many relations; joy; crafty; sociable; free; mannered; empty; legal; curiosity; advanced; friendly.
	Pleurisy; lung congestion; inflammation of lungs; pulmonary apoplexy; swollen hands.
Cancer Exalt	Pleasure; prolific; deep feelings; charitable; intuitive; receptive; deep love; family important; secure.
Leo	Speculative; grandeur; openness; arts; great energy; positive in games; fond; generous; big-hearted; noble; vain.
	Apoplexy; arteriosclerosis; swollen ankles; heart ailments due to rich diet; enlarged heart.

Jupiter

Personifications	Priests; philosophers; psychologists; psychiatrist; the wealthy; lawyer; banker; physician; official; publisher; guru; wise man; fortune hunter.

House	*Interpretation*
1st	*Childhood* Self-sufficient; optimistic; extrovert; fat; aspiring; imbalanced; sociable; well-liked; protection; indulgence; promises; vigour.
2nd	Expansiveness; growth; reliable; wasteful; generous; enjoyment; insecure; trusteeship; liberal; open; exploitable; wealthy.
3rd	Positive mind; optimism; religious influence; intelligent; flexible; versatile; changing; popular; travel; conceited; carefree; sweet.
4th	Receptive; attachment; contented; religious; psychology; family sense; impressionable; congenial; strong home; morality; fortunate.
5th	*Maturity* Creativity; artistic; self-confidence; lead; popularity; vanity; honour; achievements; dignified; intolerant; prestige; dominant.

Virgo
Det

Morality; prudent; ambitious; honest; intellectual; conscientious; critical; perfectionist; overrated; serving; work.

Enlarged or ulcerated liver; jaundice; weak back; consumption; abscess of the bowels; diarrhoea; intestinal tumours.

Libra

The law; mildness; open partnerships; advantage through marriage; benign; unfulfilled commitments; psychology.

Weak adrenals; renal abscesses; diabetes; skin eruptions; kidney tumours; amyloid kidneys.

Scorpio

Metaphysical; passionate; shrewd; striving for possessions; craving pleasure; corporate affairs; mystical.

Enlarged prostate; uterine tumours or abscesses; dropsy; strangury; urethral abscesses.

Sagittarius
Rule

Philosophy; religious; humanitarian; esoteric; nobility; foreign; jovial; liberal; psychological; superstition.

Rheumatism in hips and thighs; gout; leg pains and swelling.

Capricorn
Fall

Acquisitive; wealthy; recognised; trusty; responsible; integrity; conservatism; austere; tight; materialist.

Skin disease; melancholy; liver degeneration; weak or swollen knees; adenoid trouble.

Aquarius

Impartial; sympathetic; fellowship; human nature; occult wisdom; social reform; intolerant; astrology; broad.

Swollen ankles; high blood pressure; blood-poisoning; poor circulation.

Pisces

Deep emotions; hidden life; drugs; modest circumstances; kind; unreliable; visionary; indolent; illusory; alcohol.

Swollen feet; alcoholism; addiction; enlarged feet.

6th	Ambition; learning; teaching; teamwork; carefree; service; healing; work ethic; morality; conscientious; organisation; professional.

7th	Fortunate marriage-job; justice; popularity; temperance; charitable; social contacts; selfless relationships; judgement; spiritual.

8th	Religious; separated; legacies; funerals; sex values; overrated; proud; self-indulgent; peaceful death; materialistic; occult.

9th	*Gestation (Transcendence)* Religious; moral aspiration; foresight; plans; expansive feelings; speculative; foreign matters; inner development; justice; balance.

10th	Responsible; productive; material; practical; prominence; recognition; reliable; dignity; standing; domestic affairs; egotist; capable.

11th	Humanitarian; prominent friends; groups; help from others; liberal; obliging; collective goals; invention; ulterior motives; sociable.

12th	Altruism; contentment; solitude; generous; imaginative; inner life; compassionate; spiritual search; meditation; fantasy; crisis.

Saturn

Principles	Contraction, pessimism; negativity; stingy; concentration; focus; seriousness; economy; inhibition; reserve; unadaptable; formative energy; discipline; limitation; suffering.

Sign	Interpretation
Aries *Fall*	Selfishness; diligence; reserved; humourless; lonely; mechanical; autocratic; wilful; strong character. *Headache; colds; catarrh; deafness; chills; cerebral anaemia; toothache; tooth decay; tartar; fainting; skull fractures; emaciation.*
Taurus	Perseverance; method; constructive; money worries; ambition; hard work; father; elders; serious finances. *Diphtheria; mumps; croup; tooth decay; choking; throat stricture; stiff neck; dislocated or broken neck.*
Gemini	Intellectual; scientific; businesslike; serious; difficult; abstract; inhibited; calculating; detached; systematic. *Rheumatism; bronchitis; asthma; pleurisy; consumption; sciatica; asphyxiation; broken arms.*
Cancer *Det*	Sensitive; self-centred; elderly; paranoid; lonely; jealous; suspicious; estranged; respectful; unstable.
Leo *Det*	Limited; authoritarian; leader; simple; loyalty; hard work; loss through children; ungratified; resentful; need recognition. *Curvature of the spine; weak back; arteriosclerosis; spinal sclerosis; chronic heart disease; atrophy of the heart; weak heart; endocarditis; depression.*
Virgo	Perfectionist; hard worker; serious; materialistic; acting alone; pedantic; detail oriented; attentive; discreet. *Weak intestinal peristalsis; leukaemia; obstruction of ileum, caecum or transverse colon; gripe; appendicitis; melancholy.*

Saturn

Personifications	Doctors; bankers; workers; farmers; workers with metals; scientist; grandparents; uncles and aunts; business people; archaeologists; geologist; miner; computer programmer.

House	**Interpretation**
1st	*Childhood* Ambitious; restrained; obstinacy; responsible; cold; unfriendly; limitation; hardship; lonely; older people; defiance; selfish; serious.
2nd	Material; ordered; possessive; stability; endurance; inhibited; restricted movement; grasping; conservative; inertia; difficulty.
3rd	Difficult siblings; zealous; thorough; unadaptive; shy; disciplined; practical; scientific; critical; mechanistic; clumsy; logic; serious.
4th	Reserved; ambitious; difficult family; love; independent; defensive; repressed; economy; responsible; isolated; secure; reclusive.
5th	*Maturity* Responsible; reliable; loyal; informal; shy; conservative; repressed; unsportsmanlike; strict; serious school; inhibited sexuality.
6th	Critical; correct; responsible; methodical; pedantic; scientific; serious study; detailed; sedentary; inhibited; asexual; misunderstood.

Libra
Exalt

Industrious; conscientious; impartial; austere; reliable; managerial; corporate; meditative; businesslike; legal; enemies.

Stones; ataxia; gravel; Bright's disease; malnutrition; suppressed urine; disturbed renal function; cirrhosis of the kidneys; skin eruptions; prolapsed kidneys.

Scorpio

Resourceful; restrained; melancholy; metaphysical seriousness; cautious; corporate; legal conflict; perfectionist.

Sterility; suppressed menses; constipation; haemorrhoids; fistula; under-developed genitals.

Sagittarius

Moralising; high-minded; religious; serious traveller; prudence; law; separation from home; doubts.

Hip and thigh contusions; sciatica; dislocated hip; gout; bruises; aches; falls; lameness; broken legs; obstructed circulation; arthritis.

Capricorn
Rule

Paternal; advanced; suspicious; slow; patience; method; pessimism; diplomacy; materialistic; partial; strong; egotist.

Chronic knee trouble; rheumatism; gout; bursitis; ague; sprains; broken legs; fractures; arthritis of leg joints.

Aquarius

Serious groups; collective; ambitious; organised; responsible; mental work; detached; selfish; domineering; games.

Weak ankles; cramps in ankles and joints; bad teeth; eczema; weak ankles; arthritis; impeded circulation.

Pisces

Struggle; melancholy; restrained; older friends; retirement; deep meditation; spiritual; withdrawal; distrusting.

Rheumatism; cold feet; bunions; tuberculosis; consumption; afflicted feet; club, flat or deformed feet.

7th	Dutiful; older partner; serious relations; estrangement; impractical; loyal; inhibited; discontented; enduring; hard work; responsible.
8th	Partners' finances, emotions; lack capital; obstinate; transformations; strong; reserved; selfish; occult; concentrative; rebirth.

Gestation (Transcendence)

9th	Aspirations; serious philosophers; separation; devotion; sincere; hurt; religious; stable; unsocial; achievement; status; morality.
10th	Patience; will-power; restraint; ambitious; strong will; concentration; economy; partial; egocentric; cautious; karmic affairs; debts.
11th	Responsible; planning; reliable partner; extravagant expectations; aspirations; false friends; faithful; detached; inhibited mate.
12th	Reserved; lonely; restrained; secluded; nerves; timid; isolated; fear of failure; inferior; depressed; retiring; sacrificial; worrying.

Uranus

Principles	Originality; eccentricity; independence; rhythm; inspiration; individuality; invention; rebelliousness; dancing; perception; excitable; obstinacy; operations; accidents; changes.

Sign	*Interpretation*
Aries 1928–1934	Utopian; enthusiasm; unusual; peculiar; odd personality; free; unconventional; intuition; courage; daring; tempered. *Demoniacal complaints; injury from lightning, electricity or explosives; acute and sporadic pains in head; eye diseases; brain abscesses.*
Taurus *Fall* 1934–1942	Erratic; sudden changes; unstable finances; independent; ingenious; risk; speculative; premature; reform; original. *Spasmodic throat disorders; disturbed thyroid; wry neck; spasmodic contractions in neck; tetanus; hysteria.*
Gemini 1942–1949	Mental energy; spontaneous; inquisitive; scientific; methodical; original methods; free thinker; bizarre; comprehension. *Spasmodic asthma; convulsive hoarse; dry cough; colds; paralysis of arms and hands; nervous breakdown.*
Cancer 1949–1956	Erratic feelings; strange mother; impulsive; residence changes; rebel; freedom; excitement; psychic; sensitive.
Leo *Det* 1956–1962	Egomanic; peculiar love; children; individual; licentious; determined; organising; unrestrained; sexually free. *Palpitation; spasmodic heart action; spinal meningitis; weak valves; infantile paralysis; obstruction of blood; fainting; nervous heart complaints; irregular heart action.*
Virgo 1962–1969	Health professions; mechanical; free; subtle; original job; intellectual; revolutionary; ingenious; computers. *Flatulence; abdominal cramps; bowel cramps; spasmodic intestinal pains; nervous dyspepsia.*

Uranus

Personifications	Eccentrics; inventors; unusual people; technicians; revolutionaries; dancers & musicians; astrologers; radio–TV; electricians; healers; feminists; rebels; surgeons.

House	Interpretation
1st	*Childhood* Energetic; unusual; original; restless; odd; scientific influence; obstinacy; irrational electric; wilful; abrupt; erratic; stubborn.
2nd	Unusual objects; gains & losses; headstrong; determined; jealous; speculative; premature; unsettled; precocious; impractical; lively.
3rd	Inventive; original; precocious; creative; desultory; quick understanding; restless; intuitive; scattered; sharp; witty.
4th	Strange family; peculiar emotions; intuition; wandering; odd associations; homelessness; estrangement; impatient; rebellious; changes.
5th	*Maturity* Enterprise; boldness; creative; originality; peculiar games; dramatic; sudden affections; gambling; adventurous; quick learning; arty.
6th	Peculiar work; individual learning; quick; scientific effort; genius; occult; original; reforming; detailed; foolish; critical.

Libra 1969–1975	New relationships; divorce; irritable; affairs; free love; magnetic; quick associations; imaginative; restless. *Venereal skin eruptions; hallucinations; spasmodic kidney action; floating kidney.*
Scorpio *Exalt* 1975–1981	Regeneration; rapid change; destined struggles; violence; danger; ruthless; occult explosion; rebellious; astrology. *Miscarriages; abortions; venereal disease; difficult birth; malformed genitals; nervous afflictions of menses; epidemics.*
Sagittarius 1981–1988	Adventure; astrology; progressive education; reformed; unorthodox; Utopian; excitable; spiritual; neurotic. *Paralysis of lower limbs; obstruction of circulation of legs; thigh cramps; numbness in legs; contortions; leg accidents.*
Capricorn 1988–1996	Power; great aims; fanaticism; penetration; acquisitive; resolution; headstrong; strange career; radical. *Leg or knee accidents; cramps in knees; deformed knees; paralysis of lower legs.*
Aquarius 1996–2003	Detachment; trouble; magnification; penetration; spiritual energy; religious change; inventive talent; wayward. *Unusual diseases; cramps in ankles; spasmodic circulation.*
Pisces 2003–2011	Intuitive; peculiar methods; isolated; investigative; occult; mystical; self-willed; strange aspirations; idealism. *Deformed feet; cramps in feet and toes; paralysis of feet; contortions.*

7th	Eccentric relationships; drug experiences; rebellious; inspired; peculiar marriage view; many marriages; aesthetic; talented; rigid.
8th	Penetrating; investigating occultism; energy realised; danger; fearless; strength; tenacious; great change; rebirth; violence; superphysics.
9th	*Gestation (Transcendence)* Spiritual; enlightenment; prophecy; rebelling; religious reform; advanced ideas; progressive fanaticism; restless; unconventional; danger.
10th	Ambitious; shrewd; concentrated energy; resolute; technical ability; professional; radical ideas; sudden fall; affliction.
11th	Scientific; profound; aspirational; organising; magnification; progressive; intuitive friend; perversity; rebellious; peculiar ideas.
12th	Mystical; revelling; intuition; estrangement; strange disease; visionary; secretive; being misunderstood; yoga; seeking liberation; unreal.

Neptune

Principles	Sensitivity; psychic; impressionable; fantasy; imagination; dreams; illusion; drugs; mediumship; intuition; idealism; Utopian projections; ESP; transcendental experiences.

Sign	**Interpretation**
Aries 1861–1874	Inspiration; idealism; unselfish; highly sensitive; far distant; social welfare; confused; mad; insane; addicted.
	Insanity; trances; sleep walking; blindness; hysteria; coma; fainting; hallucinations; addiction; nightmares; obscure diseases; smallpox; sleeping sickness.
Taurus 1874–1888	Good taste; formal; unusual objects; idealistic finances; visionary; healing; natural beauty; alcoholism; addiction.
	Disorders of throat tissue; goitre; disturbed thyroid; obscure diseases of neck and throat; malformed sexual organs; septic throat; swollen throat.
Gemini 1888–1901	Nature love; mystical; magical; inspired; confusion; vagueness; scattered; poetic; quick perception; variety; worrying.
	Disorders of glands and hands; deformed hands; nervous diseases; weak-mindedness; glandular afflictions; mental disorders.
Cancer 1901–1914	Intuition; psychic force; sensitive to home/mother; cherishing; inhibited; susceptible; unstable; suffering.
Leo *Exalt* 1914–1928	Passionate; easily stimulated; acting; leading; flattery; certain; love of pleasure; misdirected affection; waste.
	Enlarged heart; suppression of heart action through drugs or narcotics; heart trouble caused by smoking.

Neptune

Personifications Psychics; sensitive people; dreamers; Utopians; tricksters; mystics; gurus; dieticians; drug dealers; anaesthetists; chemists; inventors.

House	Interpretation
1st	*Childhood* Sensitive personality; intuition; dreamy; impressionable; delicate digestion; drugs; strange appearance; peculiar relationships.
2nd	Sensitive to form; artistic; sensuous; beauty; soft; imaginative; addictive; moody; strange form; muddled; impractical; lazy; dependent.
3rd	Duality; sensitivity; fantasy; confusion; unrealistic; inspiration; wrong ideas; weak memory; misunderstanding; nicknames; siblings.
4th	Great sensitivity; spiritual perception; deep feeling; inner union; discontent; anxiety; residence changes; addictive; sacrificial.
5th	*Maturity* Beauty; peculiar pleasures; sexuality; acting; exaggerating; romantic; psychological problems; broken family; intuitions; waste.

Virgo Det 1928-1942	Fault finding; hypercritical; work difficulty; psychic communication; chaos; chemical; drugged; preoccupied. *Hypochondria; dropsy; wasting of bowels; bowel disorders from drugs or opiates.*
Libra 1942–1956	Uncertain relations; divorce; sensitive partner; drug abuse; psychedelics; strange feelings; disappointed; receptive sex.
Scorpio 1956–1970	Hidden emotions; mystery; sex urge; confusion; clairvoyance; occultism; sensationalism; depression; sickness. *Afflictions to nerves of genito-urinary tract; ill health from drug abuse; epidemic diseases.*
Sagittarius 1970–1984	Higher mind; religious regeneration; travel; foreign ideas; meditation; enlightenment; aimless; inspiration. *Rheumatism.*
Capricorn 1984–1998	Supernatural; meditation; strange objectives; deception; depression; parental sacrifice; mystic reality. *Arthritis of leg joints; lack of control over knees.*
Aquarius Fall 1998–2012	Soul unions; noble aspirations; easy temptation; social theory; group stimuli; independence; intuitive. *Blood diseases.*
Pisces 2012–2026	Mysticism; inner life; mediumistic; neurotic; metaphysical; escapist; druggist; addictive; seductive. *Overstimulated pineal gland leading to drink, drugs, delirium; overdoses; enlarged feet; disorders of feet; psychosomatic diseases.*

6th	Psychosomatic; serving; healing power; gentle; deceitful; hypersensitive; addictive; easy; despondent; magnetic energy; inspiration.
7th	Receptive; idealistic relationships; platonic; seductive; artistic; impulsive; harmonious relationships; psychic connections; oddness.
8th	Psychic; spiritual; unconscious processes; mediumistic; depressive; secretive; drugged; wasting diseases; hospitals; disappointment.

9th	*Gestation (Transcendence)* Presentiment; clairvoyance; idealism; over-active mind; dreams; unrealistic; wishes & plans; self-deception.
10th	Aspiration without application; deep ideas; uncertainty; lacking reality; family trouble; psychic experiences; scandal; mysterious.
11th	Artistic; idealistic; strange attraction; hopes; wishes; mental change; insincerity; psychic experience; notoriety; theorising.
12th	Reserve; psychic communication; reverie; art; external influences; drugs; hospitals; ill; inducement; craving; alcohol; pessimism.

Pluto

Principles	The masses; transformation; revolution; destruction; force majeure; power; magic; willpower; propaganda; coercion; media; major changes; regeneration; passages.

Sign	Interpretation
Aries 1823–1852	Self assertion in the world; power-lust; new ideas; revolutionary person; potential; courageous; dauntless; free.
Taurus Det 1852–1884	Possessiveness; materialist; endurance; utilitarian; genius with materia; art; depending on finances; productive.
Gemini 1884–1914	Inventive; mobility; comprehension; intellectual assertion; science; adventures; ruthless behaviour.
Cancer 1914–1939	Intense personal feelings; familial restraint; compulsive; paternalism; transformed family; liberated woman.
Leo 1939–1957	Revolution in self-expression; change of attitude; exteriorisation; outburst of consciousness; creativity; talent.
Virgo 1957–1972	Health revolution; mental disease; psychosomatic; holistic medicine; workers; reactionaries; punks; birth control.
Libra 1972–1984	Liberation; homosexuality; changes in partnership; social justice; regenerated civilisation; arbitration; delicate balance.
Scorpio Rule 1984–2000	Death and rebirth; regeneration; force; fanaticism; atomic warfare; world war; daemonic forces; transformation; rage.

Pluto

Personifications	Revolutionaries; mass media people; politicians; dictators; propagandists; actors and actresses; public speakers; atomic scientists; outlaws; prostitutes.

House	Interpretation
	Childhood
1st	Power drive; extraordinary energy; assertions; rage; powerful will; hardships; robust; strong parental changes; advanced; rapid growth.
2nd	Great ambition; acquisitive; great pains or losses; dependence on money; insatiable; change material situations; stewardship.
3rd	Ingenious; specialised learning; rapid speech; penetrating mind; resourceful; secretive; strong opinions; strange siblings; gossip.
4th	Strong heredity; unusual task; solitary; deep feelings; magnetic; magic; domination at home; nature love; ecology; occult; secrets.
	Maturity
5th	Dynamic emotions; authority; self-awareness; powerful will; force; dramatic expression; great achievements; creative power; talent.
6th	Healing; psychosomatic diseases; working with others; inquisitive; collecting; scientific; energetic; great criticism; fanatacism; zeal.
7th	Fateful partnerships; fame; strong unions; divorces; multiple partners; personal magnetism; dramatic changes; domineering; intuitive.
8th	Fanaticism; tragic events; record achievements; search for meaning; transforming; public death; influential; tenacious; occult; secrets.

Sagittarius 2000–	Prophecy; sagacity; exploration; travel; strive for wisdom; philosophical change; psychoanalysis; Utopian aims; religious.
Capricorn 1762–1777	New ideas; practical revolutions; great ambition; corporate; executive; inventive; obsessed; materialistic.
Aquarius 1777–1799	Democracy; mental change; scientific; advancement through friends; psychological; synthetic ideas; intellectual.
Pisces 1799–1823	Profundity; apocalyptic; universal; compassionate; Christian fanaticism; born again; mystical; astrological.

Gestation (Transcendence)

9th   Higher knowledge; spiritual regeneration; pioneering; the unattainable; travel; reform; social change; religious fanaticism; atheism.

10th   Dictatorship; struggle for recognition; practical problems; independence; danger; isolation; plans; dramatic change; willpower.

11th   Communal; Utopian communities; reforming; friendship important; sudden death; changes of attitude; exaggerated hopes; popularity.

12th   Isolation; universal; revelatory; destructive; metaphysical; secretive; tempted; suppressed emotions; strange illness; retirement; occult.

Node

Principles	Associations; alliances; sociability; communal sense; sublimation; fostering; collective influences.

Sign	Interpretation
Aries	Cultivating friendships; honours; wealth; associative urge; extrovert; social; ardent; enthusiastic.
Taurus	Gain through property; sharing resources; debt; gain by learning and property.
Gemini Exalt	Good mind; language facility; gains from siblings; publishing; writing; words create anxiety.
Cancer	Close parents; soul associations; gain by property; obliging at home.
Leo	Speculative with others; large circle of friends; sporting; clubs; society affairs; wasteful; pompous; love affairs.
Virgo	Scientific associations; teaching; institutional; research; nagging; critical of others; sensitive health.
Libra	Unable to be alone; gregarious; dependent on others; contention; communal sense; social meetings; business success.
Scorpio	Deceptive; secretive associations; esoteric organisations; sexual relations; subversive affairs.
Sagittarius Fall	Legal teamwork; administrative; orderly; communal; mental quality; prophetic dreams; psychoanalysis.
Capricorn	Responsible to others; exploitation; practical groups; unions; professional groups; authorities; social climbing.
Aquarius	Stimulating friends; many friends; social life; inseparable; grasping; helping others communally.
Pisces	Beliefs; religious communities; collectives; institutions; isolation within groups; gaining possessions.

Node

Personifications	Associations; groups; clubs; political parties; labour unions; organizations.

House	Interpretation
	Childhood
1st	Self expression; desiring to rule; recognition; social life; personal associations.
2nd	Permanent bonding; alliances; money from others; devoted people; reliable; loyalty; legacy.
3rd	Many associations; ideas from others; important contacts; superficial association; nursery school; short relationships.
4th	Family ties; prominent parental contact; confused ancestry; soul unions; dependent; attached.
	Maturity
5th	Popularity; game-playing; large schools; many loves; affectionate with family; organised; team sports.
6th	Teaching associations; science; health interests; love of animals; serving others; work relationships; honest employees.
7th	Love affairs; teams; public affairs; profit through others; gain through women and partnership; making friends easily; social.
8th	Occult organisations; associations; co-operative effort; socialism; old age home; secret relations; gifts; legacies; violent policies.
	Gestation (Transcendence)
9th	Utopian ideas; idealistic groups; legal affairs; educational interests; dreams; water journeys; political idealism.
10th	Honour; credit; great achievements; business organisations; corporate affairs; deception; material objectives.
11th	Many friendships; supportive family; ideal plans; complex relationships; compulsive joining; social life prominent; helpful.
12th	Secret associations; rest homes; hospitals; nursing staff; teams of doctors; restraint from others; philosophical interests.

Ascendant (AS)

Principles	Environment; personality; birth circumstances; people present at birth; reaction to the world; mask; way of acting; personal attitude; surroundings.

Sign	**Birth Circumstances and Environment**
Aries	Restlessness; energy; self-assertive; aggressive; impatient; surgery; forceps delivery; hurrying; ruthlessness.
Taurus	Stable conditions; security; quiet; beautiful surroundings; women present; midwife; home; domesticity; practical.
Gemini	Changes; quick birth; talking; many people present; siblings present; nerves; observers; moving around; adaptation.
Cancer	Moody; home; family contact; humid; caring; feminine; protected; simplicity; sensitivity; anaesthetics; women.
Leo	Authoritarian; confident; extrovert; active; joyous; open; prominent doctor; purposeful; bold; luxurious environs.
Virgo	Critical; hospital; doctors; nurses; naïvete; first births; virginal; nervous; stable; painstaking; hygienic; observant.
Libra	Harmonious place; balanced; teamwork; physically easy; obliging; social; talkative; craving approval; women; nurses.
Scorpio	Disharmonious; humid; hot-headed; brutal; surgical; forceps; violence; force; tragic; Caesarean; circumcision; cautious; angry.
Sagittarius	Enthusiastic; athletic; joyous; good humour; natural; easy; active; messy; lively; expansive; foreign; recognised.

Ascendant (AS)

Personality

Restless; rash; energetic; self-assertive; aggressive; impatient; quick temper; initiatory; violent; forceful; family ties; the surgeon.

Love of beauty; harmonious personality; security; property; practical; artistic; possessive; obstinate; loving; attentive; attractive; homely.

Quick responses; talkative; vivacious; adaptable; mobile; inconstant; communicative; artistic; highly strung; lively; superficial; boastful.

Sensitivity; rich home life; shyness; dependent; impressionable; sympathetic; mediumistic; gentle; addictive; unable to stand alone; dedicated.

Self-glorifying; courageous; hedonistic; ruling; generous; fun-loving; impressive; joyful; dignity; game-playing; haughty; arrogant; egocentric.

Discreet; cautious; reserved; critical; shy; precise; clean; pedantic; anxious; nervous; psychosomatic illnesses; indigestible; stable.

Balanced; harmonious personality; teamwork; attractive body; charming; flatterable; vain; saccharine; relaxed; gushy; meddlesome.

Aggressive; passionate; separate; metaphysical; reserved; paranoid; cautious; dependent; decisive; secretive; hot-blooded; sexual; magnetic.

Positive; jovial; happy; philosophical; sporty; enthusiastic; expansive; independent; social; lively; sloppy; nature-loving; hedonistic; easy.

Capricorn	Concentration; inhibition; restriction; long labour; serious; restraint; older doctor; reserved; anxious; methodical.
Aquarius	Communal; detached; serious; idealistic; restrained; cold; progressive; friendly; abstract; mechanical; unorthodox; rhythmic.
Pisces	Self-sacrificial; drugged; governed by externals; unconfident; anaesthetics; induced; isolated; psychic; dreamy; vague.

Tenacious; repressed; serious; inhibited;
materialistic; goal-conscious; hard working;
anxious; pragmatic; professional; ambitious.

Reforming; communal; detached; group-oriented;
friendly; progressive; own ideas; adaptable;
inhibited; cold; moody; changing objectives.

Sacrificial; dreamy; psychic; sensitive; vague;
depressed; comfortable; lazy; quiet; isolated;
sympathetic; lonely; simple; receptive; induced.

Midheaven (MC)

Principles	Ego-consciousness; objectives; focus; spiritual awareness; individuality; aims; profession; honour; confidence; moment of recognition; purpose.

Sign	*MC Registration Circumstances*
Aries	Intuitive; successful establishment of individuality; aware objectives; active assertion; ambitious; domineering.
Taurus	Sensitive; productive; stable; physical manifestation; substantial; tangible; secure; willed; artistic; stubborn.
Gemini	Thinking; dualistic; confused; manifold aims; changing goals; multiple professions; unstable; indecisive.
Cancer	Feeling; sensitive; protective; maternal; devoted; receptive; over-emotional; greedy; inferior; tact; simplicity; thrift.
Leo	Intuitive; extrovert; self-conscious; controlled; leading; egocentric; creative; high aspirations; organisation.
Virgo	Sensitive; concerned with health; morning sickness; orderly; diligent; critical; practical; pedantic; hypochondriac.
Libra	Thinking; harmonious; balanced; relaxed; just; co-operation; sharing; craving recognition; reliant; diplomatic; exploitative.
Scorpio	Feeling; separate; considering abortion; wilful; passionate; intense; fanatical; repressive; destructive; suspicious.
Sagittarius	Intuitive; optimistic; material; strive for security; realised; free; mobile; athletic; religious; moral; extreme.

Midheaven (MC)

Personifications   The individual; the Ego.

Ego

Ambitious; successful; individual; assertive;
confident; definite objectives; creative power;
initiatory.

Persistent aims; striving for material security; hard
to please; tenacious; egotism; materialistic;
mentality; aesthetics important; mistrustful.

Love of change; multifaceted; occasionally creative;
facile; unstable; communicative; friendly;
superficial; conflicting goals; charming.

Responsible; tactful; sensitive; dedicated;
concerned; conservative; emotional; slow; stable;
woman dominated; feminine.

Self-exteriorised; confident; open; expansive; social
climbing; optimistic; organisational; pretence;
generosity; leading; selfish; rigid.

Perfected; striving for security; lively; petty;
conservative; hypersensitivity; working hard;
service; stewardship; simple means; critical.

Advancing through others; fortunate connections;
equilibriation; co-operation; sublimation;
adaptation; exploitation; manners without.

Perseverance; mystical; independent; ambitious;
energetic; ruthless; compulsive; domineering;
purposeful; destructive; acquisitive.

Aspiring; idealistic; high standards; extended
thought; higher mind; philosophical-religious;
ambitious; changeable; Utopian; undependable.

| **Capricorn** | Sensitive; rational; pragmatic; real; selfish; egocentric; disciplined; tough; serious; inflexible; reserved; cautious. |

Capricorn Sensitive; rational; pragmatic; real; selfish; egocentric; disciplined; tough; serious; inflexible; reserved; cautious.

Aquarius Thinking; idealistic; humanitarian; detached; sociable; rebellious; frigid; scattered; friendly; vague; planning.

Pisces Feeling; solitary; isolated; lonely; sensitive to others; waiting; hoping; clarity; goal-conscious; impressionable.

Self-confident; lonely; tenacious; overworked; strong father; sober; unimaginative; prosaic; self-centred; conscientious; ambitious.

Innovative; Utopian; humanitarian; abstract; future oriented; modern; aspirational; undisciplined; new ideas; progressive action; novelty.

Passivity; hoping for results; luck; susceptible to externals; feeling alone; insular; simple; modest aspirations; occasional pleasures.

Aspect Tables

Sun Aspects

SU/SU The will to live; power; the physical body; health and energy; bodily and spiritual harmony. Lack of incentive; illness; weakness; changes in direction; being without focus. The body; father and son; grandfather to son; colleagues; man to man.

SU/MO Conscious and unconscious; relationship; inner balance; public life; success. Inner discontent; conflict; unrelated; inner tension; struggle. Man and wife; father and mother; marriage partners; friends.

Balance and economy of body liquids; 'blood and water'; serum; the eyes; facial scars or moles.

SU/ME Common sense; understanding; thoughts; practical mind; businesslike; organizational. Unclear; confusion; aimlessness; nervousness. Youngsters; intellectuals; business people.

Connective tissue; formation of granules; puberty of the male.

SU/VE Physical love; beauty; popularity; social life; aesthetics; romantic. Frigidity; ugliness; unpopular; antisocial; tasteless; cold; indulgence. Artist; beloved man or woman.

Glandular tissue; Graaf's follicles.

SU/MA Vitality; vigour; advancement; vocational success; endurance; impulsiveness. Dissidence; violence; headstrong; contentious; daring. Fighter; soldier; doctor; husband; quarreller.

Muscular tissue; cell activity; sperms; cell-inflammation.

SU/JU Health; recognition; religious; expansive; happy; successful; creative. Materialistic; indulgent; arrogant; illegal, lazy. Wealthy; healthy; prominent; socialites.

Tissue elements of the organs and glands; regenerative functions of the blood; the restoration of health.

SU/SA Separate; concentrated; absorbed; serious; hard worker; ambitious; dedicated. Selfish; inhibited; suppressive;

pessimistic; inferior; anxious; weak; negative. Serious people; elderly; sick; inhibited; cruel father; weak father; missing father.

Bone tissue; the ageing of cells; cell-sedimentation; cell-death; rheumatism; arterial sclerosis; diseases caused by mineral sedimentation; hereditary afflictions; facial moles or scars.

SU/UR   Progressive; eccentric; technological; original; free; changeable; dynamic; individual. Obstinate; self-destructive; rebellious; tense; irritable. Innovator; reformer; rebel; technician; trouble-maker.

Rhythmic functions of cells and of the body; pulse; breathing; heart neurosis; cardiac embolism.

SU/NE   Sensitive; delicate; imaginative; uncertain; refined; inspired; visionary; psychic. Insecure; weak; sick; deceptive; seducible; tasteless. Medium; romantic; dreamer; psychic; sensitive; drug addict; seducer; weak father.

Sluggish, weak or paralysed cells; water concentrations of the cell; dropsy; oedema; anaemia; drug experiences; LSD; psoric miasm.

SU/PL   Power; attainment; conscious objectives; leading; growing; autocratic; ruthless. Arrogant; forced; brutal; fanatical; destructive. Leader; fighter; revolutionary; transformer; martyr; strong father.

Regeneration of cells; the immune system; swellings; testicles; adenoids.

SU/NO   Physical associations; public; adaptive; sociable; popular; educational. Antisocial; disharmonious; unadaptable; unrelated; isolated. Associate; fellow; colleagues; witness; relative; dignitary; police.

Function of the autonomic nervous system; scars or moles on face.

SU/AS   Personal relations; physical relations; confidence; advancement; esteem; recognizable. Pushy; disharmonious; disliked; self-seeking; shy; quarrelsome; dependent. Men in the environment; contact; husband.

Function of sense organs in passive perception; facial marks.

SU/MC Individual; objective; self-knowledge; success; missionary; authority; famous. Egocentric; unclear; arrogant; conceited; uninteresting; misguided. Body and Soul; 'I'; One's own Ego.

Relationship between physical body and ego-consciousness; transforming passive perception to personal reaction; constitution.

Moon Aspects

MO/MO Emotional life; feminine relations; changeable things; pleasant moods; motherliness. Emotional suppression; moodiness; separation from mother; unemotional; tension. The feelings; the soul; mother and daughter.

MO/ME Emotional thoughts; perception; judgement; valuation; feminine ideas; discretion. Changeable; lying; gossip; criticism; calumny; ingenuous; highly strung. Intellectual women; girls; authoress; psychologist; traveller.

Water equilibrium of the nervous system; liquor cerebri; the puberty of the woman.

MO/VE Love; devotion; art; conception; romantic; cultured; marriage; graceful. Moody; shy; tasteless; sterile; irritable; loveless. Lover; expectant mother; mother; artist; woman; actor.

Glandular secretions; hormones; ferments of generation; menstruation; female capacity for conception; first conception or birth.

MO/MA Excitement; intense emotion; frankness; candid; sincere; feeling will; industrious. Impulsiveness; rash; fighting; intolerant; rebellious; irritable. Wife; woman colleague; hard worker; housewife; businesswoman.

Unconscious muscular movement; emotional reactions; blushing; function of the thyroid glund; facial marks; Basedow's disease.

MO/JU Happy; religious; social conscience; travel; faithful; recognition; positive feeling. Indifferent; negligent; rebellious; unpopular; illegal; marital problems; sloppy. Successful; generous; happy woman; females; bride; expectant mother; official women.

Liquid products of the liver and pancreas; gall bladder; digestive ferments.

MO/SA   Self-control; duty; care; attentive; circumspect; lonely;
          ascetic; critical; ambitious. Depressive; separated;
          widowed; inferior; melancholy; anxious; estranged.
          Inhibited people; sad; widow(er); single parent; female
          grandparent.

          *Chronic disturbances of the water balance; defects of the
          mucous membranes; wounds secreting watery or liquid
          deposits; bladder infections; psychical diseases; hereditary
          disease; haemorrhoids.*

MO/UR   Subconscious forces; instinct; sudden events; occult;
          intellectual specialization. Schizophrenia; emotional
          tension; overstrain; abrupt; exaggeration; anxiety.
          Restless woman; ambitious; reformists; schizophrenic.

          *Rhythm of water economy; abnormal blood pressure; colics of
          excretory organs; prostate disease; the mechanism of female
          period; schizophrenia (inherited).*

MO/NE   Refined; inner vision; imagination; inspiration;
          relaxation; romantic; idealistic. Frail; self-deception;
          unreality; weakness; addicted; seductive; supernatural.
          Sensitive; medium; impressionable people; card-readers;
          psychic; indolent; the weak.

          *Paralysed blood circulation; accumulation of water in tissues;
          deficiency of osmotic functions of cells remedied by cell salts;
          disturbance of or break in consciousness; eye diseases; released
          sexual anxiety.*

MO/PL   Extreme emotion; one-sided; fanaticism; overzealous;
          devouring; dynamic; insatiable. Fanatic; sadistic;
          obsessed; shocking; jealous; demanding; insane
          demands; upheavals. Emotional people; public relations
          people; publicists; schizophrenic; revolutionary.

          *Metabolism of body liquids; blood disease; AIDS; hepatitis;
          inherited schizophrenia.*

MO/NO   Spiritual union; inner relationships; alliances (between
          women); family ties; devoted. Estrangement; multiple
          relationships; unadaptable; frustrated; unfamilial; insular.
          Woman alliances; blood union; associates.

          *Lymphatic glands; spleen; tonsils; immune system; Hodgkin's
          disease; AIDS.*

MO/AS   Emotional relations; obliging; feminine; adaptable; personal ties; subjective ties. Hypersensitivity; disagreements; moody; changeable; overreactive; annoyed. Feminine environment; mother; alcoholics; drug addicts; lovers; personalities.

Liquids taken into the body; alkaloids; alcohol; intoxication; drug addiction; anaesthetic at birth.

MO/MC   Emotional objectives; sentiment; home; family; soul-ties; intuitive understanding. Difficult women; unprofessional; vacillation; unreliable; sentimental; wavering. Women; feeling and emotional people; governesses; mother; soul people.

Distribution of blood and liquids in the body; collapse; blood transfusion; blood donor.

Mercury Aspects

ME/ME   Movement; thinking; mind; news; opinions; perception; good comprehension; understanding; easy. Static states; subjectivity; dullness; lacking objectivity; lying; no communication. Active people; friends; confidants; mediators; intellects; teachers; siblings; the young.

ME/VE   Love thoughts; beauty sense; design; feeling intellect; hilarity; art success; writing. Vanity; conceit; hypersensitive; irresolute; squandering; luxury. Lovers; author; writer; beauty sales person; art dealer; aesthete; artist; female friends.

Glandular secretions.

ME/MA   Thought power; realised plans; resolution; repartee; enterprise; debate; settling affair. Criticism; nagging; malice; hasty action; speech difficulty; obstinate; cynical. Critic; quarreller; debater; writer.

Motor nervous system; spastic paralysis; nerve irritations; increased sensitization; reflex actions.

ME/JU   Constructive mind; erudition; literature; business sense; common sense; science; fluent. Negligence; fraud; unreliable; exaggerating; conflict; indiscreet. Speaker;

authority; negotiator; businessperson; publisher; traveller; philanthropist.

Reflex channels; skin and tendon reflexes; psycho-motor channels.

ME/SA   Mental work; concentration; deep thought; logic; organization; experience; industry. Dullness; reserve; shyness; estrangement; difficulty; hard infancy; distrust. Philosopher; intellectual; scientist; crook; logician.

Nervous system blockages; pain conducting nerves; functional relationship of the nervous system to speech and hearing.

ME/UR   Intuition; astuteness; fllexibility; independence; influence; mathematics; original mind. Scattered; madness; nerves; erratic; eccentric; contradictory. Mathematician; scientist; technician; musician; astrologer; lively people.

Depth perception; spinal cord; disturbances of equilibrium; facial pains; migraine.

ME/NE   Imagination; fantasy; deep perception; vision; presentiments; poetic; idealistic; clear. Faulty judgement; paralysis; deception; fraud; dissipated; foolish. Actor; fantasiser; dreamer; saint; liar; faith healer; psychic.

Loss of sensation; weak nerves; paralysis of nerves; mutations; chloroform; soporific drugs.

ME/PL   Persuasion; understanding; cunning; diplomacy; influence; wit; slyness. Breakdown; hasty expression; excessive opposition; over-eager; impatience; crudeness. Speaker; politician; fascist; critic; tyrant; propagandist.

Metabolism of nervous system; formation of new nervous substance; nervous irritation.

ME/NO   Joint plans; exchanging ideas; social-business meeting; correspondence; relationship. Unsociable; unpopularity; closed; blocked; disloyalty. Joiners; groupy; writer; organizer; negotiator; networker.

Relationship between autonomic and voluntary nerves.

ME/AS   Personal ideas; definition; verbal communication; meetings; intelligence; talkative. Gossip; misjudgement; anxiety; superficial; flighty. Thinker; gossip; organiser; friend; administrator; diplomat.

Reception of stimuli through sense organs.

ME/MC   Intellectual objectives; observation; self-knowledge; meditation; own aims; clarity. Aimlessness; unselfconscious; changeable; vacillation; dishonest. Expressive people; talkers; media people; MCs; job counsellors.

Motor nerves of the brain.

Venus Aspects

VE/VE   Peace; goodwill; love; desire; feeling love; humour; beauty sense; art. Unrelated; listless; tasteless; aberration; carelessness. Lover; aesthete; beauty; model; girl; actor; artist; musician; clothier; nurse.

VE/MA   Sexual love; artistry; passion; creativity; lively expression; intimacy; prolific. Asexuality; seduction; unsatisfied; infidelity; irritable; sexual disease. Lover; sexist; seducer; polygamist; active lover.

Sympathetic and parasympathetic nervous system; autonomic disturbances of function (bowels and kidneys); anomalies of menstruation; masturbation; varicose veins; haemorrhoids.

VE/JU   Joyous love; happiness; popularity; form sense; marriage; bliss; comfort; gay; hedonism. Laziness; lacking feeling; indolence; arrogance; legal conflict; indulgence. Artist; filmstar; model; socialite; expansive lover.

Hormone circulation within the body; hormone metabolism; adrenal and suprarenal glands; diseases caused by inhalation of industrial powders or metals; glandular secretions connected with specific organs.

VE/SA   Dutiful emotion; soberness; loyalty; inhibition; sacrifice; fidelity; economy; reserve. Jealousy; torment; deprivation; lonely; depressed; mother separation. Lonely people; widow(er); illegitimate children; older lover.

Malfunctioning of internal glandular secretions; glandular atrophy; enlarged glands; pulmonary emphysema; goitre.

VE/UR   Arousal; eccentricity; impulse; talent; music;
sentimentality; refinement. Repressed sexuality;
inconstancy; estrangement; unconventional; loose.
Musician; artist; eccentric lover.

Rhythm of libido and sex life; conception; birth.

VE/NE   Rapture; eroticism; mysticism; idealism; platonic affairs;
travel; refinement. Seducible; tasteless; infatuation;
dreaming; illusion; escapist. Artist; musician; dreamer;
visionary; romantic; drug dealer; addict; weak lover.

*Weakened glandular functions; pathological enlargement of
glands; weakness of sexual organs.*

VE/PL   Fanatic love; sensuality; gifted; attractive; compulsive;
devoted; talented; magnetic. Lusty; stressed love;
sadomasochism; vulgarity; excessive desire. Lover;
pornographer; menstruating woman; artist.

*First menstruation; ovaries; corpus luteum; excessive or
abnormal sex life.*

VE/NO   Love union; adaptation; universal love; ties; obliging;
artistic communities. Isolation; separation; unhappy
affair; flighty. Lover; marrieds; singles; art groupies;
gallery owner.

Autonomic supply of glandular organs.

VE/AS   Harmonious love; beauty; attractive personality;
adornment; art; taste; gentility. Bad taste; desertion;
unsociable; wasteful; indulgent. Woman; mother; wife;
lover; artist.

Harmonious proportions; physical beauty; complexion.

VE/MC   Objective love; affection; benevolence; artistic; attached;
attractive individual. Vanity; conceit; jealousy; dissipated.
Lover; artist; admirer.

Gland centre; mid-brain; third ventricle; pituitary gland.

Mars Aspects

MA/MA   Energy; activity; work; aggression; impulse; resolve; will; decision; accomplishment. Wasting energy; violence; injury; destruction. Fighter; soldier; athlete; craftsman; surgeon; police.

MA/JU   Successful creativity; joy; activity; organisation; prowess; rebellion; practicality. Conflict; estrangement; precipitancy; haste; restlessness; dispute. Manager; organizer; jurist; judge; official; athlete.

Organ activity; smooth muscular activity; the heart; completed birth and the first cry.

MA/SA   Inhibition; endurance; danger; fanaticism; spartan life; ascetic; tough. Destruction; danger; death; impotence; obstinacy; separation; tests; dispute; illness. Labourer; miner; fighter; killer.

Bone-forming processes; joints; muscles and bones as active and passive factors; tendons and sinews; inflammation of bones or bone-marrow; bone-marrow cancer; death or atrophy of an organ; paralysis of muscles controlling breathing; suffocation; the death axis.

MA/UR   Applied effort; intervention; courage; independence; operation; revolutionary; birth. Argument; obstinacy; emotional tension; stress; nerves; operation; injury; accident. Surgeon; violent people; revolutionary; reactionary; driver; fireman.

Rhythmic activity of the body; the work of the heart; injury causing blood loss; operations; cutting the skin; loss of blood; scar.

MA/NE   Inspiration; desire sensitivity; escapism; romanticism; fantasy; denial. Destruction; infection; misdirection; drugs; inferiority; smoking; paralysis; narrowness. Sick people; addict; sailor; pathologist; dealer.

Paralysis or wasting away of muscles; susceptibility to epidemic infections; the consequences or results of an infection; the normal course of disease; discharge of pus; autotoxins.

MA/PL   Superhuman force; violence; vigour; great ambition; success; obsession; research. Cruelty; assault; aggression; injury; sadism; homicide; ruthlessness. Dictator; disabled; nuclear scientist; politician; general.

Replacement of natural organs; artificial limbs or organs; dentures; plates in the skull.

MA/NO   Physical collaboration; team spirit; union; shared success; progeny; betrothal. Quarrels; lack fellowship; disrupted meetings; eunuchism; dissolution; dissociation. Collectives; communists; socialists; eunuchs.

Disturbance of life rhythms; precocity; climacteric disturbances; menopause; activity of the astral body; eunuchism.

MA/AS   Fighting spirit; forced will; teamwork; attainment; resolution; creative work; surgery. Caesarean; forceps birth; operation; fighting; aggression; conflict; dispute; quarrel. Surgeon; soldier; colleagues; boxer.

Liability to accidents; surgical operation; birth; facial marks.

MA/MC   Ego-conscious action; order; decision; success; resolution; occupation change; prudence. Excitable; stress; prematurity; purposeless; fever; fraud; agitation; murder. Organiser; leader; politician; leading personality.

Action of voluntary muscles; regulation of body heat; fever; hot flushes.

Jupiter Aspects

JU/JU   Contentment; optimism; luck; financial gain; religion; philosophy; social life. Unlucky; losses; pessimism; illegal; extravagant; materialistic; greedy; corpulence. Lawyer; judge; banker; insurer; physician; uncle; grandparent; publisher.

JU/SA   Patience; perseverance; industry; diplomacy; seclusion; duty; philosophy; calm; real estate. Vacillation; discontent; upset; failure; illness. Professor; teacher; lawyer; official; politician; relatives; tenant.

Organic defect; chronic disease; function of gall bladder and liver.

JU/UR   Optimism; fortunate ideas; perception; sudden
         recognition; bliss; invention; change. Independence;
         opposition; magnifying matters; arguments; tension;
         stress. Organisers; inventors; adventurer; optimist;
         religious zealots.

         Organic rhythm of life; peristalsis of the intestines; spastic or
         convulsive fits; colics; temporary pain.

JU/NE   Speculation; imagination; metaphysics; idealism; luck;
         ethics; generosity; profit. Susceptible; dreaming;
         unreality; enmity; insult; losses; swindlers. Speculator;
         dreamer; mystic; visionary.

         Lack of tone in body organs; atrophy of an organ; excessive
         water increase in the blood (Haemolysis); the wrong diagnosis.

JU/PL   Plutocracy; spiritual-mental power; leadership;
         regeneration; organisation; transfusion. Fanaticism;
         losses; guilt; failure; legal liability; bankruptcy;
         exploitation. Organiser; professor; teacher; speculator;
         dictator; propagandist.

         The regeneration of organs; blood transfusion; infections;
         large-scale epidemics.

JU/NO   Good contact; adaptability; tact; common interest;
         fortunate union; life force. Lack fellowship; anti-social;
         selfish; conflict; lifeless. Philosophical communities;
         fellows; partners; associates.

         Life force; Reichenbach force; kundalini; libido; orgone
         energy.

JU/AS   Agreeable; favourable influence; generosity; wealth; cure;
         success; easy birth; teamwork; Waste; friction; rebellion;
         hypocrisy; conceit; bragging. Generous people; wealthy
         people; uncles; grandparents; aunts.

         Correct diagnosis; cure; overweight.

JU/MC   Philosophical objectives; conscious aims; contentment;
         bliss; success; purpose. Risks; unclear aims; changes in
         life-style; desire for importance. Successes; philosopher;
         psychologist; priest.

         Maintenance of good health; hygiene; alcoholism.

Saturn Aspects

SA/SA   Restriction; patience; concentration; industry; crystallisation; earnestness. Hindrance; illness; developmental crisis; depression; inefficiency; sorrow; paralysis. Inhibited people; scientist; father; elderly; farmer; miner; businessperson; doctor.

SA/UR   Tension; determination; collected thinking; calmness; technical affairs; travel; endure. Emotional tension; provocation; force; backlash from past; limitation of freedom. Violent people; the dying; amputees; chronically ill.

Inhibitions of rhythm; heart block; Cheyne-Stokes breathing; unrhythmical processes; loss or operative removal of limbs or organs; chronic illness; amputation.

SA/NE   Renunciation; suffering; sacrifice; caution; method; duality; asceticism; patience; Insecurity; illness; pestilence; habit; neuroses; emotional inhibitions; insecure. Ascetics; chronically ill; elderly; druggists.

Chronic illness; hereditary disease; organic decomposition; infectious disease; illness; epidemics; inhibited weight gain; lack of fats; liver or lung disease; lack of vitality; = 0° Aries: hysteria.

SA/PL   Cruelty; hard labour; tenacity; self-discipline; adepts; martyrdom; struggling; silence. Egotism; violence; divorce; slow separation; murder; self-destruction; loss of money. Scientists; murderers; reactionaries; martyrs.

Organic underdevelopment; undescended testicle; infantile organs; organic hardening; stones; calcification; sensitivity to pollution; epidemics.

SA/NO   Isolation; inhibited union; maturity; sponsorship; mystery. Unadaptable; difficulty cooperating; death of relatives; depression; inhibition. Elderly persons; mourners.

Shock events; shock; electro-shock therapy; cure through vaccination; separation from astral body.

SA/AS Inhibited personality; difficult birth; early maturity; lonely; isolated; inmates. Depression; wrong outlook; poor family; disadvantages through others; segregation. Inmates; patients; lonely people; doctors; hospital staff; grandparents.

Seclusion from external world; skin troubles; defective tissue or organs; amputation; chronic functional disturbances of sense organs; hereditary myopia; ear inflammation; facial mark.

SA/MC Serious objectives; slow development; separation; self-preoccupation; experience. Emotional inhibition; dejection; illness; insanity; loss of consciousness; despondent. Inhibited people; patients; burden.

Feeling sick; being sick; neurosis; conscious, localized pain; ego-illness; mental or psychiatric disorders; psychoses; cancer; insanity; disintegration of the personality; dark night of the soul; loss of ego consciousness.

Uranus Aspects

UR/UR Suddenness; ambitions; enterprise; creativity; crisis change; reform; many plans. Hard conditions; change; catastrophe; nervous crises; suicidal thoughts; danger. Reformers; inventors; technicians; revolutionaries; astrologer; healer; physicist.

UR/NE Unconsciousness; inner vision; inspiration; mysticism; art; research; journeys; spirit. Instability; confusion; death; revolution; crisis; incapacity; confusion psychically. Mystics; mediums; psychics; revolutionaries.

Paralysis of rhythmic processes; nervous breakdown; heart failure; apoplexy of the brain; still-born child; miscarriage; abortion; epilepsy; lameness.

UR/PL Transformation; revolution; innovation; mobility; reform; mutation; explosion; changes. Impatience; mania; destruction; upsets; subversive activities; enforcement; explosion. Pioneers; reformers; geniuses; explorers; gunmen.

Rhythmic changes in biological processes; relationships between pulse and breathing; Chinese pulses; fever spots.

UR/NO   Shared experience; sudden attraction; unstable relations; variety; innovation; activity. Disturbance; quarrels; separation; restlessness; flighty; irritable; incidents; dreamy. Politicians; labour unions; excited family; nervous people.

Disquieting dreams; disturbance of consciousness; neuroses; rhythm of the astral body; inner vision of memory; dream-life; regularly occurring illnesses; susceptibility to the weather.

UR/AS   Environmental response; invention; new contacts; original; nervousness; rearrangement. Excitable; inconstancy; disquiet; accidents; quick changes; compulsion; rudeness. Excitable people; originals; eccentrics; technicians; neurotics.

Quickly responding nervous system; sensitised skin; sensitive nerves; headaches; trigeminal neuralgia; migraine headaches.

UR/MC   Original objectives; assertion; fortunate changes; organising; successful; stress. Tension; prematurity; unreliability; temper; upsets; sudden turns of destiny. Yogis; gurus; inventors; physicists; musicians.

Controlled breathing activity; eurhythmics; pranayama; yogic breathing; hyperventilation.

Neptune Aspects

NE/NE   Spiritual development; intellectual perception; travel; empathy; mysticism; drugs. Hypersensitivity; nervousness; confusion; health crisis; deception; addiction; deceit. Mediums; frauds; sensitives; perceptive people; spiritual people; addicts; dreamers.

NE/PL   Supernatural; intensification; active imagination; psychics; parapsychology; evolution. Confusion; torment; obsession; craving drugs or alcohol; loss; possession; falsehood. Mystics; astrologers; psychics; occultists; mediums; addicts; gamblers.

Painless stage of disease; over-indulgence of alcohol, nicotine or drugs; lack of will power for maintaining health; nervous weakness; neurosis; giving up; slow development or cure; gradual commencement of a therapy; rejected transplant; negative transfusion.

NE/NO   Idealistic associations; sensitive groups; mysticism; Utopian associations; spiritual. Antisocial; deceptive; cheating others; deception; sleeplessness; disturbed dreams. Groupies; psychic groups; mystical organisations; magic circles; covens.

           Lack of organ tone or muscle elasticity; stiffness; disturbed sleep; insomnia; psychic attack; psychedelic drugs.

NE/AS   Impressionability; sensitivity; sympathy; strangeness; refinement; idealism; water birth. Betrayal; weakness; confusion; disappointment; escapism; fraud; illusion; drugs. Anaesthetists; sensitives; mediums; addicts; psychics; mystics; weak people.

           Illusions or deceptions of the senses; crawling skin; anaesthetic birth; alcoholic; drug addiction.

NE/MC   Uncertain objectives; vagueness; peculiar ideas; Utopian; supernatural; artistic. Feigning; falsehood; acting; numbness; strange ideas; depression; deception. Utopians; parapsychologists; weaklings; actors; the mentally disturbed; psychotics.

           Depressive psychoses; mental disturbance; numbness in limbs; phantom limbs; psychic infestation; schizophrenia; psychedelic drugs or plants.

Pluto Aspects

PL/PL   Inner change; metamorphosis; transformation; propaganda; mass influence; powerlust. Ruthlessness; fanaticism; agitating efforts; weakness; coercion; indoctrination. Dictators; hypnotists; politicians; magicians; public speakers; actors.

PL/NO   Collective destiny; public figures; influencing others; group associations; movements. Tragic destiny; karma; being cramped by others; antisocial; suffering; suffocation. Crowds; mass meetings; armies; political parties; unions; multinationals.

           Embryonic growth; disturbances of pregnancy; foetal relapse; morning sickness; acute toxaemia in pregnancy, parturition or puerperium leading to convulsions or loss of consciousness.

PL/AS   Fascinating personality; ambition; magic; unusual influence; control; transformation. Changing environment; dictatorship; ruling others; repulsion; readjustment; injury. Great specialists; fascinating personalities; stars; politicians; public figures.

Physical change or transformation; commencing stage of disease; convalescence.

PL/MC   Transformed objectives; individuality; strength; growth; authority; expert knowledge. Misused power; resistance; vindictiveness; antisocial conduct; recuperation; destiny. Transformers; authorities; specialists; magicians; surgeons.

Recuperation; regaining health; decision to undergo an operation; change of therapy.

Node Aspects

NO/NO   Unions; connections; junctures; communication; approach; groups; clubs; fellowship. Limitations; antisocial; incompatibility; unsocial; unadaptive. Contacts; mediators; relatives; family; associations; colleagues.

NO/AS   Fellowship; personal relationships; family contacts; social conscience; charm; loves. Short relations; estrangements; disturbed domestic relations; antisocial; difficult. Family; associates; workmates; fellows; friends.

Memory; active unconscious processes; internal respiration; oxygen metabolism.

NO/MC   Group objectives; individual relationships; astral relationships; mutual understanding. Inconstancy; differing; individual over collective; difficult collectives; Marxists. Associations; political parties; unions; friends.

Astral body and ego-consciousness; psychic stress.

Ascendant (AS) Aspects

AS/AS   Acquaintance; location; surroundings; the place; body; social relations; personal relations. Maladjustment; feeling lost; misplaced; difficult birth. People in the environment; doctors; midwives.

AS/MC   Individual synthesis; higher self and lower self; personality and ego; integration. Impossible synthesis; irreconcilable goals; lack of direction. Synthesisers; strong personalities with direction.

Contrast between personal and hereditary qualities.

Midheaven (MC) Aspects

MC/MC   The Ego; spiritual, intellectual and social impressions; goals; objectives. Egoless; materialistic; goalless; insane. Egotists; people who live in the moment; goal-oriented people.

Appendix 2:
Astro-Medical Index

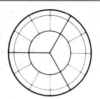

Abdominal organs. Vir.
Abnormal menstruation. Ven/Mars.
Abnormal sex. Ven/Mars=Sat or =Nep.
Abortion. Moon/Ven=Sat,=Plu; Ura/Sco.
Abscess. Jup/Mars=Moon; Lib.
Accident, car. Mars/Ura=Nep.
Accident, fatal. Mars/Sat=Plu; Mars/Plu=ASC,=MC.
Accident prone. Sun/Mars.
Accident. Mars/Plu=ASC; Mars/ASC; Plu/ASC=Mars; Ura/MC=Mars;
    Mars/Sat=Plu; Mars/Ura=Sun,=ASC,=MC; Mars/Nep=Ura;
    Sat/Ura=Mars; Mars/Nep; Mars/Plu; Mars/Node; Mars/ASC;
    Ura/Plu=Mars,=ASC.
Accidental death. Mars/Sat=Ura.
Achilles tendon. Aqu.
Acidosis. Jup/Sat=Ven; Mars/Jup.
Acne. Ari; Sun/Ari; Ven/Sat=Mars; Sun/Moon.
Active birth. Leo/,Ari/ASC; Mars/,Ura/ASC.
Acute toxaemia in pregnancy. Plu/Node.
Addiction. Nep/Ari; Sun/,Moon/,Jup/,Nep/Pis; Moon/,Mars/Nep.
Adenoids. Jup/Cap; Mars/Tau; Mars/Ven.
Adrenals. Sun/Mars=Ari,=Can; Moon/Mars; Mars; Ven/Jup; Mars;
    Lib.
Adultery. Ven/Mars=Sat.
Aging. Saturn; Sun/Sat.
AIDS. Sco; Mars/Sat=Ven,=Nep; Mars/Nep=Plu.
Alcoholism. Pis; Sco; Can; Moon/Nep; Moon/Nep=Plu;
    Nep/Plu=Moon; Sun/,Moon/,Mars/,Jup/,Nep/Pis.
Alkaloids. Moon/ASC.
Allergy. Cap.
Amnesia. Mars/Leo by Moon, Nep.
Amorous aberrations. Ven/Nep=Plu.

Amputation. Sat/Ura; Sat/ASC.

Anaemia, pernicious. Moon/Mars=Can.

Anaemia. Mars/Leo, =Moon, =Nep, Moon/Mars; Sun/Nep.

Anaesthetic birth. Moon/,Nep/,Can/,Pis/ASC.

Anaesthetics. Nep; Moon.

Anal infection. Sun/Plu.

Aneurysm. Aries, Leo; Mars/Jup.

Angina. Leo.

Anima. Moon.

Animus. Sun.

Ankles sprained. Sun/Aqu.

Ankles swollen. Jup/Aqu.

Ankles. Aqu.

Ankylosis. Mer/Sat.

Anorexia nervosa. Sat/ASC=Moon. Nep/H1, /H2.

Anxiety. Moon/Mars=Can,=Vir; Moon/Sat=Nep; Plu/ASC=Sat; Ura/Nep.

Aphasia. Sun/Ari.

Apoplexy. Tau.

Appendicitis. Sun/Jup=Mars; Mars/Jup=Ura; Ven/Mars=Nep; Sat/Vir.

Arms. Gem.

Arterial system. Sag.

Arteries blocked. Sun/Mars=Jup.

Arteries hardening. Sun/Jup=Sat.

Arterio-sclerosis. Jup/,Sat/Leo; Sat/Jup; Sun/Sat; Sat/Ven=Jup;

Arthritis. Sat/H6; Mars/Sat,=Jup; Sun/Sat,/Ura; Mars/Nep; Sun/Mars; Sun/Sat; Sun/,Sat/Sag.

Artificial organs. Mars/Plu.

Asphyxiation. Mer/Gem.

Assault. Mars/Plu=Ven; Mer/Mars=Plu.

Asthma. Gem; Mer/Ura; Mer/Mars=Ura; affl Gem.

Astral body rhythm. Ura/Node.

Astral body. Node; Node/MC.

Astral separation. Sat/Node.

Ataxia. Sat/Lib.

Athlete's Foot. Nep; Pisces.

Atrophy of glands. Ven/Sat; Jup/Nep.

Aura, Nep.

Autonomic glands. Ven/Node.

Autonomic nervous system breakdowns. Ven/Mars.

Autonomic nervous system. Sun/Node.

Autonomic vs voluntary nerves. Mer/Node.

Autotoxins. Mars/Nep.

Backache. Leo; Sun/Leo.
Bad blood. Sun/Nep=Sat.
Bad breath. Moon/Ven.
Baldness. Ari; Sag.
Basedows disease. Moon/Mars.
Beautiful child. Ven/Asc; Tau/ASC; Lib/ASC.
Beauty, physical. Ven/ASC.
Birth, active. Leo/,Ari/ASC; Mars/,Ura/ASC.
Birth, anaesthetic. Mars/Jup=Nep; Pis/,Can/,Nep/,Moon/ASC.
Birth, at home. Can/ASC; Tau/ASC; Moon/ASC.
Birth, brutal. Sco/ASC; Mars/,Plu/,Ura/ASC.
Birth, Caesarean section. Ari/ASC; Mars/,Ura/,Plu/ASC.
Birth, dangerous. Sco/ASC; Mars/,Plu/,Ura/ASC.
Birth, difficult. Mars/Jup=Sat,=Nep; Ven/Ura=Sat.
Birth, doctor. Vir/,Cap/ASC; Mars/,Sat/,Jup/ASC.
Birth, drugged. Can/,Pis/ASC; Nep/,Moon/ASC.
Birth, father present. Cap/ASC; Sun/,Sat/ASC.
Birth, forceful. Sco/ASC; Mars/,Plu/,Ura/ASC.
Birth, forceps. Ari/ASC; Mars/,Sat/ASC.
Birth, foreign. Sag/ASC; Jup/ASC.
Birth, grandparents present. Jup/ASC; Sat/ASC; Sag/ASC.
Birth, hospital. Ari/ASC.
Birth, induced. Mars/Jup=Nep; Pis/ASC; Nep/ASC; Moon/ASC.
Birth, inhibited. Cap/ASC; Sat/ASC; Aqu/ASC.
Birth, instinctive. Can/ASC.
Birth, large hospital. Plu/ASC; Node/ASC.
Birth, machines. Ura/ASC; Plu/ASC; Node/ASC.
Birth, mechanical. Cap/ASC; Sat/ASC; Aqu/ASC; Ura/ASC.
Birth, nervous. Gem/ASC.
Birth, nuns; Sag/ASC; Jup/ASC; Moon/ASC.
Birth, nurse. Vir/ASC; Can/ASC; Gem/ASC; Lib/ASC; Moon/ASC.
Birth, religious hospital. Sag/ASC; Jup/ASC.
Birth, surgical. Ari/,Sco/,Mars/,Plu/,Ura/ASC; Ven/Ura=Mars.
Birth, team. Vir/ASC; Lib/ASC.
Birth, technological. Ura/ASC; Aqu/ASC.
Birth, tragic. Plu/ASC; Ura/ASC; Sco/ASC.
Birth, unemotional. Cap/ASC; Sat/ASC; Aqu/ASC.
Birth, unorthodox. Aqu/ASC.
Birth, violent. Plu/ASC; Sco/ASC; Mars/ASC; Ura/ASC.
Birth, women present. Can/ASC.
Birth. ASC; Jup/Ura=Sun; Mars/Jup=Moon; Ven/Ura; Ura/MC=Ven;
    Sun/Moon=Jup; Moon/Ven; Moon/Jup=MC; Ven/Jup=Mars.
Births, multiple. Gem/ASC; Lib/ASC; Aqu/ASC.

Bladder cancer. Sun/Nep=Sat.
Bladder infection. Lib; Sco; Moon/Sat.
Bladder stone. Lib.
Bladder. Sco.
Blindness. Ari ecl; Sun/Moon=Mars.
Blood clots. Sun/Ven=Tau.
Blood disease. Moon/Plu; Nep/Aqu.
Blood distribution. Moon/ASC.
Blood donor. Moon/MC.
Blood infections. Moon/MC=Nep or =Plu; Moon/Sag.
Blood loss. Mars/Ura.
Blood poisoning. Jup/Mars=Nep.
Blood pressure, high. Sun/Mars; Moon/Ura.
Blood serum. Moon.
Blood. Jup.
Blushing. Moon/Mars.
Body heat. Mars.
Body tone, lack of. Jup/Nep; Nep/Node.
Body vs Ego. Sun/MC.
Body. Sun.
Bone conditions. Sun/Sat.
Bone formation. Mars/Sat.
Bone inflammation, Mars/Sat.
Bone marrow. Mars/Sat.
Bone structure. Sat; Sun/Sat.
Bones weak. Mars/Nep=Sat.
Bowels. Ven/Mars; Vir.
Brain abscess. Ura/Ari.
Brain arteries. Ari.
Brain centres. Mer/MC.
Brain disease. Ari; Mer/Ari.
Brain meninges. Ura.
Brain synapses. Mer.
Brain tumour. Ven/Ari; Sun/MC=Sat; Sun/Sat=MC; Sat/MC=Sun.
Brain. MC.
Breakdown, nervous. Mer/Nep=Ura; Ura/Plu=Sun.
Breast feeding. Can/ASC; Tau/ASC; Moon/ASC; Nep/ASC.
Breasts. Can; Moon.
Breathing, Cheyne-Stokes. Sat/Ura.
Breathing. Sun/Ura; Ura/Plu.
Bright's disease. Sun/,Moon/,Sat/Lib.
Bronchial infections. Sun/Mer=Gem.
Bronchial tubes. Gem.

Brutal birth. Sco/ASC; Mars/ASC; Plu/ASC; Ura/ASC.
Brutality. Mars/Sat=Plu.
Burns. Mars; Cap.

Caesarean section. Mars/ASC; Ari/ASC; Sco/ASC; Ura/ASC; Plu/ASC.
Calcification of organs. Sun/Sat.
Calcification. Sat/Plu.
Cancer, bladder. Sun/Nep=Sat.
Cancer, colon. Sun/Nep=Sat.
Cancer, prostate. Sun/Nep=Sat.
Cancer, throat. Sun/Nep=Sat; Moon/Tau.
Cancer. Jup/Sat=Sun; Moon/Ven; Moon/,Ven/Ura,=/Aqu; Tau; Lib;
    Pis; Sun/Plu; Sat/MC. Sat/MC.
Car accident. Mars/Ura=Nep.
Cardiac arrest. Sun/Ven=Sat.
Cardiac embolism. Sun/Ura.
Carotid artery. Tau.
Cataract. Sun/MC=Moon=Sat.
Catarrh. Moon/Sat=Jup; Sat/Ari; Sun/Plu; Ven/Ari.
Catastrophes. Mer/Mars=Ura.
Cell paralysis. Sun/Nep.
Cell. Sun.
Cerebellum. Moon; Tau.
Cerebrum. Ari.
Cervix. Sco.
Change of therapy. Plu/MC.
Cheyne-Stokes breathing. Sat/Ura.
Chickenpox. Mars/Sat.
Chills. Sat/Ari.
Chin. Tau.
Cholera. Vir.
Chronic disease. Jup/Sat; Sat/Ura; Sat/Nep.
Chronic sense organ trouble. Sat/ASC.
Chronic women's disease. Sat/Nep=Moon.
Circulation, hormone. Ven/Jup.
Circulation, paralysed. Moon/Nep.
Circulation poor. Sun/Aqu.
Circulation system. Aqu.
Circulation. Aqu.
Circumcision. Sco/,Mars/,Ura/,Plu/,Ari/ASC.
Cirrhosis. Jup affl; Jup/Sag,/Pis; Jup/Nep; Sat/Lib.
Clavicle. Gem.
Climacteric years. Jup.

Coccyx. Sco.
Colds. Sun/Nep.
Colic. Vir; Jup/Ura.
Colitis. Mars/Mer=Nep; Sco.
Collapse. Moon/ASC.
Collective Unconscious. Plu.
Colon cancer. Sun/Nep=Sat.
Colon, descending. Sco.
Colon obstruction. Sat-Vir; Sun/Ura.
Colon, sluggish. Sat/Sco.
Coma. Ari.
Commencement of disease. Plu/ASC.
Complexion, bad. Sat/ASC.
Complexion. Ven/ASC.
Conception difficult. Moon/Mars.
Conception. Moon/Ven; Cusp 9; Ven/Mars=Sun; Ven/Ura and = Moon; Sun/Ven=MC; Moon/Jup=ASC.
Congestion. Sat/Gem.
Conjunctivitis. Sun affl fire; Sun/ASC.
Connective tissue, defective. Sat/ASC.
Consciousness, disturbed. Moon/Nep.
Consciousness, loss of. Plu/Node; Jup/Sat=Ura.
Constipation. Mer/Sat; Mars/Sat.
Constipation. Moon/Mer; Sat/Nep; Sun/MC; Tau.
Consumption. Sat/Gem.
Convalescence. Plu/ASC.
Convulsions. Moon/Ari.
Convulsions. Plu/Node; Ven/Ura=Moon; Sun/Ven=Ura; Sun/Nep=Ura.
Coronary thrombosis. Sun/Sat=Plu.
Corpulence. Jup.
Corpus leutum. Ven/Plu.
Cough. Tau.
Cramp. Mars/Ura.
Cranium. Ari.
Croup. Tau.
Cure. Jup/ASC; Jup/MC.
Cystitis. Sco.

Deafness. Mer/, Sat/Tau; Moon/Mer=Sat; Sun/Ven=Sat.
Death, accidental. Mars/Sat=Ura.
Death axis. Mars/Sat.
Death, by AIDS. Mars/Nep=Plu.

Death, by drowning. Sun/Ura=Nep.
Death, easy. Mars/Sat=Jup.
Death, mysterious. Mars/Sat=Nep.
Death of a woman. Mars/Sat=Moon or =Ven.
Death of a man. Mars/Sat=Sun.
Death. Mars/Sat=Mer; Mars/Nep=Plu; Jup/Sat=Ura; Plu/MC=Sat.
Deaths, multiple. Mars/Sat=Plu.
Deceptions. Nep/ASC.
Delicate health. Sun/Nep=Jup.
Delirium. Ari; Mer/Mars=Ura.
Depression, organic. Moon/Sat=Plu.
Depression. Sat/MC=Moon; Sat/Nep=Mars.
Depressive psychosis. Nep/MC.
Depth sense. Mer/Ura.
Descending colon. Sco.
Diabetes. Nep; Jup/Sat; Ari/Lib; Can/Cap; Sun/Mer; Jup/Ura=Sun.
Diagnosis, correct. Jup/ASC.
Diagnosis, wrong. Jup/Nep.
Diarrhoea. Moon/Ven; Vir.
Diet. Vir.
Difficult birth. Ven/Ura=Sat.
Digestive disturbance. Moon/Ven,/Jup; Vir/ASC; Moon/Mars=Can.
Diphtheria. Sun/Tau.
Disease, chronic. Jup/Sat.
Disease, commencement. Plu/ASC.
Disease, hereditary. Sat/Nep=Node.
Disease, infectious. Sat/Nep.
Disease, nervous. Ura/Plu=Nep.
Disease, painless stage. Nep/Plu.
Disease. Sat/Nep=Sun; Moon/Nep.
Dissolution, quick. Mars/Sat=Jup.
Disturbed pregnancy. Plu/Node.
Disturbed sleep. Nep/Node.
Disturbing dreams. Ura/Node.
Doctor, aggressive. Ari/ASC.
Doctor delivery. Vir/ASC.
Doctor. Sun; Sat; Jup; Plu; Mer/Jup=Sun.
Dreamlife. Ura/Node.
Dreams, disturbing. Ura/Node.
Dropsy. Jup/Sco; Sun/Nep; Moon/Ven=Jup; Moon Leo/Sun; Ven/Gem.
Drowning. Sat/Plu=Nep; Mars/Plu=Nep.
Drug poisoning. Nep/ASC.
Drug sensitive. Moon/Nep.

Drugs. Nep; Jup/Nep=Mars.
Drunkenness. Sco.
Dumb. Sun/Nep=Mer.
Duodenal ulcer. Mer/Mars.
Duodenum. Vir.
Dysentery. Vir.
Dyspepsia. Moon/Sat; Ura/Vir.

Earaches, Sun/Nep,=Ari,=Gem,=Sat.
Ears, inflamed. Sat/ASC.
Ears. Aries; Taurus; Mer.
Ectopic pregnancy. Ven/Ura.
Eczema. Lib; Ven Cap; Ven/Ura; Ven/Cap.
Ego-consciousness loss. Sat/MC.
Ego-consciousness. MC; Node/MC.
Ego-illness. Sat/MC.
Electric shock. Sat/Node.
Embryonic growth. Plu/Node.
Emotional illness. Sat/Nep=Sun.
Emotional reactions. Moon/Mars.
Emotional shock. Sat/MC=Ura.
Emotional sickness. Plu/ASC=Sat.
Emotional suffering. Nep/Plu=Sat.
Emphysema, pulmonary. Ven/Sat; Mer/Ura;
Endocrine dysfunction. Sun/Sat.
Enteric fever. Vir.
Environmental influences. ASC.
Epidemics. Mars/Nep; Sat/Nep; Mars/Sat=Nep; Sco; Ura/,Nep/Sco.
Epilepsy. Ari; Sun/Nep=Mars and =Ura; Mars/Nep=Jup; Nep Can
    6th; Sun/Ura; Ura/Nep=Sun.
Episiotomy. Mars/ASC; Ura/ASC; Plu/ASC, Sco/ASC; Ari/ASC.
Equilibrium disturbances. Mer/Ura.
Eruptions. Ari.
ESP. Mer/Ura=Nep.
Eunuchism. Mars/Node.
Eurythmics. Ura/MC.
Excessive bleeding. Moon/Mars.
Excitable pregnancy. Ura/MC=Moon.
Excretion. Sco.
Expectant mother. Mars/Jup=Moon.
Eye disease. Mer Ari; 29°Tau; 6°Leo; 8°Sag.
Eyes weak. Moon/Ari.
Eyes. Sun/Moon.
Eyesight. Aqu.

Face. Mars/ASC.
Facial bones. Ari.
Facial pains. Mer/Ura.
Fainting. Mars/Leo; Sun/Ari.
Fallopian tube infections. Sun/Mer=Gem.
Fat loss. Sat/Nep=Jup.
Feeling sick. Sat/MC.
Feet weak. Moon/Pis.
Feet. Pis.
Female child. Ven/ASC; Jup/ASC; Nep/ASC; Moon/ASC.
Female disorders. Sun/Moon.
Female disturbances, periodic. Moon/Mars=Ura.
Female hormones. Moon/Ven.
Female illnesses. Sun/Plu=Moon; Moon/Ven=Sat.
Female reproduction. Moon/Mars=Sco.
Femur. Sag.
Fertility. Moon.
Fever spots. Ura/Plu.
Fever. Mars; Fire; Mars/ASC; Mars/MC; Mars/Ari.
Fibroids. Moon/Jup.
Fibula. Aqu.
Fingers. Gem.
Fistula. Sat/Sco.
Fits of weakness. Ura/Nep=Moon.
Fits, spastic. Jup/Ura.
Fits. Sun/Ver=Ura; Mars/Ura=Nep.
Flatulence. Jup/Tau.
Fluid imbalance. Sun/Moon.
Fluid retention. Moon/ASC.
Fluids. Moon.
Foetus disturbed. Plu/Node.
Food poisoning. Moon/Nep.
Food. Vir.
Forceps birth. Ari/ASC.
Forceps injury. Ari/,Mars/,Sat/ASC.
Fractures. Mars/Cap.
Frailty. Sun/Nep.
Frenzy. Mars/Ura=Nep; Mer/Mars=Ura.
Frigidity. Sat/Plu=Moon.

Gall bladder. Moon/Jup; disease. Moon/Jup=Sat; Jup; Jup/Sat.
Gallstones. Sun/Mer=Mars; Mars/Jup=Sat; Leo ASC.
Gastric mucous. Moon/Ven.

Gastric ulcer. Sat Can (/Jup).
Gastritis. Can-Cap; Sun/Mars=Moon.
Genitals, external. Lib.
Genitals, malformed. Ura/Sco.
Genitals. Mars/Nep=Ven; Sco.
Genito-urinary tract. Sco.
Getting ill. Nep/MC.
Gland atrophy. Ven/Sat.
Gland enlargement. Ven/Sat; Ven/Nep.
Glands, weakened. Ven/Nep; Sun/Ven=Nep.
Glandular activity inhibited. Sat/Nep=Ven.
Glandular secretions, abnormal. Ven/Sat.
Glandular secretions. Ven; Ven/Jup; Moon/Ven; Mer/Ven.
Glandular system. Pis.
Glandular tissue. Sun/Ven.
Goitre. Tau; Ven/Sat; Sun/Ven=Nep; Ven 6th.
Gonorrhoea. Ven/Lib; Ven/Mars=Sat.
Gout. Mer/Mars; Moon/,Ven/,Jup/,Sat/Sag; Moon/,Mars/,Sat/Cap.
Graafs follicles. Sun/Ven.
Gradual therapy. Nep/Plu.
Growth difficult. Sat/Nep=Plu.

Haemolysis. Jup/Nep.
Haemorrhoids. Sco; Moon/,Sat/Sco; Moon/Sat=Mars; Sun/Jup=Moon.
Hands. Gem.
Hardening process. Sat.
Harmonious proportions. Ven/ASC.
Hay fever. Sun/Gem; Moon/Ura; Moon/Tau; Sat/Ari; Mer/Sat.
Head arteries. Ari.
Head pains. Ura/Ari.
Headache. Ari; Sun/Mars=Ura; Sun/,Moon/, Sat/Ari; Ura/ASC.
Health, maintenance. Jup/MC.
Healthy sex. Ven/Mars=Jup.
Hearing nerves. Mer/Sat.
Hearing. Mer.
Heart activity. Mars/Ura.
Heart block. Sat/Ura.
Heart cancer. Nep/,Mars/Leo.
Heart disease. Sun/Mars; Sun/,Moon/,Mars/,Sat/,Plu/Leo.
Heart failure. Ura/Nep.
Heart muscle. Mars/Jup.
Heart palpitations. Sun/Leo,/Aqu.
Heart rhythm. Mars/Ura.

Heart weak. Moon/Nep=Leo.
Heart. Sun.
Heartburn. Moon/, Jup/Leo.
Heat regulation. Mars/MC.
Hepatitis. Mars/Jup=Moon.
Hereditary disease. Sat/Nep=Node; Moon/Sat; ASC/MC.
Hereditary myopia. Sat/ASC.
Hernia, hiatus. Moon/Ura.
Hernia. Ven/Mars; Vir.
Hiatus hernia. Moon/Ura.
High blood pressure. Sun/Mars.
High fevers. Fire.
Hip joints. Sag.
Hips. Sag.
Hodgkins disease. Moon/Node.
Home birth. Can/ASC; Tau/ASC; Moon/ASC.
Hormone circulation. Ven/Jup.
Hormone metabolism. Ven/Jup.
Hormones. Moon/Ven.
Hospital birth. Ari/ASC.
Hospital retention. Sat/Nep=Node.
Hospital staff. Sat/Nep=Node.
Hospital. Sun/Nep=Node or =ASC; Mars/Nep=Node.
Hygiene. Jup/MC.
Hyperactivity. Mars/Jup; Mars/Nep.
Hyperaemia. Sun/Gem.
Hyperaesthesia. Sun/Aqu.
Hypersensitive nerves. Nep/Plu=Ura; Sun/Nep=MC;
    Moon/Nep=Mars.
Hypertension, Ven/Mars; Jup/Sat=Mars.
Hyperthyroid. Sun/Plu=Mars,=Ura,=Tau,=Sco.
Hypnosis. Plu/ASC=Mer.
Hypochondria. Nep/Vir; ASC/Vir.
Hypoclycaemia. Moon/Jup=Sat,=Lib,=Vir,=Pis; Moon/Mer;
    Moon/Ven.
Hypotension. Jup/Sat=Mars.
Hypothyroid. Sun/Plu=Tau,=Sco.
Hysteria. Sun/Ari; Ura/Tau; Ven/Ura=Moon; Sat/Nep=Sun in Aries.

Iliac arteries. Sag.
Illness, chronic. Sat/Ura.
Illness, female. Mars/Sat=Moon.
Illness, from others. Nep/ASC=Sat.

Illness, male. Mars/Sat=Sun.
Illness, process of. Sat/ASC=Sun.
Illness, recurring. Ura/Node.
Illness, resistance to. Mars/Sat=MC.
Illness, serious. Sat/Nep=Plu.
Illness, sudden. Mars/Sat=Ura; Moon/Ura=Sat; Sat/Nep=Ura.
Illness. Jup/Sat=Ura; Sat/Node=Nep; Sat/Nep; Mars/Sat=ASC,=
    Mer,=Ven; Mars/Nep=Ura; Sat/Plu=Jup; Sun/Nep=Sat,=Jup; Sun/
    Moon=Sat; Sun/Jup=Sat; Illness.
Illusions. Nep/ASC.
Immune system. Plu; Moon/Plu; Moon/Node.
Impotence. Mars/Sat Sco.
Incestuous assault. Mars/Plu=Sun.
Increased blood water. Jup/Nep.
Indigestion. Jup/Can; Vir.
Induced birth. Nep/ASC; Nep.
Industrial inhalation. Ven/Jup.
Infantile organs. Sat/Plu.
Infection defence. Moon/Node.
Infection, sexual. Moon/Nep=Mars.
Infection, urethral. Sun/Plu.
Infection, vaginal. Sun/Plu.
Infection. Jup/Nep=Plu; Jup/Plu=Nep; Mars/Nep=Sun,=Moon,=Ven;
    Sun/Nep.
Infectious disease. Sat/Nep.
Inflamed mid-ear. Sat/ASC.
Influenza. Sun/Nep.
Ingested liquids. Moon/ASC.
Inhibited glandular activity. Sat/Nep=Ven.
Inhibited weight gain. Sat/Nep=Jup.
Injuries. Ura/ASC=Mars.
Injury from forceps. Ari/ASC; Mars/ASC.
Injury, heavy. Mars/Ura=Sat.
Injury, minor. Mars/Ura=Jup.
Injury with blood loss. Mars/Ura.
Injury. Mars/Ura and =Sun; Moon/Plu=Mars; Moon/Ura=Mars; Plu/
    ASC=Mars; Sat/Ura=Mars;=Plu; Ura/MC=Mars; Ura/Plu.
Inner tension. Mer/Sat=Ura.
Insanity. Mer/Mars=Ura; Ura/Plu; Nep/Ari; Sun/Ari.
Insomnia. Mars/Nep=ASC; Mars/Ari; Moon/Ari; Sun/Nep.
Institutionalisation. Nep/Node=Mars.
Internal respiration. Node/ASC.
Intestinal peristalsis. Jup/Ura.

Intestines. Vir.
Involuntary reflexes. Mer/Mars.
Iron. Mars; Moon/Mars.
Isolation. Sat/ASC.

Jaundice. Mer/Sag.
Jaw. Tau.
Joints. Mars/Sat.
Jugular vein. Tau.

Kidney congestion. Ven/Ari.
Kidney disease. Ven/Sat=Moon; Lib; Moon/Sat; Sun/Nep=Ven.
Kidney disease. Mars/Nep=Ven.
Kidney floating. Nep/Lib.
Kidney stone. Lib; Sun/Sat;=Lib; ASC/Cap; Sat/Lib.
Kidneys. Lib; Ven; Ven/Mars.
Kundalini. Jup/Node.

Lack of body tone. Nep/Node.
Lack of fats. Sat/Nep=Jup.
Lack of resistance. Mars/Sat=Nep.
Lameness. Moon/Sag; Ura/Nep=Mars.
Large hospital. Plu/ASC; Node/ASC.
Laryngitis. Tau; Moon/Mars(=Taurus).
Larynx. Tau.
Legs, neuralgia. Mer/Cap.
Legs, rheumatism. Jup/Sag.
Leprosy. Ura/Cap.
Lethargy. Ven/Ari.
Leukaemia. Moon/Nep=Sat; Sat/Vir.
Libido. Ven/Ura.
Life force. Mars/Ura=Plu; Ura/Plu=ASC; Jup/Node.
Limbs, artificial. Mars/Plu.
Limbs, loss of. Sat/Ura.
Liquid distribution. Moon/ASC.
Liver disease. Moon/Jup,=Sat; Jup/Sat=Sun; Sat/Nep=Jup.
Liver enlarged. Jup/Vir.
Liver, secretions. Moon/Jup.
Liver ulcerated. Jup/Vir.
Liver. Jup/Sat; Jup.
Localised pain. Sat/MC.
Loss of consciousness. Plu/Node.
Loss of ego-consciousness. Sat/MC.

Loss of limbs. Sat/Ura.
Loss of senses. Mer/Nep.
Lower jaw. Tau.
Lumbago. Lib; Sun/Sat=Ura.
Lung disease. Mars/,Sat/,Ura/,Nep/Gem; Sat/Nep=Jup.
Lungs. Gem.
Lymph cancer. Moon/Node=Plu.
Lymph glands swollen. Sun/Nep.
Lymph glands. Moon/Node.
Lymph. Moon.
Lymphatic system. Pis; Moon.

Madness. Mars/Ura=Nep.
Magnetic sexuality. Ven/Mars=Node.
Maintenance of health. Jup/MC.
Malaria. Sat/Node.
Male child. Mars/ASC; Sat/ASC; Sun/ASC.
Male hormones. Sun/Mars.
Malnutrition. Vir.
Marks, facial. Sun/ASC; Moon/Mars.
Mastoiditis. Sat/Tau; Moon/Sat; Mars/Sat.
Masturbation. Ven/Mars.
Measles. Ari; Ven/Mars=Sat.
Medical students. Vir/ASC; Mars/ASC; Mer/ASC.
Memory. Node; Ura/Node.
Meninges of the brain. Ura.
Meningitis. Sun/Ari.
Menopause. Moon/Ven=Sat.
Menses difficult. Tau.
Menses excessive. Ven/, Mars/Sco.
Menses suppressed. Sat/Sco.
Menstrual cycles. Moon/Ura.
Menstrual disorders. Sco.
Menstrual troubles. Moon/Mars=Plu.
Menstruation, abnormal. Ven/Mars.
Menstruation, first.Ven/Plu.
Menstruation. Moon/Ven; Moon/Mars; Moon/Sat (Sco).
Mental defect. Sun/Nep=Mer.
Mental disturbance. Nep/MC.
Mental dullness. Moon/Mars.
Metabolism, high. Fire; Air; Sun; Mars; Jup.
Metabolism, hormone. Ven/Jup.
Metabolism, low. Water; Earth; Tau; Cap; Moon; Ven; Sat.

Metabolism, nerve. Mer/Nep.
Metabolism of liquids. Moon/Plu.
Mid-brain. Ven/MC.
Midwife, aggressive. Ari/ASC.
Midwife. Tau/ASC; Can/ASC; Lib/ASC; Ven/ASC; Moon/ASC;
   Nep/ASC.
Migraine. Mer/Ura; Mer/Nep; Moon/Mars; Sat/Ura; Ari; Vir/ASC.
Miscarriage. Moon/Ven=Sat,=Plu; Ura/Sco.
Mole, facial. Sun/Node.
Mole. Sun/Moon.
Moodiness. Jup/Sat=Sun; Moon/MC=Ura.
Mother. expectant. Mars/Jup=Moon.
Motherhood. Ven/Plu=Moon; Sun/Ven=Ura.
Motor nerve system. Mer; Mer/Mars; Mer/MC.
Mouth. Mer.
Mucous membrane defects. Moon/Sat.
Mucous. Pis; Ven/Ari.
Multiple births. Gem/ASC; Lib/ASC; Aqu/ASC.
Multiple sclerosis. Leo/Aqu; Ura/Nep=Sat; Mer/Nep,=Ura; Sat/Ura.
Mumps. Moon/Ven=Mars; Ven/Tau.
Murder. Mars/Sat=Plu; Mars/Sat=Mer.
Muscle paralysis. Mars/Nep.
Muscle rupture. Mars/Ura.
Muscles, voluntary. Mars/MC.
Muscles. Mars; Sun/Mars.
Muscular dystrophy. Moon/Mars.
Muscular movement, unconscious. Moon/Mars.
Muscular tissue. Mars/Jup.
Myopia, hereditary. Sat/ASC.

Nails, Vir.
Narcotics. Moon/Nep, /Sat, /Sun; Moon/Pisces.
Nasal polyps. Sun/Tau.
Neck. Tau.
Nephritis. Lib; Mars/Lib.
Nerve irritation. Mer/Mars.
Nerve substance, new. Mer/Plu.
Nerve weakness. Sun/Nep=Mer; Mer/Nep.
Nerves, hypersensitive. Nep/Plu=Ura.
Nerves, overstrained. Mer/Ura=Plu.
Nerves, pain-conducting. Mer/Sat.
Nerves, shattered. Sat/Plu=Nep.
Nerves. Mer; Sun/Ura; Mer/Ura; Gem; Moon/Ura=Nep; Ura/ASC.

Nervous breakdown. Mer/Nep=Ura; Ura/Gem.
Nervous crises. Sun/Plu=Mer.
Nervous disease. Sat/Nep=Mer; Ura/Plu=Nep; Nep/Gem.
Nervous diseases. Mer/Sat=Ura; Mer/Ura=Nep.
Nervous equilibrium. Moon/Mer.
Nervous irritation. Mer/Nep; Mer/Nep=Sat; Mer/Plu.
Nervous love. Ven/Nep=Mer.
Nervous metabolism. Mer/Nep; Mer/Plu.
Nervous overexcitement. Ura/Plu=Sun.
Nervous paralysis. Mer/Nep.
Nervous system, sympathetic. Ven.
Nervous system, motor. Mer/Mars.
Nervous system blocks. Mer/Sat.
Nervous system, para-sympathetic. Ven.
Nervous system. Ura; Gem.
Nervous tension. Moon/Sat=Ura.
Nervous unrest. Ura/MC=Mer.
Nervous weakness. Nep/Plu=Mer.
Nervousness, excessive. Mars/Plu=Mer.
Nervousness. Moon/Mer/Ura.
Neuralgia in knees. Mer/Cap.
Neuralgia. Ari.
Neuritis. Mer/Mars, /Ura, /Nep; Sun/Mer=Fire.
Neurosis. Ura/Plu=Nep.
New nerve substance. Mer/Nep.
Nightmares. Nep/Ari.
Nose bleed. Jup/Tau; Mars Tau.
Numbness of limbs. Nep/MC.
Nutrition. Jup.

Obesity. Jup/H6,/Vir; Moon/Jup=Ura; Jup/Ari.
Occipital region. Tau.
Odyle force. Jup/Node.
Oedema. Moon/Ven=Mars.
Old age. Sat.
Operation. Mars/ASC; Mars/Ura=Sat,=MC; Mars/Plu=MC;
  Ura/MC=Mars.
Operations, avoid. Sun/Moon.
Operations, successful. =Moon/Ven.
Optic nerve. Ari.
Organ atrophy. Mars/Sat.
Organ calcification. Sun/Sat.
Organ death. Mars/Sat.

Organ loss. Sat.
Organic activity. Mars/Jup.
Organic decomposition. Sat/Nep.
Organic defects. Jup/Sat.
Organic rhythm. Jup/Ura.
Organic troubles. Ven/Sat=Sun.
Organic underdevelopment. Sat/Plu.
Organs, artificial. Mars/Plu.
Organs. Jup.
Orgasm. Ven/Ura; Jup/Ura.
Osmotic functions disturbed. Moon/Nep.
Ovaries. Sun/Ven; Ven/Plu.
Overeating. Jup/Tau.
Overindulgence in alcohol, nicotine, drugs. Nep/Plu=Sun,=Moon.
Overstrained nerves. Mer/Ura=Plu.
Overweight. Moon/Ven.
Oxygen respiration. Node/ASC.

Pacemaker. Sun/Ura; Ura; Aqu.
Pain, facial. Mer/Ura.
Pain, localised. Sat/MC.
Pain-conducting nerves. Mer/Sat.
Painless stage of disease. Nep/Plu.
Palpitation. Leo.
Pancreas, secretions. Moon; Moon/Jup.
Para-sympathetic nervous system. Ven.
Paralysis, muscle. Mars/Nep.
Paralysis, nervous. Mer/Nep.
Paralysis of breath. Mars/Sat.
Paralysis of limbs. Sun/Sag.
Paralysis, spastic. Mer/Mars.
Paralysis. Nep; Moon/Nep=Sat; Ura/Nep; Ura/Nep=Mars.
Parasites. Nep; (Can).
Parkinson's disease. Sat/Ura; Mer/Mars; Ura/Sat.
Pathological gland enlargement. Ven/Nep.
Peculiar diseases. Nep/Plu=Sun.
Pelvis. Sag.
Penis. Sco.
Perception, passive. Sun/ASC.
Peristalsis, intestinal. Jup/Ura.
Peristaltic action. Vir.
Peritonitis. Mer/Mars; Vir.
Pernicious anaemia. Moon/Mars=Can.

Phlebitis. Ven/Mars.
Physical attraction. Node/MC=Mars.
Physical beauty. Ven/ASC.
Physical breakdown. Sun/Plu=Mars.
Physical change. Plu/ASC.
Physical harm. Nep/ASC=Sun.
Physical love. Ura/MC=Ven.
Physical violence. Ura/ASC=Mars.
Physique, sensitive. Nep/Plu=Sun.
Pimples. Mars/Cap.
Pineal gland. Ari; Nep.
Pituitary gland. Ura; Ven/MC. Anterior=Sat; Posterior=Jup.
Pituitary malfunction. Moon/Ven=Sat,=Can,=Cap.
Plane crash. Mars/Ura=Nep.
Pleurisy. Gem; Moon/Mer=Mars; Sun/Gem.
Pneumonia. Moon/Gem; Moon/Ura=Mars; Moon/Nep=Sat.
Poison gas. Mars/Sat=Nep; Sat/Plu=Nep.
Poison. Mars/Sat=Nep; Sat/Plu=Nep.
Polio. Sun/Nep=Plu. Sun/Plu=Nep; Sun/Ura.
Pre-birth scan. Aqu/ASC; Ura/ASC.
Pregnancy, acute toxaemia. Plu/Node.
Pregnancy, disturbed. Plu/Node.
Pregnancy, excitable. Ura/MC=Moon.
Pregnancy, problem. Sun/Moon.
Pregnancy vomiting. Plu/Node.
Priapism. Sco.
Process of illness. Sat/ASC=Sun.
Procreation. Mars/Jup=Ven; Ura/MC=Ven; Moon/Mer=Mars; Ven/
   Jup=Mars; Ven/Mars=Sun,=Plu.
Promiscuity. Ura/MC=Ven.
Prostata. Moon/Ura.
Prostate cancer. Sun/Nep=Sat.
Prostate disease. Sco.
Prostate enlarged. Jup/Sco.
Prostate. Sco; Sun/Plu.
Prostatitis. Sun Sco; Sun/Sat=Mars.
Psoriasis. Mer/Mars=Sat.
Psychic stress on the soul. Node/MC.
Psycho-motor channels. Mer/Jup.
Psychosis, depressive. Nep/MC.
Psychosis. Sat/MC=Moon.
Puberty, female. Moon/Mer.
Puberty, male. Sun/Mer.

Pulmonary disease. Mars/Nep=Jup; Sun/Sag.
Pulmonary emphysema. Ven/Sat.
Pulse. Sun/Ura; Ura/Plu.
Pus. Mars/Nep.
Pylorus. Vir.

Rape. Mars/Plu=Ven; Mer/Mars=Ven; Sun/Ven=Ura,=Plu;
    Ven/Plu=Mars.
Rebirthing. Nep/ASC.
Rectum. Sco/
Recuperation. Plu/MC.
Recurring illness. Ura/Node.
Red blood cells. Mars; Moon/Mars.
Reflex actions. Mer/Mars; Mer/Jup.
Regenerated cells. Sun/Plu.
Regenerated organs. Jup/Plu.
Regeneration. Plu.
Reichenbach force. Jup/Node.
Removal operation. Sat/Ura.
Renal stones. Mars/Sco.
Renunciation. Moon/Mars=Ura.
Respiration, internal. Node/ASC.
Respiration, oxygen. Node/ASC.
Respiratory afflictions. Sun/Jup=Gem,=Sag.
Rheumatic fever. Moon/Leo; Leo/Aqu; Sun/Sat=Ura.
Rheumatism. Jup/Sag; Sun/,Moon/,Mer/,Sat/Cap; Sun/Sat.
Rhythm disturbed. Mars/Node.
Rhythm. Ura.
Rhythmic changes. Ura/Plu.
Rhythmic inhibitions. Sat/Ura.
Rhythmic paralysis. Ura/Nep.
Ringworm. Ari.

Sacrum. Sag.
Sadness. Moon/Sat=MC.
Scaled skin. Moon/Sat.
Scapula. Gem.
Scar, facial. Sun/Node; Sun/Moon; Mars/Ura.
Schizophrenia, inherited. Moon/Plu; Moon/Ura.
Schizophrenia. Nep/MC=Ura.
Sciatic nerve. Sag.
Sciatica. Mars/Jup.
Sciatica. Sat/Gem; Sun/Mer=Ura,=Fire; Sun/Sag.

Scrotum. Sco.
Seclusion. Sat/ASC.
Secretions, abnormal glandular. Ven/Sat.
Secretions, glandular. Ven/Jup.
Seducible. Ven/Plu=Nep.
Self-illness. Sat/MC.
Sense organs. Sun/ASC.
Senses, loss of. Mer/Nep.
Sensitive physique. Nep/Plu=Sun.
Sensitivity. Sun/Nep=MC.
Sensitised skin. Ura/ASC.
Sensory loss. Mer/Nep.
Sensual stimuli reception. Mer/ASC.
Sensuality, pronounced. Ven/Mars=MC.
Sex, abnormal. Ven/Mars=Sat or =Nep.
Sex drive, periodic. Sun/Ven=Ura.
Sex drive, weakened. Sun/Ven=Nep.
Sex, healthy. Ven/Mars=Jup.
Sex organs, weak. Ven/Nep; Sun/Nep=Moon.
Sex, pathological expression. Ven/Mars=Sat or =Nep.
Sex, strong. Ven/Mars=Plu.
Sex union. Ven/MC=Mars.
Sexual aberration. Sun/Nep=Ven; Ven/Nep=Mars; Ven/Plu.
Sexual desire. Sun/Ven=Ura.
Sexual goals. Ven/Mars=MC.
Sexual inhibition. Sat/Node=Moon.
Sexual rhythm. Ven/Ura.
Sexual union. Sun/Moon=Mars.
Sexual weakness. Sun/Nep=Mars; Moon/Nep=Mars.
Sexuality, magnetic. Ven/Mars=Node.
Sexuality, unhealthy. Ven/Sat=Sun.
Sexuality, unrestrained. Mer/Plu=Ven; Mer/Nep=Ven.
Sexuality. Mars; Sun/Ven=Plu; Ven/Mars=MC.
Shattered nerves. Sat/Plu=Nep.
Shin bone. Aqu.
Shock, emotional. Sat/MC=Ura.
Shock events. Sat/Node.
Shock. Jup/Sat=Ura.
Shoulders. Gem.
Sick associations. Mars/Sat=Node.
Sick family. Mars/Sat=Node.
Sickness, feeling of. Sat/MC.
Sickness. Moon/Sat=MC; Sat/MC=Sun.

Sinews. Mars/Sat.
Sinusitis. Moon/Mars; Jup/Sat=Mars; Sun/Plu.
Skin complaints. Sun/Mer.
Skin crawling. Nep/ASC.
Skin responses. Mer/Jup.
Skin sensitised. Ura/ASC.
Skin trouble. Sat/ASC; Mars/Nep=Sat.
Skin. Cap; Lib.
Skull fractures. Sat/Ari.
Sleep, disturbed. Nep/Node.
Sleeplessness. Nep/Node.
Sleepwalking. Nep/Ari.
Sleepwalking. Moon/Nep.
Slow progress. Nep/Plu.
Smallpox. Ari.
Smoking. Mer/Nep; Mars.
Solar plexus. Nep.
Soul sickness. Moon/Sat=Nep.
Soul stress. Node/MC.
Spasms. Sun/Ura; Sun/Nep=Ura.
Spastic fits. Jup/Ura.
Spastic paralysis. Mer/Mars.
Speech defect. Sun/Nep=Mer.
Speech inhibition. Sun/Sat=Mer.
Speech nerves. Mer/Sat.
Speech organs. Mer.
Speech. Mer.
Sperm. Sun/Mars.
Sphincter. Sco.
Spinal cord. Leo; Mer/Ura.
Spinal marrow. Ura.
Spinal meningitis. Ura/Leo.
Spine curvature. Sat/Leo.
Spleen. Leo; Vir; Moon/Node.
Stamina lack. Nep/Plu=Mars.
State of illness. Sat/Nep=MC.
Sterility. Sat/Sco.
Sterility. Vir; Sun/Moon; Moon/Jup=Sat; Sun/Mer=Sat;
    Ven/Sat=Moon.
Stillbirth. Ura/Nep.
Stones, kidney. Sun/Sat;=Lib; Moon/Sat; Mars/Sco.
Stones. Sat.
Strained nerves. Mer/Ura=Plu.

Strangulation. Mars/Sat.
Stress. Sun/Nep=MC; Sun/Ura.
Strong sex life. Ven/Mars=Plu.
Stuttering. Mer/Tau.
Subconscious. Node.
Sudden desire. Ura/MC=Ven.
Sudden illness. Sat/Nep=Ura.
Suffering, emotional. Nep/Plu=Sat.
Suffering. Sun/Nep=Plu; Mars/Sat.
Suffocation death by. Mars/Sat.
Suffocation, Mars/Tau; Plu/ASC=Mer.
Suicide. Mars/Sat=Plu; Mars/Plu; Sat/Plu=Mars.
Suprarenals. Lib; Mars; Ven/Jup.
Surgeon. Sun; Mars; Ura; Plu.
Surgery, avoid. Moon/Ura.
Surgery, female. Mars/Ura=Ven.
Surgery. Ari/ASC.
Surgical birth. Ari/ASC; Ven/Ura=Mars.
Swelling. Sun/Plu.
Sympathetic nervous system. Ven.
Synovial fluids. Pis.
Syphilis. Lib; Sco.

Tachycardia. Sun/Mars.
Tapeworm. Nep; Vir; Nep/Can.
Tarsus bones. Pis.
Teeth bad. Sun/Aqu.
Teeth. Ari; Sat in Aries; Sun/Sat.
Temper, violent. Moon/Mars=Ura.
Tendon reflexes. Mer/Jup.
Tendons. Mars/Sat.
Tension, nervous. Mer/Sat=Ura; Moon/Sat=Ura.
Testicle undescended. Sat/Plu.
Tetanus. Mars/Tau; Ura/Tau.
Thalidomide. Nep/H9; Nep/MC; Nep/CP.
Therapeutic process. Plu/MC.
Therapy change. Plu/MC.
Thighs. Sag.
Throat cancer. Sun/Nep=Sat.
Throat. Tau.
Thrush. Lib; Sco.
Thymus. Gem; Sun.
Thyroid gland. Tau; Moon/Mars.

Thyroid imbalance. Sun/Ven.
Tibia. Aqu.
Tics. Mer/Ura.
Toes. Pis.
Tongue. Tau.
Tonsillitis. Ven/Tau.
Tonsils removal. Moon/Node=Mars or =Ura.
Tonsils. Tau; Moon/Node.
Toothache. Ari; Sat/Ari.
Toxins. Mars/Nep=Sat.
Trachea. Gem.
Trance. Ari.
Transformation. Plu/ASC.
Transfusion, successful. Jup/Plu.
Transfusion, unsuccessful. Sun/Nep=Plu; Nep/Plu=Sun.
Transplants. Mars/Plu.
Trigeminal neuralgia. Ura/ASC.
Tuberculosis. Gem; Jup/Sat; Sun/Sat=Mer; Sun/Sat; Sun/Mer=Sat.
Tumour, brain. Sat/MC=Sun.
Tumour. Sun/Sat=Jup; Mars/Jup.
Typhoid. Vir.

Ulcer, duodenal. Mer/Mars.
Ulcer. Sat, Ura, Mars in Cancer affl Sun or Moon.
Ulcers, stomach. Cancer; Mars/Can; Ura/Can.
Ulcers. Moon/Jup=Mars; Moon/Mars=Can,=Vir,=Pis.
Unconsciousness. Ura/Nep=Sun.
Undergoing a therapy. Plu/MC.
Undescended testicle. Sat/Plu.
Unhealthy sex life. Ven/Sat=Sun.
Unrest, nervous. Ura/MC=Mer.
Unrestrained sexuality. Mer/Nep=Ven.
Unrhythmical processes. Sat/Ura; Ura/Nep=Sun.
Uraemia. Moon/Lib.
Urethral infections. Sun/Mer=Gem; Sun/Plu.
Urinary infections. Sco.
Urinary tract. Lib; Ari; Sco.
Uterine infections. Sco.
Uterus. Sco.

Vagina. Sco.
Vaginal infection. Sun/Plu.
Vaginitis. Ven/Mars.

Varicose veins. Ven/Mars; Sun/,Moon/,Mer/,Ven/,Mars/,Sat/,Aqu;
  Ven/Jup.
Vasomotor system. Lib.
Veins. Ven; Ven/Ura=Moon; Ven/Mars=Sun.
Vena cava. Leo.
Venereal disease. Sco; Mars/Nep; Ven/Mars=Sat; Moon/Ven=Mars;
  Ura/Sco.
Venous system. Sun/Ven.
Venticle, third. Ven/MC.
Vertigo. Ari affl by Ura.
Violence. Moon/Ura=Mars; Sun/Plu=MC; Mars/Ura;
  Sat/Ura=Mars,=Plu.
Violent birth. Plu/ASC; Sco/ASC; Mars/ASC.
Violent insanity. Mer/Mars=Ura.
Violent temper. Moon/Mars=Ura.
Vital force. Leo.
Vitality weak. Mars/Sat=Nep; Sat/Nep=Sun; Ura/Nep.
Vitality. Sun; Sun/Moon.
Vocal cord. Tau.
Voluntary muscles. Mars/MC.
Vomiting in pregnancy. Plu/Node.

Wasting diseases. Mars/Nep.
Water danger. Sat/Plu=Nep.
Water equilibrium. Moon/Mer.
Water retention. Moon/Nep.
Weak nerves. Mer/Nep.
Weak procreation. Ven/Sat=Sun.
Weak vitality. Mars/Sat=Nep.
Weakened glands. Ven/Nep.
Weakness, nervous. Nep/Plu=Mer.
Weakness. Mars/Nep=Sun,=Sat,=ASC.
Weakness. Mars/Sat=Nep; Moon/Nep=ASC; Moon/Ura=Nep;
  Sun/Nep=Jup.
Weather susceptibility. Ura/Node.
Weight loss. Sat/Nep=Jup.
Will, weak. Sun/MC=Nep; Nep/Plu.
Woman doctors at birth. Can/ASC; Lib/ASC; Moon/ASC.
Wounds, secreting fluids. Moon/Sat.
Wounds. Ura/ASC=Mars.

Yoga. Ura/MC.

Appendix 3: *Ebertin Correspondences between Body Parts and Zodiac Degrees (from* Anatomische Entsprechungen der Tierkreisgrade)

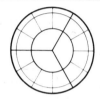

Aries (0° to 30°)

 1 Cerebrum
 2 Mid-brain – mesencephalon
 3 Cerebellum (abscess)
 4 Pineal gland (goitre)
 5 Right and left eye (hair)
 6 Orbital cavity (eye socket)
 7 Ear (jaundice)
 8 Cheekbone
 9 Crystalline lens of eye
10 Eyeballs
11 Optic nerve
12 Tongue
13 Corpus callosum (rheumatism)
14 Frontal lobes of the brain
15 Lateral lobes of the brain (suicide, stroke)
16 Pons varioli
17 Spinal cord canal
18 Nerve connections
19 Corpus callosum cerebri
20 Hyoid bone and tongue
21 Eye muscle
22 Cheek muscle
23 Masticatory muscle
24 Cheekbone muscle

25 Sternocleidomastoid muscle
26 Cranium
27 Fornix (tuberculosis)
28 Mid- and hind-skull
29 Auditory canal (bronchitis)
30 Parotid gland, throat

Taurus (30° to 60°)
 1 Throat and pharynx
 2 Palate
 3 Throat cavity
 4 Uvula
 5 Throat or laryngeal cavity
 6 Larynx
 7 Vocal chords
 8 Cervical nerves
 9 Jugular vein
10 Cervical vein (alcoholism)
11 Neck nerves connecting with the spinal cord (neurasthenia)
12 Neck nerves connecting with the spinal cord (neurasthenia)
13 Neck nerves connecting with the spinal cord (neurasthenia)
14 True vocal cords
15 Epiglottis
16 Carotid artery (abscess)
17 Thyroid gland (tonsils)
18 Lymph vessels (appendix)
19 Maxillary artery
20 Occipital bone (goitre)
21 Sinus artery
22 Hyoid muscle
23 Teeth (rheumatism)
24 Upper jaw
25 Lower jaw (alcoholism, tonsils, glands, suicide)
26 Nasal bone
27 Cervical vertebrae
28 Triangular muscle
29 Trigon (visual sense)
30 Trapezius

Gemini (60° to 90°)

 1 Trachea
 2 Esophagus

3 Upper right pulmonary lobe (appendix)
4 Lower right pulmonary lobe (anxiety, pulmonary inflammation)
5 Lower left lung lobe (anxiety, lung trouble)
6 Upper left lung lobe
7 Apex of the lungs (heart)
8 Bronchial tubes (eyesight)
9 Pulmonary artery (rheumatic fever)
10 Hilus lung root (typhoid fever)
11 Thymus gland
12 Tracheal membrane
13 Pulmonary veins
14 Clavicle (collarbone)
15 Scapula (shoulder blade)
16 Costal pleura
17 First rib (Bright's disease, kidneys)
18 Second rib (asthma)
19 Laryngeal muscles
20 Third rib
21 Arm muscles
22 Upper arm (appendicitis, insanity)
23 Spine
24 Elbows
25 Radius (gout, neurasthenia)
26 Wrist bones, (suicide)
27 Finger joints
28 Metacarpal bones (tuberculosis)
29 Fourth rib
30 Fifth rib

Cancer (90° to 120°)

1 Sixth rib
2 Seventh rib
3 Eighth rib (sight)
4 Ninth rib
5 Tenth to twelfth rib
6 Diaphragm
7 Thoracic canal
8 Hyacus (paralysis)
9 Pylorus
10 Gastric fundus
11 Gastric veins (alcoholism)
12 Large gastric curvature
13 Small gastric curvature

14 Abdominal stomach walls
15 Gastric nerves (suicide)
16 Pancreas
17 Pancreatic opening
18 into common duct
19 Head of pancreas
20 Upper arterial groove
21 Lower arterial groove
22 Gastric mucosa and Epithelion membrane
23 Gastric blood vessels
24 Blood vessels of
25 digestive organs
26 Mammary glands
27 Nipples
28 Rib cartilage
29 Spleen
30 Twelfth dorsal vertebra

Leo (120° to 150°)

1 Left coronary artery
2 Aorta
3 Right artery
4 Left carotid artery
5 Right carotid artery
6 Entrance of pulmonary artery (eyesight)
7 Left coronary vein
8 Vena cava (anaemia, hearing)
9 Upper vena cava (alcoholism)
10 Jugular vein
11 Clavicular vein
12 Spinal column
13 Right heart chamber
14 Left heart chamber
15 Right atrium
16 Left atrium
17 Right auricle
18 Right cardiac cavity
19 Ventricular septum (spine)
20 Mitral valve
21 Left atrium
22 Left auricle (appendix)
23 Left auricle (rheumatism)
24 Papillary muscle

25 Pericardium (alcoholism, abscess)
26 Myocardium
27 Heart ligaments (goitre)
28 Heart valves
29 Cardiac septum (neuritis)
30 Dorsal spine

Virgo (150° to 180°)

 1 Duodenum
 2 Small intestine
 3 Caecum (appendix)
 4 Ascending colon (large intestine) (asthma)
 5 Transverse colon
 6 Descending colon
 7 Rectum
 8 Abdominal cavity
 9 Right hepatic lobe (rheumatic fever)
10 Left hepatic lobe (gall, typhoid fever)
11 Ligament of Trietz (gall)
12 Abdominal aorta
13 Hepatic arteries
14 Gall bladder artery
15 Wart
16 Hepatic groove
17 Abdominal muscle
18 Serrate groove
19 Left hepatic groove
20 Bile duct
21 Gall bladder duct (typhoid fever)
22 Gall bladder
23 Hepatic cartilage (spine)
24 Tendons of liver
25 Liver (cancer, gout, arthritis)
26 Abdominal vein (suicide)
27 Hip veins (tuberculosis)
28 Hepatic veins
29 Back lobes of liver
30 Hepatic duct

Libra (180° to 210°)

 1 Kidney, pelvis
 2 Renal cortex
 3 Adrenals (abscess)

 4 Kidney surfaces (goitre)
 5 Malpighi's Pyramid
 6 Pubis
 7 Nervous system (jaundice)
 8 of the kidney
 9 and
10 renal
11 pelvis
12 Left renal system
13 Right renal system
14 Left inquinal gland
15 Right inquinal gland
16 Renal arteries
17 Adrenal arteries (kidney illness)
18 Fatty capsule of kidneys
19 Great renal calyx
20 Small renal calyx
21 Renal hilus
22 Renal veins
23 Adrenal veins
24 Vascular circulation
25 of the renal cortex
26 Vascular system
27 of the skin (tuberculosis)
28 Urinary bladder (hair)
29 Right ureter (bronchitis)
30 Left ureter

Scorpio (210° to 240°)

 1 Urethra opening
 2 Urethral meatus
 3 Prostate or uterus
 4 Right side of uterus or testicles
 5 Left side of uterus or testicles
 6 Right epididymus, uterine cavity
 7 Left epididymus, right Fallopian tube
 8 Scrotum, left Fallopian tube
 9 Spermatic duct, vagina (alcoholism)
10 Corpus cavernum oseum (neurasthenia)
11 Penis, labia majora
12 Seminal vesicles
13 Glans penis, vulva, labia minora
14 Foreskin

15 Cowpers glands
16 Cochlear head, right ovary (abscess)
17 Testicular lobes, left ovary
18 Efferent ducts, hymen (appendicitis)
19 Uterine ligaments, Hallers Netz
20 Ligaments of penis, Bartholin's gland (goitre)
21 Sphenoidal cavity
22 Ethmoid bone and ligaments
23 Nasal bone, Fimbria of Fallopian tubes (rheumatism)
24 Nasal septum
25 Coccyx, ovarian ducts (tonsillitis, alcoholism)
26 Perineum
27 Anus
28 Mucous membranes
29 –
30 Nasal muscles

Sagittarius (240° to 270°)

 1 Pelvic bone
 2 Hip bone
 3 Ischium (tailbone)
 4 Thigh bone
 5 Right large femoral artery
 6 Left large femoral artery (anxiety)
 7 Right surface femoral artery (heart)
 8 Left surface femoral artery (sight)
 9 Right lymphatic vessel (rheumatic fever, eye diseases)
10 Left lymphatic vessel (typhoid fever)
11 Adductor muscle
12 Large tibial vein
13 Rosen vein (rheumatic fever)
14 Surface femoral vein
15 Right hip veins
16 Left hip veins
17 Sciatic nerve
18 Right femoral *kreiser* (asthma)
19 Left femoral *kreiser*
20 Right head of femur
21 Left head of femur
22 Right trochanter (insanity, appendicitis)
23 Left trochanter (spinal problems)
24 Hollow of knee, popliteal fossa, cartilage
25 Condyle of right femur (neurasthenia, gout)

26 Condyle of left femur (suicide)
27 Gluteal muscles
28 Right leg muscle
29 Left leg muscle
30 Pear-shaped muscle

Capricorn (270° to 300°)

1 Right patella
2 Left patella
3 Cutaneous nerves of upper leg (eyesight)
4 Cutaneous nerves of tibia
5 Cutaneous nerves of knee
6 Right adductor muscle
7 Left adductor muscle
8 Lymph vessels of knees (paralysis)
9 Veins of knee
10 Ligaments of right knee
11 Ligaments of left knee
12 Right knee joint
13 Left knee joint
14 Right knee cartilage
15 Left knee cartilage (suicide)
16 Right knotty protuberance
17 Left knotty protuberance
18 Right knee ligaments
19 Left knee ligaments
20 Tendons of right knee
21 Tendons of left knee
22 Muscle endings
23 From upper to lower legs
24 From upper to lower legs
25 Connections between femur
26 and tibia
27 Deep lying nerves
28 Artery of right knee
29 Artery of left knee (bronchitis)
30 Adductor muscles

Aquarius (300° to 330°)

1 Right shinbone nerve (fatty degeneration)
2 Left shinbone nerve
3 Right fibula

4 Left fibula
5 Nerve of right fibula
6 Nerve of left fibula
7 Vein of lower right leg
8 Vein of lower left leg (anaemia)
9 Skin of right lower leg (alcoholism)
10 Skin of left lower leg
11 Right crural band
12 Left crural band
13 Artery of right lower leg (rheumatism)
14 Artery of left lower leg
15 Lymph vessel of right lower leg
16 Lymph vessel of left lower leg
17 Nervous system (Bright's disease)
18 of
19 the
20 spinal
21 chord
22 Right gastrocnemius, cecum (appendicitis)
23 Left gastrocnemius (rheumatism)
24 Right tibial muscle
25 Left tibial muscle (alcoholism, abscess)
26 Right fibula
27 Left fibula (goitre)
28 Right tibia
29 Left tibia (neuritis)
30 Connections

Pisces (330° to 360°)

1 Right heelbone
2 Left heelbone
3 Nerves of right foot (appendicitis)
4 Nerves of left foot (asthma)
5 Right cuboid bone
6 Left cuboid bone
7 Right anklebone
8 Left anklebone
9 Right metatarsus (rheumatic fever)
10 Left metatarsus (typhoid fever)
11 Lymph vessels of foot
12 Artery of right foot
13 Artery of left foot
14 Right surface veins

15 Left surface veins
16 Cruciate ligaments of right foot
17 Cruciate ligaments of left foot
18 Right extensor digitorum
19 Left extensor digitorum
20 Right fibula muscle
21 Left fibula muscle (typhoid fever)
22 Right Achilles heel (insanity, appendicitis)
23 Left Achilles heel (spine)
24 Right capsular joint
25 Left capsular joint (cancer, gout)
26 Nerves of lower foot
27 Phalanges of right foot (acute nephritis)
28 Phalanges of left foot (tuberculosis)
29 Toe nails of right foot
30 Toe nails of left foot

Appendix 4:
Dating Houses, Signs, Planets and Sensitive Points

The Ascendant is the reference point in the horoscope from which all ages in life are determined. Events in gestation are measured in months before conception, while events in childhood and maturity are in years and months of age. There are two basic ways to date the house cusps, sign cusps and planet positions.

The easiest way is to make a dating disk by having a transparent acetate photocopy made of Figure 65. Such acetate sheets are available

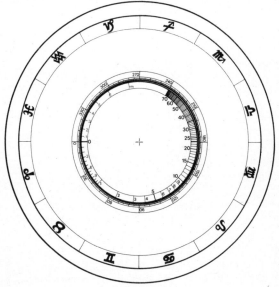

Figure 65

at most photocopy establishments. The dating disk shows dates from conception to old age. The advantage of using such a disk is that when the birth position on the disk is aligned with the Ascendant in a horoscope, the dates of houses, signs and planets can be seen instantly. Events in gestation and childhood are shown quite accurately. The only drawback is that the dating is only accurate to within one degree after the age of about 7 years old. For most purposes this degree of accuracy is sufficient, however.

A more accurate way is to use the Time Scale Tables in Table 8. The operation is quite basic and can be learned very quickly.

In the sample blank horoscope shown in Figure 65, you can see that the innermost ring is numbered from 0° at the beginning of Aries by 30° increments through the signs of the zodiac. This is called 'absolute longitude'. Absolute longitude is simply the measurement of any position in a horoscope from 0° Aries, the spring equinox point. Thus:

Absolute Longitude	Zodiac Sign
00°– 30°	Aries
30°– 60°	Taurus
60°– 90°	Gemini
90°–120°	Cancer
120°–150°	Leo
150°–180°	Virgo
180°–210°	Libra
210°–240°	Scorpio
240°–270°	Sagittarius
270°–300°	Capricorn
300°–330°	Aquarius
330°–360° (0°)	Pisces

If a planet is at 15° Sagittarius, its absolute longitude would be 240° for zero Sagittarius, plus 15° equals 255°. A planet at 6° Cancer 20' would be 96°20' absolute longitude. A planet at 26°20' Aquarius would be 300° for zero Aquarius plus 26°20', equals 326°20'.

Once the absolute longitude of a planet is determined, you need to calculate the number of degrees from the ASC. In the sample horoscope the ASC is 24° Virgo, which translates to 174° absolute longitude (150° + 24° = 174°). The 5th House cusp is 28° Capricorn, which translates to 298° absolute longitude. To determine the age of the 5th cusp, subtract 298° − 174° = 124° from the ASC. Enter the Time Scale Table and find the age equivalent. Opposite 124° is the age of 7 years 6 months. Franklin Roosevelt therefore entered the 5th House at the age of 7 years and 6 months old.

When a planet to be dated is in the early signs, the subtraction cannot be made. For example, to date the registration of Saturn, which registers at 6° Taurus (36° absolute), you cannot subtract 174° from 36°. In this case you must add 360°. Thus the position of Saturn is 396° − 174° = 222°, which is equivalent to the age of 53 years and 6 months old.

To determine the date of planets or cusps in gestation, the same process is used. To date the registration when the cusp of Leo was entered during Roosevelt's gestation, the position of the cusp of Leo is 120° + 360° = 480° − 174° = 306°, which is equivalent to the age of 13 weeks after conception. As the archetypal gestation is 40 weeks, the time before birth is 40 − 13 = 27 weeks before birth.

The conception point cannot be located accurately because of the uncertainty of the time lapse between actual fertilisation and the beginning of the development of the cellular body at the 9th House cusp. In principle, however, the shorter the duration of the 9th to 12th houses (as indicated by the distance from the 9th cusp to the ASC), the shorter the length of gestation.

Dating Sensitive Points

In addition to dating the house and sign cusps and the planets, it is often helpful to date the sensitive aspect points of the planets, the ASC and the MC. Using a straight edge and the table there is an easy way to do this. The sensitive aspect points of a planet at, for example, 16° of any sign will all register at 16° of the other signs. Likewise, when the number of degrees of a planet from the ASC is determined in the Time Scale Table, by placing a ruler along the same line all the sensitive dates will be shown. If, for example, a planet is dated at 31 years and 6 months old, aligning with 195°, by placing a ruler along that line you can see that its earlier registrations are 9 years 5 months old (the sensitive sextile), 2 years 5 months old (the sensitive trine), 0 years 3 months old (the sensitive opposition), and 5 weeks after conception (the sensitive sextile). For the other aspect sensitive points, align your ruler with the equivalent line of the bottom tables (165° or 225°), and find that the sensitive semi-sextiles are at 56 years and 8 months and 17 years and 4 months old, etc. Obviously the 45° and 135° aspects require more addition and subtraction to determine.

Table 8   Life★Time Astrology Time Scale

Degrees from ASC	Week	Degrees from ASC	Week	Degrees from ASC	Year	Month	Degrees from ASC	Year	Month
240°	4	300°	12	00°	00	00	60°	1	8
241		301		01			61		
242		302		02			62		
243		303		03			63		
244		304		04			64		
245	4	305	13	05	0	1	65	1	11
246		306		06			66		
247		307		07			67		
248		308		08			68		
249		309		09			69		
250	4	310	15	10	0	2	70	2	2
251		311		11			71		
252		312		12			72		
253		313		13			73		
254		314		14			74		
255 **9th**	5	315 **11th**	16	15 **1st**	0	3	75 **3rd**	2	5
256		316		16			76		
257		317		17			77		
258		318		18			78		
259		319		19			79		
260	5	320	18	20	0	4	80	2	9
261		321		21			81		
262		322		22			82		
263		323		23			83		
264		324		24			84		
265	6	325	20	25	0	6	85	3	2
266		326		26			86		
267		327		27			87		
268		328		28			88		
269		329		29			89		
270	7	330	22	30	0	7	90	3	6
271		331		31			91		
272		332		32			92		
273		333		33			93		
274		334		34			94		
275	7	335	24	35	0	9	95	4	0
276		336		36			96		
277		337		37			97		
278		338		38			98		
279		339		39			99		
280	8	340	26	40	0	11	100	4	5
281		341		41			101		
282		342		42			102		
283		343		43			103		
284		344		44			104		
285 **10th**	9	345 **12th**	29	45 **2nd**	1	0	105 **4th**	5	0
286		346		46			106		
287		347		47			107		
288		348		48			108		
289		349		49			109		
290	10	350	32	50	1	3	110	5	6
291		351		51			111		
292		352		52			112		
293		353		53			113		
294		354		54			114		
295	11	355	35	55	1	5	115	6	2
296		356		56			116		
297		357		57			117		
298		358		58			118		
299		359		59			119		
300	12	360	40	60	1	8	120	6	10

Degrees from ASC	Year	Month	Degrees from ASC	Year	Month	Degrees from ASC	Year	Month
120°	**6**	**10**	**180°**	**23**	**5**	**240°**	**75**	**11**
121	7	1	181	23	11	241	77	5
122	7	2	182	24	4	242	78	11
123	7	4	183	24	10	243	80	6
124	7	6	184	25	4	244	82	0
125	7	8	185	25	10	245	83	6
126	7	10	186	26	4	246	85	4
127	8	0	187	26	11	247	86	11
128	8	2	188	27	5	248	88	8
129	8	4	189	28	0	249	90	5
130	8	6	190	28	6	250	92	2
131	8	8	191	29	1	251	94	0
132	8	10	192	29	8	252	95	10
133	9	0	193	30	3	253	97	8
134	9	3	194	30	11	254	99	7
135 5th	9	5	195 7th	31	6	255	101	7
136	9	7	196	32	2			
137	9	10	197	32	9			
138	10	0	198	33	5			
139	10	3	199	34	1			
140	10	5	200	34	9			
141	10	8	201	35	5			
142	10	10	202	36	2			
143	11	1	203	36	10			
144	11	4	204	37	7			
145	11	7	205	38	4			
146	11	10	206	39	1			
147	12	1	207	39	11			
148	12	4	208	40	8			
149	12	7	209	41	6			
150	**12**	**10**	**210**	**42**	**3**			
151	13	1	211	43	2			
152	13	4	212	44	0			
153	13	8	213	44	10			
154	13	11	214	45	9			
155	14	2	215	46	8			
156	14	6	216	47	7			
157	14	9	217	48	6			
158	15	1	218	49	5			
159	15	4	219	50	5			
160	15	8	220	51	5			
161	16	0	221	52	5			
162	16	4	222	53	6			
163	16	8	223	54	6			
164	17	0	224	55	7			
165 6th	17	4	225 8th	56	8			
166	17	8	226	57	10			
167	18	1	227	58	11			
168	18	5	228	60	1			
169	18	10	229	61	3			
170	19	2	230	62	6			
171	19	7	231	63	9			
172	20	0	232	65	0			
173	20	4	233	66	3			
174	20	9	234	67	7			
175	21	2	235	68	11			
176	21	7	236	70	3			
177	22	1	237	71	7			
178	22	6	238	73	0			
179	22	11	239	74	5			
180	**23**	**5**	**240**	**75**	**11**			

Appendix 5:
Rectifying Approximate Birth Times

The discovery of the Critical Rotational Pattern brought many valuable improvements in astrological accuracy, as well as an inroad to radionics. Initially the sensitivity of the pendulum can be used to rectify the horoscope, that is, to correct the birth time. In the United States, many countries of Europe, and Scotland, the birth time is recorded by law on birth certificates, often to the nearest minute. This ensures that astrology work has a high level of accuracy when done properly. In England, however, there is no such recording of correct birth times. Often clients identify their time of birth by saying that it was 'exactly as tea began', or 'just as my father left for work in the morning'. While not doubting the regularity of English families, the real accuracy of such times is very much in doubt. In the context of Life★Time Astrology, an inaccuracy of one degree on the Ascendant throws the timing of events in life off by eight months at the age of 30 years old. Since it takes about four minutes of time for the ASC to move one degree, an inaccuracy of only fifteen minutes in a birth time can change the ASC by more than four degrees, or more than two years in the dating of life events. It became necessary for me to develop a system for rectification which was capable of rectifying inaccurate or questionable birth times.

Initially it is possible, when a birth time is slightly inaccurate, to correlate the events in life as a series of dates so that they can be compared to their equivalent astrological combinations. In the accompanying example, the birth time was known to have been between 12 noon and 1 o'clock in the afternoon, and the issue was to determine exactly when the birth occurred. For the purpose of rectification it is first necessary to have a series of live events which are best if they are overt physical events which can be dated indisputably, for example accidents, injuries, broken bones, operations or other medical emergencies. These are preferable to those which, while important in other ways, such as marriages, changes of residence or career moves, are more attached to the outer chronicle of one's life. A list of events which happened in the client's life follows:

Event	Age
Heart murmur	12–13yrs
Heart operation (near death)	18yrs
Daughter born	23yr 1mo
Daughter born	25yr 2mos
Son born	28yr 11mos
Divorce	38yr
Remarriage	39yr
Appendicectomy (near death)	41yr 9mos

Horoscopes are erected for the earliest and latest times given, of 12:00 noon and 13:00 pm, but it is best if a time directly in the middle of the span is taken as a model upon which to work, i.e. 12:30 pm. A list of planetary positions and sensitive points are developed and compared to the list of events as given. It can immediately be seen that the actual times compare favourably with the 12:30 pm model. The comparison is made between times actually supplied and the planetary positions or sensitive points and their dates (Figure 66).

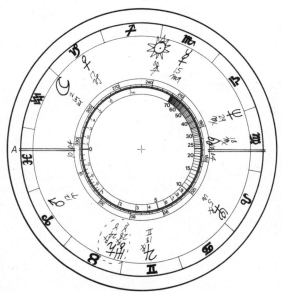

Figure 66

The heart murmur was vaguely dated as being sometime around 12 or 13 years old, and we notice that the natal Pluto registers in September 1953, at which time she was just two months short of 12 years old. The predicted date is before the actual date.

The operation during which her heart almost stopped was in the end of 1959, and in February 1959 there was a sensitive square from Saturn and in January 1960 a sensitive sesquiquadrate (135°). Ebertin in CSI considers the Mars/Saturn contact 'the death axis', specifically through 'the death or atrophy of an organ'.[1]

There follows the birth of three children from 1964 to 1967. The astrological indications for children vary greatly as their effect upon the mother can range from being so easy that they do not show at all to interrupt the flow, to the trauma of long labour when Saturn or Neptune are involved, to overt danger and surgery when Mars, Uranus or Pluto are implicated, particularly with the hard aspects. It is also important to recognise that the birth is seen in the mother's horoscope *relative to the way she perceives it.* In some cases there can be a Caesarean section which goes without the powerful destructive aspects one might associate with surgery, simply because the mother is accustomed to having children that way. The critical point is that the state of health is relative to the individual. When trauma is a part of life, small traumas can go unnoticed.

In our case, none of the births was traumatic, and they therefore do not appear to be significant for rectification purposes.

She was divorced in November 1979 and remarried in November 1980, corresponding to the trine Moon in March 1978 and the sextile Pluto in October 1980. The new relationship began well before the divorce. The Moon/Pluto combination is very appropriate for emotional changes of a profound kind with the additional qualities of 'an extremely emotional life',[2] and is often correlated to times when psychology and psychotherapy are either studied or practised.

She had an appendicitis operation in July 1983, very near but before the registration of the sesquiquadrate in November 1983.

She dislocated her shoulder in April 1984, just before the registration of the inconjunct (150°) Ascendant in March 1984, but sandwiched between the sesquiquadrate Saturn in November 1983 and the opposition Mars in January 1986. The dislocated shoulder is related to the earlier heart operation.

Since the majority of events as dated using 12:30 pm in the print-out happen earlier than actual by about one year, the ASC moves ahead by about two degrees, making the new birth time 12:38 pm. At this point the rectified chart can be correlated to the rest of the life events.

Appendix 6:
Astrological Computer Services in the UK

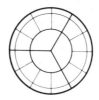

The calculation of the horoscope, while not a difficult process, does take many hours to learn and much practice to do accurately. In any event, in this age of computers it is pointless to learn the calculation routines. The author suggests that you utilise one of the many astrological computer services available in the UK to have your birth horoscope calculated accurately.

1 Orion Enterprises
   26 Grafton Square, London SW4 0DB, (01)-720-8107.

2 Alhena Enterprises
   Hillcroft, Chevin Avenue, Silver Mill Hill, Otley, W. Yorkshire LS21 3BH, (0943)-462-324.

3 Linkplus Limited
   23 Park Hall Road, London N2 9PT, (01)-444-5104.

4 Equinox
   21 Whittlesey Street, London SE1, (01)-928-2960.

5 Findhorn Astrological Services
   Cluny Hill College, Forres IV36 0RD, Scotland.

6 ASCROL
   Box 219, Griesbach Road, London W9, (01)-263-8783.

7 Starword Research
   53 Loughborough Road, Quorn, Loughborough LE12 8DU,
   (0509)-42076.

Conversion Formulae for Pocket Calculators

The position of any planet at a given date may be determined by a simple formula with a pocket calculator. We can calculate degrees from the ASC into years of age, or vice versa.

Degrees from the ASC into Years Decimal

Years Decimal = ((x + 120)/120) INV LOG − 10) * .0766

Where x = number of degrees from the ASC in true longitude
Where * = multiply

The answer is given in Years Decimal as 25.75 years would be twenty-five years and .75 of a year, or 9 months. To find the month during the year multiply the decimal times 12 months. (.75 year times 12 months = 9 months)

Years Decimal into Degrees from the ASC

Degrees from the ASC = ((y/.0766) + 10) LOG * 120 − 120 + ASC

Where y = Age in Years Decimal
Where * = multiply
Where ASC = Ascendant in true longitude (degrees from 0 Aries)

The answer is given in true longitude in the horoscope. To find degrees from the ASC, do not add the ASC at the end of the formula.

The author thanks Ad Strack van Schijndel of Holland for these formulae.
   Chester Kemp has developed programs for calculating horoscope information and for the Log Time Scale for use with Casio calculators. For further information contact him at 8 Orchard Road, Hounslow, Middlesex, England.

Appendix 7:
Astrological Computer Programs

Astrological programs are available which calculate the horoscope and produce a list of Life★Time dates in life from conception to 99 years old. The two versions available from the author run on Commodore 64 format and the small Sharp PC-1402 with its printer CE-126P. Write to:

> Life★Time Service Ltd
> 1 Coniger Road
> Fulham
> London SW6 3TB
> (01-736-3367)

Life★Time Interpretation

Life★Time Service Ltd offers a beautiful, professionally presented computer horoscope of about twenty-five pages, laser-printed, in a four-colour cover and including a full colour horoscope diagram printed by laser.

The Life★Time Interpretation describes events from before conception to the age of 99 years old including:

- The nature of your conception and gestation time.
- The events and quality of your Ascendant/Rising Sign as it derives from your birth and the people present.
- The registration of all ten planets, their aspects and the life events they have created.
- More than 100 sensitive point events throughout your life which show when early influences return to affect you.

The accuracy of the interpretation depends upon a correct birth time. Please check and find the most accurate birth time you can, even if this means finding your birth certificate or hospital records. Make sure whether you were born am or pm, and that the time between midnight and 1.00 am is written as 00.34 am Do not convert to standard time, daylight savings or summer time, or war time – the correct local time is sufficient. If you do not know your time it is, unfortunately, not possible to benefit from the Life★Time Interpretation. Please allow four weeks for processing and delivery of your finished interpretation.

Life★Time Interpretation

Life★Time Service Ltd, 1 Coniger Road, Fulham, London SW6 3TB
Phone (01)-736-3367 Fax (01)-731-0015

Please send my Life★Time Interpretation for £29, reflecting a £10 discount for having purchased this book.

Name   _____

Address   _____

            _____

Birthdate   Day _____ Month _____ Year _____

Birthtime   __ : __ AM/PM (Using 24-hour day)

Birthplace   City _____ Country _____

Notes

1 The Modern Health Crisis

1 Grossinger, Richard, *Planet Medicine*, Boulder, 1982.
2 Ibid.
3 Quinn, Janet F., 'The Healing Arts in Modern Care', in D. Kunz, *Spiritual Aspects of the Healing Arts*, Wheaton, Illinois, 1985.
4 Witte, Alfred, *Rules for Planetary Pictures: The Astrology for Tomorrow*, Hamburg, 1928.
5 Ebertin, Reinhold, *Combination of Stellar Influences*, Aalen, 1972, pp. 16–17.

2 Astrology as a Healing Art

1 Collin, Rodney, *The Theory of Celestial Influence*, London, 1954.
2 Mann, A. T., *Life★Time Astrology*, London, 1984; San Francisco, 1988.

3 The New Healing Paradigm

1 Adapted from: Wilhelm, Richard (trans.), *The I Ching or Book of Changes*, Princeton, 1950.
2 Seymour, Percy, *Astrology: The Evidence of Science*, Luton, 1988.
3 Cotterell, Maurice, *Astrogenetics: The New Theory*, London, 1988.
4 Schwaller de Lubicz, R. A., *Symbol and Symbolic: Egypt, Science and the Evolution of Consciousness*, trans. by Robert and Deborah Lawlor, Autumn Press, Brookline, 1978.
5 Schwaller de Lubicz, R. A., *Symbol and Symbolic: Egypt, Science and the Evolution of Consciousness*, trans. by Robert and Deborah Lawlor, Autumn Press, Brookline, 1978.
6 Santillana, Giorgio and Dechend, Hertha von, *Hamlet's Mill: An Essay on Myth and the Frame of Time*, Godine, Boston, 1977.

7 Hall, Manley Palmer, *Secret Teachings of All Ages*, Crocker, San Francisco, 1928, showing a diagram from the work of Athanasius Kirscher's *Oedipus Aegyptiacus*.
8 Grof, Stanislav, *Beyond the Brain: Birth, Death and Transcendence in Psychotherapy*, State University of New York Press, New York, 1985.

4   Life★Time Astrology

1 De Nouy, Pierre Lecomte, *Biological Time*, London, 1936.
2 See Rupert Sheldrake's books about morphogenetic fields and the transmission of characteristics beyond heredity.
3 Sheldrake, Rupert, *A New Science of Life*, London, 1981.
4 Huber, Bruno and Louise, *Man and His World*, trans. by Lore Wallace, New York, 1978.
5 Rudhyar, Dane, *The Astrology of Personality*, New York, 1963.
6 Nauman, Eileen, *The American Book of Nutrition and Medical Astrology*, San Diego, 1982.
7 Ibid.

5   The Wheel of Therapies

1 Rudhyar, Dane, *Astrology and the Modern Psyche*, Reno, 1976.
2 Jung, Carl G., *The Practice of Psychotherapy*, CW 16, London, 1954.
3 Jung, C. J., *Psychology and Alchemy*, CW 12, London, 1953, p. 132.
4 Grossinger, Richard, *Planet Medicine*, Boulder, 1982, pp. 199–200.
5 Grof, Stanislav, *Beyond the Brain: Birth, Death and Transcendence in Psychotherapy*, pp. 98–102.
6 Assagioli, Roberto, *Psychosynthesis*, London, 1975.
7 Grossinger, Richard, *Planet Medicine*, p. 390.
8 Weaver, Herbert, *Divining the Primary Sense*, London, 1978.
9 See particularly the works of David Tansley, *Chakras, Rays and Radionics*, 1984 and *Raypaths and Chakra Gateways*, London, 1985 and the chapter on 'Astro★Radionics' later in this book.
10 Bailey, Alice A., *Esoteric Healing*, New York, 1953, pp. 119–20.
11 Townley, John, *Astrological Cycles and Life Crisis Periods*, Maine, 1977.
12 Ebertin, Reinhold, *Combination of Stellar Influences*, pp. 102–3.
13 Ibid., pp. 104–5.
14 Ibid., pp. 158–9.

6   Astrological Diagnosis

1 Mann, A. T., *Life★Time Astrology*, London, 1984.
2 *The Sunday Times*, 31 January 1988, p. 1.
3 Nauman, Eileen, *The American Book of Nutrition and Medical Astrology*, San Diego, 1982, p. 52.

4 Ebertin, Reinhold, *Combination of Stellar Influences,* pp. 160, 186
5 Grof, Stanislav, *Beyond the Brain.*
6 Dossey, Larry, *Space, Time and Medicine,* Boulder, 1982.
7 A midpoint is one of the two zodiacal points where two planets are equidistant.

7   Astro★Radionics

1 Tansley, David V., 'Healing Through Patterns in Radionics and Radiesthesia', in the *Journal of the British Society of Dowsers,* vol. XXVIII, no. 193, Ashford, September, 1981.
2 Tansley, David V., *Radionics: Science or Magic?,* Saffron Walden, 1982.
3 Tansley, David V., his early works include *Radionics – Interface with Ether Fields, Radionics and the Subtle Anatomy of Man,* and *Chakras, Rays and Radionics.*
4 Ebertin, Elsbeth and Reinhold, *Anatomische Entsprechungen der Tierkreisgrade,* translated list by Mary L. Vohryzek, Freiburg, 1976.
5 Boericke, William, *Homoeopathic Materia Medica,* 9th edn, Philadelphia, 1927.
6 Ibid., pp. 79–83.
7 Whitmont, Edward, *Psyche and Substance,* Boston, 1980.
8 Ebertin, Reinhold, *Combination of Stellar Influences,* pp. 160–1.
9 Ibid., pp. 156–7.

8   Healing the Future

1 Wellspring publication, London, 1986.
2 Ibid., p. 2.
3 A source of powdered acidophilus is available through Wellspring Vitamins Ltd, 133 Beaufort Street, London SW3.

Appendix 5   Rectifying Approximate Birth Times

1 Ebertin, Reinhold, *The Combination of Stellar Influences,* p. 156.
2 Ibid., p. 108.

Bibliography

Achterberg, Jeanne, *Imagery in Healing: Shamanism and Modern Medicine*, 1985, New Science Library, Boston.

Arroyo, Stephen, *Astrology, Psychology and the Four Elements*, 1975, CRCS, Vancouver.

Bailey, Alice A., *Esoteric Healing*, 1953, Lucis Publishing, New York.

Beard, Ruth M., *An Outline of Piaget's Developmental Psychology*, 1969, Routledge & Kegan Paul, London.

Cade, C. Maxwell and Coxhead, Nona, *The Awakened Mind*, 1979, Wildwood House, London.

Capra, Fritjof, *The Tao of Physics*, 1975, Wildwood House, London.

Collin, Rodney, *The Theory of Celestial Influence*, 1954, Robinson & Watkins, London.

Collin, Rodney, *The Theory of Eternal Life*, 1950, Robinson & Watkins, London.

Conway, David, *The Magic of Herbs*, 1973, Jonathan Cape, London.

Cornell, H. L., *Encyclopedia of Medical Astrology*, 3rd rev. edn, 1972, Samuel Weiser, New York.

Cotterell, Maurice, *Astrogenetics*, 1988, Brooks, Hill Robinson, Saltash, Cornwall.

Cramer, Diane, 'A Review of Current Medical Astrology Books', Winter 1985–6, NCGR Journal, Stamford, CE.

Culpeper, Nicholas, *The Astrological Judgement of Diseases*, 1655, repr. 1959, AFA, Tempe, Arizona.

Davies, Paul, *The Cosmic Blueprint*, 1987, Heinemann, London.

Dethlefsen, Thorwald, *The Challenge of Fate*, 1984, Coventure, London.

de Vries, Marco, *The Redemption of the Intangible*, 1981, Institute of Psychosynthesis, London.

Dossey, Larry, *Beyond Illness*, 1984, Shambhala, Boulder.

Dossey, Larry, *Space, Time and Medicine*, 1982, Shambhala, Boulder.

De Nouy, Pierre Lecomte, *Biological Time*, 1936, Methuen, London.

Ebertin, Elsbeth and Reinhold, *Anatomische Entsprechungen der Tierkreisgrade*, 1976, Freiburg.

Ebertin, Reinhold, *The Combination of Stellar Influences*, 1972, Ebertin-Verlag, Aalen.

Flanagan, Geraldine Lux, *The First Nine Months*, 1970, Heinemann, London.

Gauquelin, Françoise, *Psychology of the Planets*, 1982, ACS, San Diego.

Gauquelin, Michel, *Spheres of Destiny*, 1980, J. M. Dent, London.

Greene, Liz, *Relating*, 1977, Coventure, London.

Grof, Stanislav, *Beyond the Brain*, 1985, State University of New York Press, Albany.

Grossinger, Richard, *Planet Medicine*, 1982, Shambhala, Boulder.

Guirdham, Arthur, *A Theory of Disease*, 1957, George Allen & Unwin, London.

Gurudas, *Flower Essences*, 1983, Brotherhood of Life, Albuquerque, New Mexico.

Hahnemann, Samuel, *Organon of Medicine*, (1810), first integral English translation, 1983, Victor Gollancz, London.

Hamaker-Zondag, Karen, *Astro-Psychology*, 1980, Weiser, New York.

Harmon, J. Merrill, *Complete Astro-Medical Index*, 1975, Astro-Analytics Publications, Van Nuys, California.

Harvey, Ronald, *Mind and Body in Astrology*, 1983, L. N. Fowler, Chadwell Heath, Essex.

Hastings, Arthur (ed.), *Health for the Whole Person*, 1981, Bantam, New York.

Heindel, Max and Foss, Augusta, *A Guide to Healing*, 1929, Rosicrucian Fellowship, Oceanside, Ca.

Heindel, Max and Foss, Augusta, *The Message of the Stars*, 1927, Rosicrucian Fellowship, Oceanside, Ca.

Inglis, Brian and West, Ruth, *The Alternative Health Guide*, 1983, Michael Joseph, London.

Jansky, Robert Carl, *Astrology, Nutrition and Health*, 1977, Para Research, Rockport, Mass.

Jung, Carl Gustav, *Psychological Types*, 1923, Routledge & Kegan Paul, London.

Kunz, Dora (ed.), *Spiritual Aspects of the Healing Arts*, 1985, Theosophical Publishing House, Wheaton, Ill.

LeShan, Lawrence, *Holistic Health*, 1984, Turnstone Press, London.

Mann, A. T., *Life★Time Astrology*, 1984, Allen & Unwin, London.

Mann, A. T. (ed.), *The Future of Astrology*, 1988, Unwin Hyman, London.

Mann, A. T., *The Round Art: The Astrology of Time and Space*, 1979, Dragon's World, London.

Meyer, Michael, *A Handbook for the Humanistic Astrologer*, 1974, Anchor Books/Doubleday, Garden City.

Nauman, Eileen, *The American Book of Nutrition and Medical Astrology*, 1982, ACS, San Diego.

Prigogine, Ilya and Stengers, Isabelle, *Order out of Chaos*, 1984, New Science Library, Boulder.

Rosenblum, Bernard, *The Astrologer's Guide to Counseling*, 1983, CRCS, Reno, Nevada.

Rudhyar, Dane, *The Astrology of Personality*, 1963, Doubleday, Garden City.

Seymour, P. A. H., *A Causal Mechanism for Gauquelin's Planetary Effect*, 1986, privately published paper, Plymouth.

Sheldrake, Rupert, *A New Science of Life*, 1981, Blond & Briggs, London.

Stein, Zane, *Interpreting Chiron*, 1983, Association for Studying Chiron, Lansdale, Pa.

Steiner, Rudolf, *Spiritual Science and Medicine*, (1948) 1975, Rudolf Steiner Press, London.

Szanto, Gregory, *Astrotherapy*, 1987, Arkana, London.

Tansley, David V., *Chakras, Rays and Radionics*, 1984, C. R. Daniel, Saffron Walden.

Tansley, David V., *Radionics: Interface with Ether Fields*, 1975, Health Science Press, Bradford, Devon.

Tansley, David V., *Radionics: Science or Magic?*, 1982, C. R. Daniel, Saffron Walden.

Vithoulkas, George, *The Science of Homoeopathy*, 1980, Grove Press, New York.

Vogh, James, *Astrology and Your Health*, 1980, Granada, London.

Watson, James, *The Double Helix*, 1968, Weidenfeld & Nicolson, London.

Weaver, Herbert, *Divining the Primary Sense*, 1978, Routledge & Kegan Paul, London.

Westlake, Aubrey, *The Pattern of Health*, 1973, Shambhala, Boulder.

Westlake, Aubrey, and Rae, Malcolm, *The Radiesthetic Faculty*, 1973, privately printed, Godshill.

Whitmont, Edward, *Psyche and Substance: Essays on Homoeopathy in the Light of Jungian Psychology*, 1980, North Atlantic Books, Richmond, California.

Wilber, Ken, *The Atman Project*, 1982, Theosophical Publishing House, Wheaton, Ill.

Wilber, Ken, *The Spectrum of Consciousness*, 1977, Theosophical Publishing House, Wheaton, Ill.

Wilber, Ken, Engler, Jack and Brown, Daniel P. *Transformations of Consciousness*, 1986, New Science Library, Boston.

Zukav, Gary, *The Dancing Wu Li Masters*, 1979, Rider & Hutchinson, London.

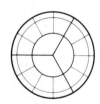

Index